"Lots of people have helped advance the sport of whitewater paddling. Ken Whiting has proved he is one who stands out among them. Since becoming the World Freestyle Champion in 1997, through his thoughtful teaching, Ken's enthusiasm for whitewater has helped countless paddlers achieve their own whitewater goals."

– SCOTT MACGREGOR, RAPID MAGAZINE

"Ken's done it again! Like the paddle or helmet, this book is an essential for every boater!"

– EUGENE BUCHANAN, EDITOR, PADDLER MAGAZINE

"My fiance and I got into kayaking in general last March, then decided to take the big step and try whitewater kayaking. I can assure you that the sheer joy and sharp technique in your books and videos has everything to do with both our progress in learning and our happiness in achieving. Keep up the good work!"

– GEORGE BALDWIN

"I just picked up your latest instructional playboating video — what a great offering! I had an epiphany learning that almost ALL of these moves could be practiced/performed on flatwater (ie. helix, tricky whu)."

– DAVE GARDNER

"Love the new book! Excellent photos and great explainations."

– MARK SIMPSON

"The book is great; it is laid out in a clean and concise format, Paul's photos are awesome and illustrate the moves well. You lay out a nice foundation of strokes and balance work and follow it up with great explanations of the moves and their sequences."

D1404155

ALSO BY KEN WHITING:

BOOKS

- The Playboater's Handbook 2 -

DVD'S

- Whitewater Kayaking with Ken Whiting -
- Playboating with Ken Whiting -

THE ULTIMATE GUIDE TO

Whitewater
Kayaking

BY KEN WHITING AND KEVIN VARETTE

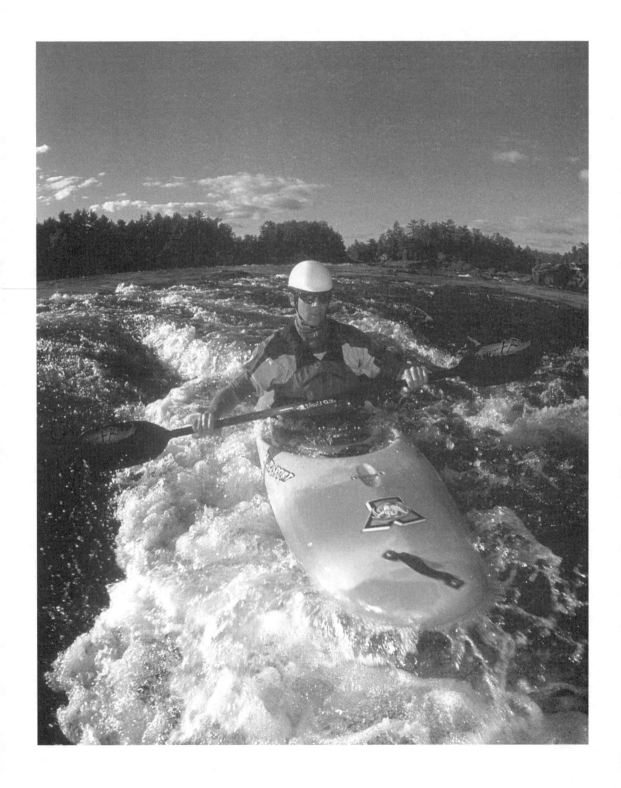

THE ULTIMATE GUIDE TO

Whitewater Kayaking

BY **KEN WHITING** AND **KEVIN VARETTE**

PHOTOS BY PAUL VILLECOURT
ILLUSTRATIONS BY PAUL MASON

 THE HELICONIA PRESS

Published by

THE **HELICONIA PRESS**

1576 Beachburg Road
Beachburg, Ontario
K0J 1C0
www.helipress.com

This book was printed in Canada by Custom Printers, Renfrew, Ontario.

First Edition

ISBN 1-896980-12-0

Written by: Ken Whiting and Kevin Varette
Photography by: Paul Villecourt except as noted: Jock Bradley, Ruth Gordon, Andrew Watkinson
Illustrations by: Paul Mason
Cover and book design: Ken Whiting
Editor: Jane Karchmar, Kevin Varette
Layout: Tara Yourth, Custom Printers of Renfrew Ltd.

Front Cover: Ken Whiting at Butcher's Knife on the Ottawa River. (Photo by Paul Villecourt)
Back Cover: Ken, Kevin, and the gang at S-turn on the Ottawa River.

National Library of Canada Cataloguing in Publication

Whiting, Ken, 1974-
            The ultimate guide to whitewater kayaking / by Ken Whiting and Kevin Varette.

ISBN 1-896980-12-0

        1.   Kayaking. 2. White-water canoeing. I.
             Varette, Kevin, 1973-
             II. Title.

GV788.W465 2004   797.122'4   C2004-902638-0

About Safety

The publisher and the authors do not take responsibility for the use of any of the materials or methods described in this book. Whitewater kayaking is an activity with inherent risks, and this book is designed as a general guide, not a substitute for formal, professional instruction. By following any of the procedures described within, you do so at your own risk.

Contents

ACKNOWLEDGEMENTS

This book is the culmination of all that we have learned about whitewater kayaking over an immensely fulfilling 15 year period. As you may already know, or as you're going to find out, kayaking is as much about the experiences you share as it is about any of the skills or techniques you acquire. It's a journey, for many a lifelong one, and what it has to offer is hard to find anywhere else. This particular part of our journey was inspired and supported by so many friends, family and colleagues that we can't name you all in this brief acknowledgement. You know who you are, because our lives on and off the river would be that much different if it weren't for you. So thank you.

In particular, we'd like to thank our loving families, who have once again not only put up with us but actually found it within themselves to encourage our behaviour.

We must also acknowledge the invaluable assistance of Paul Villecourt (as usual) for his amazing photographic talent, Paul Mason for his energetic drawings that give so much more life to this book, Tim Gordon for his general wisdom, Ruth Gordon for her positive attitude and all of our contributors whose writings have put the final touches on an image we only hoped might actually materialize.

Finally, we want to remind you of something to hold onto. As we progress as a society, our wants and needs diverge further and further from the simplicity of nature, not because we are necessarily malicious or ignorant, just because we are human. When you choose to take on a sport like kayaking, aside from all it has to offer you, that choice is scoring one point for nature in a battle that, for the most part, seems quite bleak.

So our final acknowledgement is to you. Just imagine if everyone in the world had as strong a tie to her liquid gold as you have or will soon have... the world would be a better place.

INTRODUCTION TO KAYAKING

For newcomers to the sport, the first thing to know is that all you need to become a kayaker and to keep improving are a good attitude and a healthy appetite for fun. Contrary to what is commonly believed, this is not just a fringe activity reserved for adrenaline junkies, testosterone-laden extremists, and suicidal risk-takers with nothing to lose. If you're already doing it (in a controlled environment with relatively sane people), you'll probably agree. Let it be known, however, that any paddler would be lying if he said he didn't enjoy the ego boost consistently afforded to him as wide-eyed onlookers stand stupefied by the execution of such awesome manoeuvres that must have taken years to learn (not)! Anyhow, it's important to dispel this myth of extremism at the outset, because it has kept far too many people (young and old) from discovering the hidden treasures awaiting them on the water. Let the truth be known that kayaking is PURE FUN! The reality is that you can learn to do it in a short period of time, and continue doing it safely for as long as you're mobile. Whether you're new to paddling or are already on your way, know that this something you will enjoy for a long, long time!

For you paddlers, a few words about progression, conceptual understanding, and keeping it fun. Now that you're self-sufficient out there, it's time to ask yourself if you're content to just sit back and cruise. One of the most wonderful things about paddling is that it doesn't let up; an endlessly rewarding learning process lies in store for paddlers of all kinds who are keen to take it on. We've dedicated much of our teaching careers to elevating paddlers (actually, to helping paddlers elevate themselves) out of their "intermediate ruts" and into the world of advanced techniques. The foundation is in

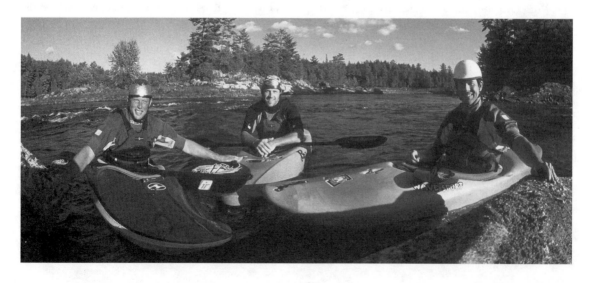

discovering and truly understanding the concepts upon which the advanced skills are based. From here, it's a matter of practising the right exercises and staying focused on the basics as you push your own personal envelope. Most importantly, however, make your way through this process without expecting to conquer the world in a day! A lifetime of paddling awaits you, and the real measure of success after each paddle is how much fun you had!

The past decade has been full of exciting changes and growth for whitewater paddling. Paralleling its close cousins, skiing and snowboarding, this growth has fuelled technological advances in equipment design, which have made it much easier, more comfortable, and more fun to progress, regardless of your shape or size. While this has led to substantial leaps in terms of what can be done in a kayak, it has also made the sport much easier for beginners to learn. Alongside this progress we are quickly evolving in both the analysis and instruction of techniques and concepts. Kayaking is now an everyday component of phys-ed programs, summer camps, and outdoor clubs. More and more cities around the world are building paddling parks to accommodate the growing interest and demand. It also continues to branch out into increasingly specialized areas including playboating (the most popular), classic river running, creek boating, expedition paddling, competitive freestyle, slalom and downriver racing, c-boating, squirt boating, and surf kayaking—all of which we take a look at in this book.

Whitewater kayaking is much more than just a physical activity, though; any paddler you talk to will have their own version of why. However, most would agree that it's an ongoing journey with many incredible discoveries en route. It will in myriad ways challenge you, strengthen you, reward you, connect you, mystify you, and, most importantly, free you. In a shrinking world increasingly characterized by the pressures of industrialized chaos, there's much to be said for pure escapism! The act of kayaking demands 100% of you, so as you focus on your strokes, balance, edging, timing, and the constantly changing river, there is simply no space for intrusions—you are free. No cell phone, no e-mail, no "real world" stressors whatsoever—just you being with the water.

Oh, and the people you'll find yourself surrounded by—well, in our experience, they're okay, too. You may find yourself hanging out with a schoolteacher or a fourteen-year-old student, with a young doctor or a retired farmer, with a mother of three, or maybe someone just like you. The thing is, when you run into one of these people in the real world, whether they know you or not, you share something very special that industrialization can never touch.

There is only one way to arrive at the place you are now and you think to yourself, "Please just let this last a little longer!" Then again, you'll inevitably find that the days that you paddle, the rest of your world seems a little brighter. So get out there and try it, but be warned—addiction rates are extremely high and we accept no liability for the ensuing consequences!

ABOUT THE AUTHORS

KEN WHITING

During the summer of 1989, Ken picked up a kayak paddle for the first time. He was fourteen years old at the time, and was taking a five-day kayaking course on the Ottawa River. Little did Ken know that this week of paddling would set the course of his life. Four years later he postponed his plans for university and satisfied his need to play by travelling, paddling, and working as a raft guide in Australia. Ken's addiction to whitewater only grew from this experience.

In 1994, Ken's competitiveness broke through the surface as he began frequenting, and winning, freestyle competitions across the continent. Three years later, in 1997, he reached his ultimate goal by winning the World Freestyle Kayaking Championships. Winning the World's was a major turning point in Ken's life, as shortly afterwards he made the decision to develop a career within the whitewater industry that he loved so much. In 1998, Ken wrote and published 'The Playboater's Handbook', a reference for freestyle kayaking technique. Following the great success of the book, Ken teamed up with Chris Emerick, a talented American videographer, and began producing instructional videos as well. To this point,

Ken has produced six best-selling and award-winning instructional kayaking books and videos, including his latest releases 'Playboating with Ken Whiting', 'Whitewater Kayaking with Ken Whiting', and 'The Playboater's Handbook 2'.

Ken's projects also provide him with a great means of exploring different parts of the world. He has paddled on well over 200 different rivers in fifteen different countries, including Japan, Honduras, Guatemala, Chile, Peru, Argentina, New Zealand, and Australia, as well as throughout Europe and North America. Nowadays, Ken and his beloved wife Nicole live in the small, rural town of Beachburg, only minutes from the put-in to the Ottawa River. Every winter, they head down to Chile's Futaleufu Valley to escape the great Canadian cold.

Ken has clearly become one of the most influential whitewater paddlers in the world, and was recognized so by Paddler Magazine as one of their "Paddlers of the Century." He continues to develop industry-leading instructional tools, and is a contributing editor to a wide variety of outdoor/paddlesports magazines. Ken teaches with one of the world's premier kayak schools, Liquid Skills, and with Kayak Futaleufu, running kayak trips in Chile. For more info on Ken's latest activities, visit www.playboat.com.

KEVIN VARETTE

Originally from Ottawa, Ontario, Kevin Varette currently lives with his family just a short walk from the rapids of the Ottawa River, where he grew up paddling from the age of fourteen. He is one of Canada's foremost kayak instructors and a founding partner of both Liquid Skills kayak school and Kayak Futaleufu vacations.

A five-time member of Canada's National Freestyle Team, including the top Canadian finish at the 2001 World Championships in Spain, Kevin's unique capacity for working with others is combined with world-class skills and experience. He has paddled, competed, and guided around the globe, including the U.S., Central America, South America, Africa, New Zealand, and Australia. Since 2000, he has been spending his summers teaching at Liquid Skills and his winters guiding for Kayak Futaleufu in Patagonia, Chile.

Kevin initiated a coaching program for Canada's juniors in 2001, has sat as Freestyle Chair for Whitewater Ontario, has taught countless volunteer clinics, has written many instructional articles and has contributed to the sport in myriad ways throughout his career. Along with his fiancée, Tagget, and children, Noa (seven), Lucie (three) and their latest (and last!) creation, Finn (three months), Kevin plans on remaining a fixture on the Ottawa River for the foreseeable future.

Outside of kayaking, he has a degree in psychology, a diploma in Adventure Tourism, a certificate in Life Coaching, several certifications in mountain guiding, and is starting a Masters degree in physiotherapy in September 2004. Kayaking has been a fundamental part of his life and his passion is to share everything the sport has to offer with as many people as he can.

CONTRIBUTORS

Tao Berman

It's hard to think about extreme kayaking without considering Tao Berman. With three world waterfall running records, and countless first descents, Tao has pushed the limits of extreme kayaking more than anyone. His accomplishments don't end there. He is also one of the best freestyle kayakers in the world, and has won a number of major competitions to prove it, including the 2002 Pre World Freestyle Championships in Austria. This extraordinary combination of nerve and skill has placed Tao in a class of his own. For more information about Tao and his latest activities, visit www.taoberman.com.

Anna Levesque

Anna Levesque is the producer of the celebrated whitewater kayaking instructional video for women, Girls at Play. The World Freestyle medallist, five-time Canadian Freestyle team member, and Nike ACG athlete works to promote women in kayaking by teaching women's clinics and leading women's paddling trips abroad. To learn more about Anna and women in kayaking go to www.watergirlsatplay.com.

Dunbar Hardy

Dunbar Hardy is a co-owner and lead instructor of Tarkio Kayak Adventures (www.teamtarkio.com) based in Missoula, Montana. He is also an accomplished freelance photographer and writer, as well as a senior contributor for Kayak Session Magazine. Dunbar is recognized as one of the most experienced and accomplished expedition paddlers/leaders in the world. He has participated in first descents and expeditions in such places as Mexico, Honduras, Guatemala, Costa Rica, Panama, Venezuela, Ecuador, Peru, Chile, Argentina, New Zealand, Nepal, Bhutan, Morocco, Italy, France, Switzerland, and Russia. Dunbar is currently working on a book of his travels and paddling adventures from around the world. For more information on Dunbar's activities, visit www.dunbarhardy.com.

Brendan Mark

As the 2003 World Squirtboating Champion, and a long-time kayaking instructor, Brendan Mark was the obvious choice to write the squirtboating segment of this book. Still a committed athlete, Brendan spends his summer months bouncing around North America, visiting competitions, festivals, and teaching clinics for the Liquid Skills Kayak School. Brendan has also been an innovator of whitewater kayaking instructional techniques, introducing squirtboats as a highly effective means for teaching general paddling and playboating techniques. For more information on what Brendan is up to, visit www.trickywhu.com.

Phil DeRiemer

Phil DeRiemer is a renowned whitewater professional, with over twenty years of experience teaching, guiding, and exploring from a kayak. For four of those years he lived between rivers, his truck, and a storage shed. This itinerant lifestyle made him an obvious choice to write the section about self-contained trips. His knowledge and experience on the topic stems from numerous self-contained adventures, including a traverse of Baffin Island, Peru's Paucartambo River, an early self-supported trip on the Grand Canyon of the Stikine, and explorations in the Sierra Nevada mountains near his home in California. He and his wife Mary are owners of DeRiemer Adventure Kayaking, offering kayaking trips in the U.S. and abroad. www.adventurekayaking.com

Mary Hayes DeRiemer

Mary Hayes DeRiemer is a renowned kayaker with a unique ability to communicate her passion for the sport and technical wizardry to others. She has been teaching kayaking since 1982 and has been leading international kayaking trips for almost as long. Mary currently leads kayaking trips in Ecuador, the Grand Canyon, the Rogue River in Oregon, and the Middle Fork of the Salmon in Idaho. She teaches for DeRiemer Kayaking, which she and her husband started in 1993. Mary is also a contributing writer for Canoe and Kayak Magazine, and an American Canoe Association instructor/trainer educator. For more information about Mary and DeRiemer Kayaking, visit www.adventurekayaking.com.

Paul Mason

Paul Mason is the son and former paddling partner of the late Bill Mason. Paul is a diehard openboater, and hopes his paddling buddies will still speak to him after drawing all these kayaks. As a freelance cartoonist, Paul has created artwork for a variety of applications including: educational posters, comic strips, editorial cartoons, murals, books, and his popular personal commemorative cartoons. See more of Paul's work at redcanoes.ca.

Paul Villecourt

Paul Villecourt is a French photographer and whitewater paddler who is dedicated to capturing the sensations of adventure and outdoor sports. His passion for whitewater has taken him and his camera to all corners of the world. Paul is regarded as one of the finest whitewater photographers in the world, and his work has been published in virtually every outdoor magazine in Europe and North America. For more info, visit www.outdoor-reporter.com.

GETTING STARTED

Because whitewater kayaking is a technical sport with specialized equipment and some inherent risks, we highly recommend learning through a reputable kayak school or club. There are too many stories of people going out for their first time with friends and getting scared or frustrated when they should really be leaving that experience craving the next, and confident in their ability to succeed. This book provides you with the most cutting edge instructional techniques and concepts that will serve as invaluable references as you progress, but it's not a replacement for on-water instruction. There's no shortage of kayak schools, paddling clubs, associations, and organizations available to help get you started. By using the Internet, asking at retail stores, or even going to a local river, you should have no trouble getting going on the right path.

I THINK KEN MEANS PADDLING EQUIPMENT.

F. Mason

1

EQUIPMENT

**TOOLS OF THE TRADE • THE KAYAK • PADDLE
PERSONAL GEAR • ACCESSORIES**

"No matter what anyone tells you, try before you buy." (Jeff Strano)

TOOLS OF THE TRADE

As with any physical activity, your body is your most important tool. The healthier, stronger and more flexible you are, the more you'll be able to accomplish. This doesn't mean that you need to be Arnold Schwarzenegger or that whitewater kayaking is necessarily a high-impact sport. In fact, it's amazing how far good technique will get you. In the same breath, power and flexibility will pave the way to getting the most out of your kayak. It should go without saying that warming up and stretching are invaluable ways of keeping the body healthy. Unfortunately, many paddlers completely ignore their lower bodies. The lower body is actually just as important as the upper body to warm up for a day on the water. In particular, tight hips will impede your boat tilts, and tight hamstrings can dramatically

Keeping your body strong and flexible will improve your paddling and make your time in a kayak much more comfortable.

affect your ability to lean forward. Keeping your body strong and limber will definitely help improve your paddling, but it will also make sitting in a small kayak a lot more comfortable.

Like many outdoor sports, kayaking requires an initial investment of specialized equipment, and there are retail stores, outfitters, and on-line forums packed with stuff to sell you. In terms of performance, your boat and paddle are the two pieces that are key to make informed decisions about. The rest of the gear is to keep you safe, comfortable, and functional. In general, though, you are best off to try out whatever equipment you can before buying. Let's have a look . . .

THE KAYAK

KAYAK ANATOMY

Hull and deck: The bottom and top of the kayak.

Bow and stern: The front and back portions of the kayak.

Cockpit: The hole through which a paddler enters the kayak.

Grab loops: The loops at the bow and stern ends that are used for carrying the kayak and for towing swimmers.

Security bars: Metal bars that are permanently attached to the kayak just in front and just behind the cockpit. These are the strongest points on the kayak and get used for rescues, or when locking a kayak up.

Foot pegs/bulkhead: Adjustable foot support systems in the bow of the kayak.

Thigh hooks: Contoured pieces of plastic that support the upper leg and provide the leverage from which to rock the kayak back and forth.

Back band: An adjustable support for the lower back.

Support wall: A wall of foam that provides structural support, and runs vertically, separating the kayak into two equal halves.

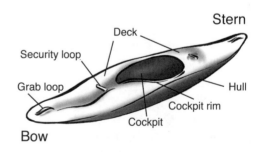

2

Drain plug: A screwable plug that provides an easy way of letting water out of the kayak.

Sidewalls: The sides of the kayak, between the hull and the deck.

What are Kayaks Made of?

For a long time, whitewater kayaks were made only of cloth and resin (commonly referred to as "composite" materials). Composite kayaks are made with layers of fibreglass, Kevlar or graphite cloth, glued together and stiffened by resin. These composite kayaks are very strong and light. The only downside is that if they were to hit a rock hard enough, they would crack. It was for this reason that there was much excitement when the first plastic kayak hit the market in 1970. Since that time, plastic has been the material of choice for recreational whitewater kayaks, although it is still possible to find some composite boats on the market. Plastic (polyethylene) kayaks are incredibly durable, long lasting, and relatively cheap to produce in comparison to composite boats. When they hit rocks hard, they may dent, but will seldom break. These dents will usually pop out after a little time spent in the sun.

BOAT DESIGN AND SELECTION

The days of long, skinny kayaks shaped like logs with a hole carved into the top of them are gone, and along with them the

performance characteristics that a log offers! Boat design is now a sophisticated process that makes use of professional designers, athletes, flashy software

The Dancer (on the left) was once the most popular introductory kayak. Nowadays, paddlers are learning in kayaks almost half the length. These kayaks allow paddlers to progress at astonishing speeds.

packages with digital simulations, and multi-prototype trial runs. Today's boats are shorter (from 1.5m to 3m, or 5 ft to 9 ft), wider (about 40 cm, or 25 in), flat-hulled, and far more thoroughly outfitted than their predecessors. These fundamental changes have afforded the paddler with substantially increased manoeuvrability, stability, and control.

Rocker

Rocker is the curvature from bow to stern, as viewed from the side. As a general rule, the more rocker a kayak has, the more quickly it will turn. It will also travel through rapids more easily and surf waves with greater ease because the ends won't get caught by the incoming water.

Rocker is the curvature of a kayak's hull from bow to stern, as viewed from the side.

Hull Shapes

Planing Hulls: These are flat hulls that create a very wide footprint in the water. They are the most common form of kayak hull because they are the most stable, and surf waves incredibly well. The edges of the "planing" hull are bevelled up to the sidewalls at varying angles of aggressiveness. The more bevel, the "softer" the edge, and

therefore the more forgiving and less tippy the boat will be when its side is exposed to the current.

Displacement Hulls: These are rounded hulls. These were once the standard for whitewater kayaks, but have been largely replaced by the preferred planing hull. Displacement hulls track most effectively and are easily tilted on edge, but they aren't as stable or as manoeuvrable as planing hulls.

Boats designed specifically for playboating (surfing and performing various other acrobatics) will typically be shorter, have wider planing hulls, larger sidewalls, and more aggressive edges to maximize performance and manoeuvrability. These boats will also tend to have less volume in the bow and stern to allow the ends of the boat to be forced under water easily when desired. Boats designed for more all-around river running are typically a bit longer for increased speed. They also have narrower hulls that carve a better track in the water, more bevelled (and therefore forgiving)

Playboats (left) have wider, flatter hulls and more aggressive edges, while more all-around boats have narrower hulls, more rounded edges (right).

Cost

New boats typically range from about US $850–$1200. The used boat market is substantial, so it's fairly easy to find discounted prices at retail stores, on-line forums, kayak schools, or around local paddling spots. One thing to consider is that as boats come with increasing amounts of design and outfitting features, there are more things to look out for when purchasing previously owned models. Buyer beware!

edges, and more volume in the ends (to prevent them from submerging). As you can see, your intended use for the boat is important in making a choice.

One of the most remarkable areas of progress in design has been the inside of the boats. Specially contoured and adjustable seats, thigh hooks, foot braces, and lower back support systems have become the norm in all new models. It used to take us so long to outfit boats with mini-cell foam, a grater and sloppy cement that we'd have a party and make an evening out of it! Today, you can unwrap your boat, make some minor adjustments, and paddle away—too easy!

In concept, the snugger you are, the more responsive the boat will be to your every movement and the better your posture will be. In reality, there's a comfort/control tradeoff and everyone has their limits. You will figure out your own soon enough!

PICKING A BOAT

"When choosing a boat, the first thing you should ask yourself is, 'What type of boating do I really want to do?'" (Shane Benedict)

Now that you're aware of the basic design features, it's time to get out there and test-drive. If you're just starting, you'll want to take lessons; while you're there, ask your instructors for advice and, most importantly, try out different boats. Manufacturers now produce most models in a variety of sizes so you shouldn't have too much trouble getting relatively comfortable in one. The decision should be made based on the following factors: your intended use for the boat, your size and weight, your comfort level in the boat, your budget, and any personal preferences. Remember that you will be improving fairly quickly, so pick a boat that has at least some features you will appreciate as your skill level progresses. Many retail stores or outfitters will allow you to rent a boat as a demo and then allocate the rental cost toward the purchase if you're still keen. By doing this, you maximize your trial time and will have made the most informed decision possible. Good luck!

THE PADDLE

In whitewater kayaking, the paddle becomes an extension of your upper body, so the most logical choice is to use one that feels good to you. Designs vary slightly, but the general anatomy of paddles is the same. The two blades are attached to a shaft that can be straight or bent in various ways. The blades may be symmetrical or asymmetrical in shape, but all have a slightly concave power (front) face and a non-power (back) face.

The most influential factor in choosing a paddle is your size. You need to consider the length of the paddle, the width of the shaft, and the size of the blades. Smaller paddlers should look for a paddle with slightly smaller blades and with a narrower shaft that makes it easier to grip. The stronger you are, the larger the paddle blades you will be able to control. Using a paddle that is too long or too large will cost you some control and could put an undue amount of stress on your body.

Paddles are conventionally measured in centimetres. In general, a paddle 196–200 cm in length is good for paddlers between 5'8" and 6'1". For paddlers between 5'3" and 5'8", a paddle 192–196 cm in length should work great.

Next, you'll need to consider the offset of your blades. The offset, or "twist," refers to the difference in angles between the two blades. Traditional kayak paddles have blades that are offset at ninety degrees so that as one blade pulls through the water, the other slices efficiently through the air. For whitewater kayaking, a thirty- or forty-five-degree twist is most popular. Many of us are even using paddles with no offset at all! A lower offset means less repetitive twisting of the wrist, which can help prevent tendonitis and can facilitate some moves.

Paddles come in a variety of materials, ranging from aluminum and plastic to fibreglass and carbon fibre. Finding the right one for you is a personal choice that depends on your budget and weight preference. Durability is also a concern, so we would recommend staying away from aluminum for whitewater paddling.

Cost

The range of dependable paddles have price tags in the neighbourhood of US $150 to $400.

Paddle blades can be offset very differently. The offset, or 'twist', of a paddle ranges from between 0 and 90 degrees.

PERSONAL GEAR

Safety and comfort are the main considerations when choosing your personal gear. Of course, style is always a factor, but gear manufacturers are pretty in tune with the times. You're likely to find yourself in a variety of paddling and weather conditions, so our general advice is to shop comparatively, but to buy good gear. It will go a long way towards making your paddling experiences safer and more enjoyable, particularly in cold conditions.

HELMETS

Helmets are available in plastic and composite materials (such as fibreglass and Kevlar), and a variety of designs ranging from aesthetically plain to off-the-wall. You want to be sure that the helmet you buy is sturdy and shaped so that it protects your forehead and temples. Give it a good squeeze on its sides to gauge its sturdiness. It also needs to fit snugly enough so that it won't move around on your head, especially when upside down in whitewater. They'll often require a little

fine-tuning of the inner foam lining to provide this comfortably snug fit, and will usually come with foam inserts that can be attached to do so. Another consideration is the sun protection factor that the helmet offers, as the river is a great place to get fried. Many helmets have brims that do a reasonable job of keeping your face safe. Cost: US $50 to $200.

PFDS

Needless to say, your personal flotation device is an essential piece of safety equipment, so be sure to go for a quality product. Manufacturers have struck an appealing balance between flotation and low-profile designs that don't obstruct movement by keeping the bulkiest part of the PFD low on the torso, away from the shoulders and upper chest. Specialized rescue vests offer a releasable harness system and various other safety features that are recommended for more advanced river running (see the "Rescue" segment of this book). Talk to someone at the store who has been trained in Coast Guard Approval Ratings, and read the labels inside the PFDs so you're informed about what you are buying. Paddling "vests" are not rated as "life preservers"—this is to say that they are not designed to float your head above the surface when you're unconscious. They do offer various amounts of flotation; at least fifteen pounds of buoyancy is a common recommendation for the average person. Cost: US $75 to $250

SPRAY SKIRT

The spray skirt is responsible for sealing off the cockpit of your kayak and keeping water out of your boat as you paddle. This is a pretty important job, so when shopping for a spray skirt, you should be looking for one that is comfortable, effectively keeps water out, stays on, and will last. Most companies now offer them with a reinforced layer around the outside of the skirt, where the cockpit rim puts the greatest stress on the material.

A Kevlar-reinforced skirt is a bit more expensive, but you'll find it lasts much

longer. A stiff rubber "rand" (the part that tucks under the cockpit rim) will stay on much better than an elastic bungee cord, but make sure that it is not so stiff that you have trouble putting it on or taking it off. On the other hand, we are now finding that bungee cord rands are more effective at keeping water out of some cockpits. This is another reason to try out as many different skirts, and ask as many questions, as you can. Another thing to check out is whether the seams have been taped on the inside and outside for a better seal. Finally, make sure you pick a size that is snug around your waist—it will stretch! Cost: US $75 to $200.

DRESSING FOR WARM CONDITIONS

Some people are lucky enough to actually have to find ways to "deal" with warm temperatures! Most often, the dilemma is how to keep water out of the boat while staying cool and protected from the sun. It's best to have some form of light short-sleeved under layer and either a "shorty" splash top or dry top outer layer. Shorts of any kind are fine for the lower body.

There is a variety of specialized materials designed for paddling now. Lightweight polypropylene (available in many brand names and styles) is the classic under layer, but there is now an assortment of other pieces to choose from, such as rash guards and fuzzy rubbers. To keep water out of your boat, your best bet is some type of splash top or even a short-sleeved dry top. Short-sleeved dry tops can be quite warm on a hot summer day, but they do a great job of

A short sleeve 'spash top' keeps water out of the boat, while keeping you cool and protected from the sun.

a short sleeve rash guard works great under a short sleeve 'splash top'.

neoprene are available in both short-sleeved and long-sleeved tops and bottoms (as it gets colder, you'll want to start covering your legs). For an even warmer layer, micro fleece tops are available in all sorts of thicknesses. Layering is always the best option as it allows you to fine-tune your temperature throughout the day. In other words, as a general rule, wear more than is necessary as you are much better off being too warm than too cold. Being cold on the river will zap your energy, your enthusiasm, and your ability to enjoy your paddle. Cost: US $40 to $120.

keeping the water out and letting you play uninterrupted for longer. Cost: Rash Guards: US $40–$85; Shorty Splash Tops and Dry Tops: US $50–$300.

DRESSING FOR COLD CONDITIONS

"A good dry top is worth its weight in gold if you are in a cooler environment. Staying warm is just as important as a pfd or a helmet." (James Mole)

Under Layers: As with under layers for any outdoor sport, it's preferable to have a material that wicks moisture away from the skin, as opposed to absorbing it and holding it against you. As mentioned above, various blends of lightweight polypropylene, polyester, spandex and

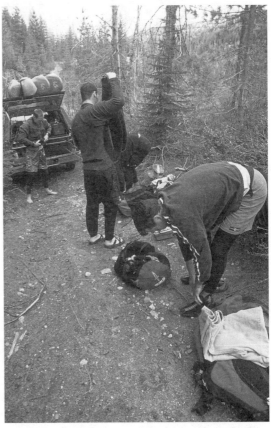

Getting ready for an early spring day of paddling.

9

Outer Layers: Long-sleeved splash tops or pants and dry tops or pants are most effective in cold conditions. They are constructed using different thicknesses of rip-stop nylon with various types of breathable or non-breathable water-resistant treatments. Dry tops and dry pants have tight latex or neoprene gaskets at the wrists, ankles, and neck to prevent water entry.

A long sleeve dry top has latex gaskets on the wrists and at the neck to keep you warm and dry.

Because latex wears quickly in the sun, the gaskets should be protected by other material. You can cut rings off the gaskets along pre-marked lines to customize the fit, but be careful, as they rip easily. Use a sharp knife or pair of scissors and avoid nicking the gasket. Remember, the material will stretch a little and you can always make another cut, so don't go too big too fast! Gaskets can be replaced by gluing a new one on if the need ever arose. You can find them in some retail stores; or order them directly from the manufacturer. The seams of dry tops and pants should be taped for the best seal. For the absolute driest and warmest day on the river,

consider a dry suit. They don't come cheap, but they provide an unrivalled level of comfort on even the coldest and wettest days. Cost: Tops: US $65–$300; Pants: US $65–$250; Dry suit: US $500–$1000.

ACCESSORIES

Nose plugs—great little pieces of gear that can make life a lot more pleasant for some paddlers. By preventing water from shooting unmercifully through the sinuses, you'll not only save yourself a running nose for the following few days, but you'll probably find yourself much more relaxed when underwater, which can make a big difference when going for a roll! Be sure to get specialized kayaking plugs that won't come off. Cost: US $5 to $10.

Nose plugs may not be the most flattering piece of equipment, but they can save you some real discomfort.

Earplugs—always a great idea, as they will help prevent ear infections and the longer-term issue of exotosis, which is the closing of the eardrum in response to cold water shock. There are now earplugs on the market with small holes or valves that allow you to hear quite clearly while keeping all water out. Cost: US $6 to $50.

River shoes or booties—it's always important to wear a good pair of water shoes that provide traction on wet rocks. Not only do they keep your feet warm and serve as protection to you both in and out of your kayak, they will allow you to move around quickly on shore to help others if the need ever arises. Cost: US $50 to $100.

Sunglasses—if you plan on spending a significant amount of time on the water, then you'll want to invest in a good pair of sunglasses. The reflection of the sun off the water is intensified and can be very damaging to the eyes. Make sure that your glasses are attached to you so they won't fall off. Some companies now make sunglasses specially designed for sports like kayaking. Cost: US $20 to $200.

ACCESSORIES FOR COLD CONDITIONS

Pogies, mitts or gloves—to keep your hands warm. Pogies are hand covers (if you see nylon ones, don't buy them) that attach by Velcro onto the paddle shaft. Gloves and mitts tend to be a little warmer, while pogies allow your hands to be in direct contact with the paddle. People stand behind all three, so try them out! Cost: US $15 to $50.

Skull cap—a thin, insulating layer that fit under your helmet. Since we lose such a relatively large amount of body heat from our head, this simple piece of gear can have a huge impact on your comfort level on the river, and is never a bad idea to bring along in cooler conditions. Cost: US $20 to $35.

Some people would argue that it's never too cold to paddle; you just need the right gear.

(2)

BEFORE HITTING THE WATER

THE MENTAL GAME • CUSTOMIZING YOUR KAYAK • CARRYING YOUR BOAT
GETTING IN AND OUT • PUTTING ON YOUR SKIRT • USING YOUR PADDLE

*"Only half of kayaking has to do with hard skills. The other half is mental,
and your mental state is controlled by your level of confidence."* (Tao Berman)

THE MENTAL GAME

We were taught early on that good paddling technique is as important as having strong paddling muscles. What we weren't taught right away is that kayaking is as much a mental game as it is a physical one, and that in order to improve you need to develop both of these elements. Since you're reading this, you have already shown the mental capacity to be a great paddler, because at some point you made the decision to explore a sport that is falsely considered by many to be reckless and dangerous. Whether you're already paddling or just getting into the sport, you've probably already learned that whitewater kayaking is like any other outdoor adventure sport in that it can be as dangerous and exciting, or as relaxed and enjoyable, as you choose it to be.

The mental game is a dynamic and unique attribute of this sport. Early on, you need to teach yourself to do many things that are counter-instinctual, such as keeping your head down while rolling, getting more aggressive as the current gets stronger, and using rocks as your friends. As your mental game improves, your confidence could progress more quickly than your actual physical skills. This of course can result in poor decisions that create dangerous situations. On the other hand, you may end up with skill sets that surpass your mental game. It's a lot easier to gauge where your physical skills are, but it's very important that you take the time to consider how your mental game is doing. Remember that the goal is to have fun with one of Mother Nature's most incredible natural playgrounds. How you do that is a very personal thing and should not be dictated by how others feel.

CUSTOMIZING YOUR KAYAK

As a general rule, your boat should fit like a good pair of shoes: snug yet comfortable. Let's take a closer look at how you should be sitting in your kayak, along with some outfitting considerations that will give you the most control and comfort in your boat. When sitting in your kayak, your legs should be in front of you with your knees bent and legs splayed out and under the thigh hooks. Your feet should be resting comfortably against their supports. When sitting upright like this on the water, your kayak should be "trimmed out," which means that the bow and stern should be equally out of the water. If you find your

stern is lower in the water, you'll need to move yourself forward in your kayak by sliding the seat forward and/or tightening the back band slightly. If you find your bow is lower in the water, or that you're short on foot room, you'll need to move the seat backwards slightly or loosen the back band.

The outfitting of your kayak will have a large impact on both your control and your comfort in your boat. When outfitting a kayak, you need to consider the support that is provided to your feet, legs, butt, hips, and lower back.

Foot Supports

Depending on the model of your kayak, it will have either foot pegs, a movable bulkhead, or a foam bulkhead system.

Foot pegs are small plates that slide forward and backward along a track to accommodate different leg lengths. These are the most easily adjusted form of foot support, although sand has a tendency to get caught in the track, making their adjustment more difficult over time. The downside of foot pegs is that they provide a smaller platform to push on and with any serious head-on impact this can easily result in broken toes or even ankles. They also offer more potential for your feet to get temporarily stuck while trying to exit.

A movable bulkhead is a wall of plastic that slides forward and backward and then gets locked into place. There are a number of different bulkhead systems available. Playboats will often have a bulkhead system that focuses on providing your heels with support, whereas river runners or creekboats will often have a bulkhead that provides support for the whole foot. Movable bulkheads are the safest and most reliable form of foot support and can be customized for comfort with foam.

Foam bulkheads are basically chunks of foam that are stuffed into the bow of the kayak, creating a wall of support for your feet. Foam bulkheads can be quite comfortable and aren't a bad option. The downside is that the foam does compress, which means that the fitting will become looser over time and will require adjustments. This compressed foam can also have the effect of pushing out the plastic in the bow of your kayak, which sometimes creates additional volume in the end, where you won't need or want it.

Leg Supports

Your legs should fit comfortably under the thigh hooks with even pressure across your thigh. Most thigh hooks can now be adjusted to fit a wide range of leg girth and length, but older outfitting will require some customized padding. Though it is most important that your thigh hooks provide your legs with a surface to squeeze against for support and to pull up against for edging, it's also very important that your legs are supported from the outside and from underneath. This outside support provides additional control and helps reduce hip discomfort.

Butt Support

There's no doubt that your butt is one of the most padded parts of your body, but this doesn't mean that it won't appreciate a little tender loving care. Many seats now come equipped with seat padding, but if yours doesn't, then placing a quarter inch of mini-cell foam on your seat will make for a much more comfortable day on the water. Some paddlers who are short in the torso will glue considerably more foam to their seat to raise their centre of gravity and give themselves more control over their edging. This can be very helpful for some, but beware that you don't raise yourself too high, as this will make you very tippy.

Back Support

Back support is absolutely critical for both comfort and performance. Back bands are by and large the most functional and effective systems and should be used in any kayak. The back band should fit above your hips and be tightened enough to prevent you from sliding backwards without impeding your ability to lean right back. The best back bands are those held in place with heavy-duty webbing and with rounded hardware that won't create weak points or potentially cut any of the straps.

Outfitting has come a long way over the years. Most kayaks now come with quick and easy adjusting thigh hooks, seats, hip pads, back bands and bulk heads.

Hip Support

Much of the control you have over your kayak stems from the hips, so it's vital that they're well supported. It's also very important that your hips aren't being squeezed too tightly, as this can cause your legs to fall asleep or just be downright painful. Your hip padding should be snug enough to prevent your butt from sliding from side to side, but no tighter. It's also very helpful if your hip pads cup over your hips and upper thighs, providing some support from above. This provides additional edge control over your kayak and helps keep your butt from falling out of the seat when you're upside down. Of course, you need to be sure that your hip support still allows an easy escape from the kayak if needed. Generally, if you can get into your kayak without too much effort, then you can be almost sure that you'll be able to get out more easily when the need arises and the adrenaline is flowing.

Some other things that you might want to make a permanent feature in your boat are a sponge to remove any water from your kayak, and a screwdriver that will allow you to tighten the screws on your kayak or make any small adjustment to your outfitting.

CARRYING YOUR BOAT

Carrying your boat is a bit of an art form! First off, bend your knees when you lift up the boat. They are light enough that it's tempting to just reach down for them, but heavy enough to do some lower back damage.

One way to carry the boat is by resting the inside of the cockpit rim on your shoulder and holding onto it with the same hand for control. Keep your PFD on for some shoulder padding, especially for long carries.

Other cultures have taught us to carry boats on our heads as well. This is achieved by turning the boat backwards and adjusting its angle so that the back band rests comfortably on your forehead. Again, one hand can be used to balance the boat while the other carries gear.

You can also throw some teamwork into the mix. Having one person at either end holding onto the grab-loops, with the gear thrown into the cockpits, makes for quite a civilized carry.

Finally, if you have to carry your boat for any major distance, you may want to try a specialized carrier that lets you throw your kayak on your back like a pack.

GETTING IN AND OUT

Kayaks are relatively small spaces, so getting in and out of them is best achieved using technique and not just brute force. The key is to keep your legs straight for as long as possible as you are sliding in. Once you are in far enough, drop one knee at a time under their respective thigh hooks. This should allow your legs to bend outward enough that your butt can drop down into the seat. Getting out is actually much easier. With your hands on the sides

Using your paddle as a brace on shore is a good method of getting out on a rocky shoreline.

of the cockpit at about your hips, push down and back. Keeping your legs straight, you should be able to slide them right out of the boat. If you're having trouble with either technique, try temporarily pushing the foot braces forward or loosening off the back band to create more room.

The river environment will frequently throw a twist into things; realistically it won't be often that you're getting in and out on a nice sandy beach! You'll learn a few of your own tricks as you gain experience, but here are some general tips that may help you.

When getting in or out while the boat is in the water, don't sit too far back on the boat—it will inevitably sink the stern and foil your attempt. In some situations, you can use the paddle as a brace by placing it perpendicular to the boat with one blade on shore and the shaft resting behind the cockpit. This works well when the water is not fluctuating much, but can be frustrating if it is! A common choice on the river is to

The best place to get in your boat is on a flat, stable rock from which you can then slide into the water.

17

find a friendly looking rock as close as possible to the water to launch from. The same applies for getting out: try to find a rock that you can either slide up onto slightly (backwards is easiest) or brace your paddle upon. Get out quickly, remembering to keep your legs straight and your weight as forward as possible. As soon as you manage to get one foot out and on solid ground, the rest of the process gets a whole lot easier.

PUTTING ON YOUR SKIRT

Today's skirts, particularly those with a Kevlar-reinforced trim and a stiff rubber rand, can be hard to put on. The best technique is to start at the back of the cockpit. Make sure the rand is tucked securely under the cockpit rim behind you, and then tuck it in a little further out towards the sides to make sure it will stay put when you go for the big push. Once it's secure at the back, grab the front of the

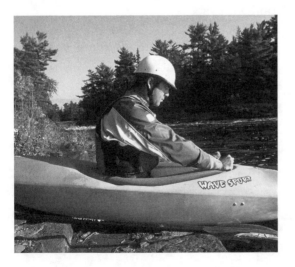

skirt with both hands and stretch it out over the front of the cockpit rim with what will likely take a big grunt. As you do this, make sure the grab loop remains outside of the boat! Once the front is latched, work one hand down each side to tuck in the rest of the rand. Skirts vary in size and stiffness, but they all take some effort to get on. It can be tough at first, but you'll get used to it! One trick that tends to help is wetting the skirt before getting in. This seems to soften up the neoprene, making it a bit more flexible.

USING YOUR PADDLE

As we mentioned earlier, the paddle evolves into an extension of your arms and is probably the piece of gear you'll become most intimate with. You're more likely to go through a few boats than you are to change paddles, especially once you've found your match. We've already discussed how to choose a paddle, so now let's look at how to use it.

First of all, being left- or right-handed has an important impact on your paddling, as it dictates which is your control hand. Quite simply, for a right-handed paddler, the control hand is the right; for a left-handed paddler, the control hand is the left. Having said this, it's becoming increasingly more common for all paddlers to learn with right-handed control paddles. The reason for this is simple: left-handed control paddles are very uncommon, so finding a replacement is highly unlikely in the event that you

For a right-handed control paddle, the right hand is the control hand and stays glued to the paddle. The left hand is the "greased" hand and loosens up between strokes to allow the shaft to rotate within it.

break, forget, or lose your paddle. Your "control" hand is the hand which grips the shaft firmly at all times, which is why we also call it the "glue" hand. This control hands grip should never change. This applies to paddling, bracing, rolling, playboating and running waterfalls. It's your reference point for how the paddle will react and you need to be able to rely on it automatically. After taking a stroke with the blade closest to this control hand, loosen your grip with the opposite hand (commonly referred to as the "grease" hand) to allow the shaft to rotate within it.

This rotation is necessary to accommodate the "feather", or "twist" of your paddle, and lets you place the next blade in the water squarely. This loosening of the "grease" hand, and the rotation of the shaft within it, continues between each stroke.

The most efficient and powerful grip on the paddle is with your hands a few inches from the blades. You can check your grip both by looking out at your hands and by lifting your paddle up onto your head, where the angle that your arms are bent should be about 90 degrees. Having your hands too far out makes for very awkward strokes, while having your hands too far in toward the center will cost you substantially in the amount of force you can apply at the blades.

Most paddles will have some degree of an oval shape to the shaft at the control hand to help "index" your grip. This lets you grip your paddle correctly without having to look down at your hand. You can add to the index by taping some additional material in a position underneath the knuckles of your control hand. The oval shape of the shaft also helps to prevent the shaft from turning in your control hand. You can supplement your control hand's grip with grip tape or paddle wax.

LET'S SEE PG. 1 HOW TO KAYAK

③

ESSENTIALS

**THE WET EXIT • EMPTYING THE BOAT • THE THREE GOLDEN RULES
PADDLING POSTURE • SHOULDER SAFETY • EDGING
AN INTRODUCTION TO SPIN MOMENTUM • SKIDDING VS. CARVING
BRACING BY MARY DERIEMER**

"Bad habits only get harder to break!" (Ken Whiting)

THE WET EXIT

This is the process of exiting the boat when it flips. Getting out when upside down is actually the easiest position in which to do so, since gravity is working in your favour. In any entry level course we teach, wet exits are the first topic covered, so that students know they're not locked in the boat!

The motions are the same as getting out in other situations. Your first move is to lean forward, which will protect your face and

chest. Now pull the skirt's grab loop to break the seal between skirt and boat. You'll then drop your knees down to straighten your legs, slide your hands back alongside the cockpit rim to about your hips, lean forward and push. As you come out, you should be doing a partial front somersault. Your instinct may be to lean back and reach up to the surface with your face for a breath, but you'll quickly learn to bypass this instinct! Try leaning back in

Tucking forward, reach for your skirts grab loop.

Having pulled the grab loop and popped your skirt, place your hands out to the side of your hips to push out of the kayak.

Stay tucked forward as you push yourself out of the kayak

As you break free from the kayak, roll to the side and to the surface.

your chair now. What do you notice it does to your butt? It lifts it up. In a kayak the effect is that your thighs and knees are pushed up against the thigh hooks, which can impede your exit. The last tip (excuse the pun!) is to go slowly. This entire process will take less than five seconds and the more relaxed you are, the more smooth your exit will be.

EMPTYING THE BOAT

When emptying a boat full of water a little technique can make a big difference, but any way you slice it, emptying the boat is one of the most tiring parts of learning to paddle. First of all, getting the boat to shore can be challenging, especially when you're in moving water and/or far away. In this case, you'll likely need some help. If you're close to the bank, leave the boat upside down (where it's full of air and thus lighter) and push it to shore. Now try to get one end up out of the water. Just by raising one end, water will have drained from at least half of the boat. Take care in getting the end up on shore, especially if the boat is full, as it can be very heavy. If you have friends nearby, this may be a good time to call them forth! Now lift the lower end to dump the bulk of the water out through the cockpit. To drain the rest of the water, you can prop the centre of the boat up on your knee and rock it back and forth. If it has a drain plug then you can unscrew it and stand the boat up vertically. A sponge will also come in handy for getting the final drops out.

Propping one end of your kayak is a great means of emptying out your kayak.

EMPTYING A BOAT ON THE WATER

The boat-over-boat technique is a method of emptying a boatful of water from a kayak. It's a useful skill to have when a capsized boat is far from shore and the water isn't too rough. It involves dragging the upside down kayak over your own cockpit and rocking the boat back and forth to dump the majority of the water out. If the kayak has float bags in the stern, then it is easiest to do this by pulling the bow over your kayak first. Either way, it will certainly be useful to have the swimmer help push the boat across your kayak. Once the boat is empty, you can flip it upright and off your kayak. At this point you can tow the boat to shore or provide the swimmer with an aided re-entry, which we discuss in more detail in the rescue chapter.

Pull the upside down kayak over your cockpit.

Rock the upside down boat back and forth to empty the water.

THE THREE GOLDEN RULES

The Three Golden Rules will apply to your paddling from here on. Whether you're running your first river or surfing a huge wave, you need to separate your body movements, use the power of your torso, and maintain control of your kayak with an active blade. These three rules will serve as a checklist for you to refer back to as long as you paddle. You will notice them being applied to virtually every technique we discuss in this book. Let's have a closer look . . .

1. SEPARATE YOUR BODY MOVEMENTS

The best kayakers have mastered the art of letting their upper and lower bodies work independently of, yet cooperatively with, each other. This means there needs to be a distinct separation of movements at the hips. Early on you'll become comfortable

Separating the movements of your upper and lower body movements applies to your forward and backward leans, your lateral edging, and your upper body rotation.

with this separation as it applies to leaning forward and backward. As you progress, it will become a key ingredient of balancing your boat on edge and staying ahead of your boat as it spins.

2. USE THE POWER OF YOUR TORSO

To make the most of each stroke, you need to use much more than just your arm and shoulder muscles. Whether you're propelling the boat or turning it, your goal is to harness the power available from your entire upper body. We refer to this as torso rotation. It is the way you get your front and side (oblique) stomach muscles involved with your strokes. Using these larger muscle groups will maximize the strength of each stroke, and will improve your stamina as your efforts are spread over more muscles.

There are three components to torso rotation: the winding up of the body, the planting of a pivot blade, and the unwinding of the body. To wind up, turn your upper body at the hips in the direction you want to go. At this point, your stomach and chest should no longer face the direction that your kayak does. Once your body is wound up, plant your paddle blade completely in the water as a pivot. As you push or pull on this pivot blade, draw on your stomach muscles to force the body back to its (unwound) position of rest.

This act of using the stomach muscles to return your body to its position of rest is what we refer to as unwinding the body. One applicable analogy is that of an elastic band. The further you stretch it, the more it will sting when it makes contact! Similarly, the more you wind up, the more power you will have available to you. It would be excessive to fully wind up your body for every single stroke, but your stomach muscles should always be involved.

Using the power of your torso means winding up your upper body for strokes.

Torso rotation is also an important way of protecting your shoulders from injury. As a rule of thumb, you want to keep your hands in front of your upper body. By turning your whole torso, you can reach as far back as you want with a blade and still be in a safe position, while at the same time harnessing more power for your strokes.

3. MAINTAIN CONTROL WITH AN ACTIVE BLADE

Today's short boats are incredibly responsive. As such, they're very easy to manoeuvre, but are more susceptible to being pushed around by even the smallest river features. Whereas longer boats can cruise through waves and different currents with less effort, smaller boats don't track or maintain their speed as well. The only way to truly control them is to have an active blade in the water. This means it's important to get your next stroke in the water as soon as the one you're taking is

Unwinding your body as you push or pull on your paddle, lets you draw on the power of your stomach muscles.

Keeping an active blade in the water is the only way to be in control of your kayak.

finished. Having a blade in the water allows you to take an active role in deciding what your boat will do, rather than reacting to the things that happen to it. Keeping this rule in mind will help you paddle in a straight line, carve smooth eddy turns, punch through crashing waves, and perform increasingly advanced moves.

PADDLING POSTURE

Paddling posture refers to the different ways your body positioning can help with the control and balance of your kayak. As with most dynamic sports, posture plays an important role in paddling performance. For example, if you're familiar with skiing, you know what it feels like to stray from the proper body position. When you get caught leaning back, your weight is on the tails of the skis and you lose control. When you fall over to one side, you go into survival mode trying to recover. When your

weight is too far forward, odds are your tips dig in, or you go for a nasty yet acrobatic tumble. Similarly in kayaking, the goal is to maintain control of your centre of gravity to prevent crashing and burning. There are two aspects to paddling posture: lateral balance (edge to edge) and body position. Both rely on the first Golden Rule of upper-lower body separation.

Lateral Balance

Lateral balance involves keeping your weight over the centre of the boat and not off to one side. In flat water this is fairly straightforward, but in whitewater it requires that you be loose at the hips and allow the boat to tilt on edge without your upper body doing the same. A classic analogy of this technique is the belly dancer, who can wildly fling the hips while remaining perfectly still in the upper body. Whitewater can act in many ways to rock your boat from edge to edge, but if your

A moderately aggressive position provides the most flexibility, balance, and control.

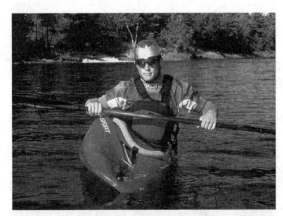

Lateral balance involves keeping your weight centered over your kayak, which means staying loose at the hips.

hips are loose and your body stays over the boat, you'll be fine. It's when you stiffen up or let your weight fall to one side that you're likely to take the plunge!

To get a feel for this while sitting in a chair, try taking your feet off the floor and leaning over onto one butt cheek. How long can you balance like this? Notice how you are bending at the waist and keeping your head over the chair to avoid falling. Now, try letting just your head tip out to the side a little. What happens?

Body Position

Body position refers to your lean along the length of the boat, again assuming separation at the hips. In this context, an aggressive position is a strong forward lean; a neutral position is sitting straight up; and a defensive position is leaning back. Acknowledging that you will inevitably spend some time recovering, the goal is to paddle as often as possible in the position that best prepares you to deal with dynamic situations. You want to sit in a position that

If you stiffen up, or let your weight (head) fall to one side, you're likely to flip.

allows you the most flexibility, balance, and control to minimize the amount of time you spend recovering. This default body position in kayaking is sitting with a moderately aggressive lean. To achieve this, sit up straight with your butt against the back band and then bend slightly forward at the hips. Pretend a rope secured to the bow of your boat was attached to your belly button and someone pulled the slack right out of it. It is not a slouch—your stomach muscles need to be turned on and ready.

The most common problem paddlers have is "getting in the back seat." When this happens, your weight shifts onto the stern edges, which causes them to sink slightly and exposes them to all the weird and wonderful effects of river currents. The back seat position also compromises your control, making it difficult to take efficient strokes or balance the boat on edge.

SHOULDER SAFETY

The shoulder dislocation is to kayaking what a blown knee is to skiing. Why is this injury so dreaded? The pain factor doesn't seem to drive the fear into paddlers' hearts; it's more the thought of having to go through surgery, of sitting idle through months of therapy, of the shoulder never again being as strong as it was. Unfortunately these are substantiated concerns, as a shoulder dislocation is often accompanied by damage to the joint that requires real care, and sometimes surgery, to heal. These are all good reasons for us to take a good look at how to keep your shoulders safe.

It goes without saying that having well-conditioned muscles around the shoulder will go a long way towards keeping the joint in place. It should be noted that paddlers often have much stronger back shoulder muscles than front, as these are the muscles used primarily for forward paddling. Seeing as the majority of shoulders dislocate forwards, your goal should be to make the front muscles equally as strong as the back. This is where back paddling practice comes in. But even with Superman's shoulders, a dislocation can easily happen, though there are two simple rules that, when followed, will go a long way towards keeping your arms intact. The first: don't overextend your arms. The second: maintain a "power position" with your arms. Let's look at both of these in more detail.

Keeping the hands clearly in front of your shoulder line keeps you in your "power position", which is safest for your shoulders.

1. The idea of not overextending your arms is a simple concept to appreciate, but it isn't always so simple to apply. When you're getting tossed around in whitewater, the desire to keep your head above the water can easily override any safe paddling practices. Try to stay as relaxed as possible and fight the urge to use massive "Geronimo" braces.

2. So what is the "power position"? When looking at your body from above, let's imagine an invisible line that passes through both shoulders. We'll refer to this as the "shoulder line." Now imagine another line that divides your body into two equal sides. We'll call this the "midline." The power position simply involves keeping your hands in front of your shoulder line and preventing your hands from crossing your midline. In so doing, you'll maintain a rectangle with your arms, paddle, and chest. With this rectangle formed, you get

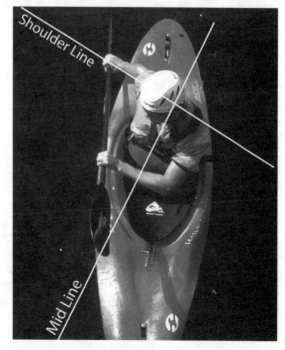

Letting a hand fall behind your shoulder line puts your shoulder in a vulnerable position.

the most power from your paddle, and your shoulders stay in the safest position.

When your hands move behind your shoulder line your arm is in a very vulnerable position. Does this mean that you can't safely reach to the back of your kayak? Not at all! But what it does mean is that in order to reach to the back of your kayak you'll need to rotate your whole torso so that your arms stay in the power position. This act of rotating your whole torso is fittingly named torso rotation. Torso rotation is not only responsible for keeping your shoulders safe, but it is one of the Three Golden Rules of whitewater paddling (see "Three Golden Rules" section).

EDGING

Much of your time kayaking will be spent on one edge or the other, depending on what you're doing. Peeling out into the whitewater, ferrying across the current, side-surfing in a hole, or paddling through

a wave train all require you to keep balanced while the boat is tilted on edge. To tilt a boat on edge, shift your weight slightly over to one butt cheek (as in the chair exercise) and lift the opposite knee. Remembering the importance of keeping your weight centred over the middle of

Staying loose at the hips is the key to edging. This lets you keep your head and weight over the kayak, even when your kayak is being aggressively edged.

EDGING PRACTICE

As you progress, it becomes more and more important to be able to tilt the boat on edge quickly and transfer from one edge to another comfortably. You can practise this on the water in a stationary position by staying balanced while rocking the boat from edge to edge. Try to make waves form off both sides of your boat. You can also practise paddling in a straight line with your boat on edge. Try to keep a steady forward stroke going while holding your boat on one edge. Play with the full range of tilts, from gentle to aggressive, to get a feel for the various positions. Recall that the flared-out sidewalls of newer boats are designed to provide secondary stability and make balancing on edge easier (so use them!). Now try switching to the other edge without losing your paddling rhythm. This is a great drill for improving your balance and edge control while strengthening your stomach muscles.

your boat, try balancing on that edge. You should feel your stomach and side muscles working to keep your weight in and forward, and your leg muscles holding the boat in its tilted position.

AN INTRODUCTION TO SPIN MOMENTUM

A couple of the most prominent features of the newer kayak designs are their shorter lengths and their flat hulls. While these combine to make the boats more manoeuvrable (and fun!), these two features can also leave you spinning in circles without the right technique. A boat with forward speed left to coast on its own will skid out to one side and quickly lose its momentum because it doesn't have a centre line or keel in the water to keep it on track. It follows that whenever you give a boat forward or backward speed, you're also giving it potential 'spin momentum'. This is true of any boat left to coast, but the difference with these kayaks is that their spin momentum will take over immediately because that is what they are designed to do! Of course, turning or spinning your boat also establishes momentum in one direction. Once established, spin momentum will continue turning the boat until there is no energy left or until something is actively done to change it.

SKIDDING VS. CARVING

Now that you understand the concept of spin momentum, it's important that we look at the different ways it will turn your kayak. Modern whitewater kayaks are designed to turn very effectively in two different ways. Their wide, flat hulls allow them to skid, while the sharp edges allow them to carve. Both of these features come in really handy in different situations. Just as with downhill skiing or snowboarding, the key to carving is getting on edge and preventing your tail end from sliding out. Most paddlers have a tougher time carving than spinning out because it requires balancing on edge.

When your kayak is kept flat, it skids to a stop.

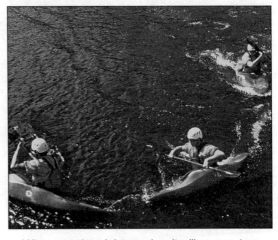

When your kayak is on edge, it will carve a turn.

BRACING

by Mary DeRiemer

YOUR BODY: THE SECRET TO BRACING

Is there a connection between what the body and paddle do when bracing? What you'll discover is that your body rights the boat! The paddle's job is to help centre your body over the righted boat. In a bomber brace, these two actions occur simultaneously. Both the body motion and the correct way to move the paddle are counter-intuitive. To make the learning process easier, first let's isolate the body motion.

Believe it or not, the head bone's connected to the hipbone; the hipbone's connected to the knee bone; and the knee

By dropping your head toward the water you 1) lower your center of gravity; 2) disengage the knee that's pulling the boat over' and 3) engage the knee that rights the boat.

bone is connected to your boat! Therefore, it's what you do with your head that is the overriding factor in whether the brace you're doing is effective and effortless.

Here's to illustrate. Sit on the floor as though you're in your kayak. Tilt your "boat" on edge by lifting one cheek off the floor. Balance yourself by keeping your hands in the air below and in front of your shoulders on either side of your body. Notice that your spine curves toward the high hip/knee in an effort to counterbalance. When the river puts you in this position, the instinctive response is to keep the head as far above the water as possible. This, however, only serves to pull up harder on the knee that's already too high for balance. This negative spiral continues until, despite all efforts with the paddle, your head succeeds in pulling your boat far enough off balance that it causes you to flip. The river provided the initial instability; your head caused your flip!

To right an over-edged boat, the knee that's going underwater must pull up to level things out. Knowing that the head bone is circuitously connected to the hip/knee bones, you can switch the direction that the head moves by pulling up on the correct knee!

What? Drop your head into the fall? Yep, by dropping your head toward the water you: 1) lower your centre of gravity; 2) disengage the knee that's pulling the boat over; and 3) engage the knee that rights the boat.

There are two ways to drop your head into the fall. You can tilt your ear laterally toward your shoulder, or you can turn your face toward the side of the boat. If your neck is sensitive, the latter is sufficient to initiate righting the boat and is much less stressful on your neck.

The hinge point of the righting motion is at the waist, in a lateral movement. A way to get full use of this righting motion is to drive the ribcage inward laterally, toward the spine. Remember, though, the head and knee are the "ends" of this hinge. So to get the fullest range of motion, use the head to pull the knee up.

Practise this movement with a slight edge in your living room river right now. Get into the position described in the second paragraph. We call this "riding the rail" when it occurs on the river. You now have nanoseconds in which to respond correctly! Drop your head toward and pull up on the lower hip/knee simultaneously. The "boat" responds. Your balance is regained as your cheeks flatten evenly on the floor. Wa-hoo! You now know the secret to an effortless brace.

HIGH BRACE

She's up! She's down! Yes, she is up! A proficient high brace can recover a boat from the upside-down position! The best boaters use their high brace when others are going for the roll setup. What makes this possible is a paddler's experience and timing, allowing her to simultaneously dink her head, pull up on the lower hip and knee, and use her paddle to safely and effortlessly recover. First a reminder—it's the body that rights the boat. That said, you need to practise how to move the paddle correctly. Once this movement is natural, put the dink together with the paddle to practise your new and effortless brace.

With your boat flat, assume your moderately aggressive posture. Hold your paddle shaft horizontally across the boat in front of your body. This evenly distributes the weight of your upper body so as not to overweight the bracing side of the boat. Rolling the knuckles back, place the powerface on the surface of the water just out from your knee. Keep the inside hand low so that the shaft remains as horizontal as possible. Now, slide your blade in toward your knee a few inches. Then clear the blade from the water by rolling your knuckles forward to slice the blade free. Practise the movement of the paddle with your boat flat and stable until the motion becomes natural.

When learning to brace, our instinct is to use the paddle first. Be sure to synchronize the movement of the paddle with the dink. Tilt your boat a mild two degrees, and practise the two movements simultaneously until smooth and fluid. Once your muscles are ingrained with this new habit (this might take some time), edge the boat a little more. Be sure to stay synchronized and fluid before adding more edge. Why? Because the high brace is potentially the stroke most dangerous in its effect on the shoulder.

If the blade drifts behind the hip, the shoulder joint is placed in its weakest and most vulnerable position. Unfortunately, pulling back and down on the paddle is our instinct! A forceful flip onto a poor form high brace is enough force to cause muscle tears and even dislocation. Moving

Make sure not to overextend your arms or reach back behind your hip.

The high brace involves rolling your knuckles back so that you use the power face of your paddle against the water.

Dropping your head toward the fall lets you completely upright your kayak with your lower body.

SAFETY TIP FOR THE HIGH BRACE

To prevent your paddle from drifting too far behind your hip and putting your shoulder at risk, you can finish the high brace by sculling your paddle forward to your toes. Sculling means pushing your paddle through the water with the blade angled such that it climbs towards the surface. In this case, you'll roll your knuckles back and push your paddle forward.

the head away from the flip, which is another dangerous instinct, further increases the potential for injury. Keep your shoulders safe by: 1) keeping the bracing paddle in front of the body in the area of the knee; 2) moving the horizontal paddle inward toward the boat, not backward as in a forward sweep, 3) while simultaneously dropping your head toward the fall.

Many paddlers have only a high brace and end up overusing it. Using the high brace in inappropriate places can get the paddler in trouble in two ways. It can end up becoming a crutch or kickstand, and cause the paddler to get stuck in a state of imbalance and then flip anyway. If a paddler in a hole tries to back up on a high brace, the resulting blade face and arm position opens him up to the possibility of shoulder injury. Used in this way, the high brace is a weak, ineffective, and potentially dangerous stroke. So let's go on and learn my favourite, the low brace.

LOW BRACE

One of the most valuable strokes for any kayaker is the low brace. Watch your local hole guru at play, and you will notice that this is the brace most often used. Hmmm, what's at play here? (Besides the guru.)

First, there are two ways to use any brace—to recover when unbalanced and to move around while staying balanced. The low brace is the strongest one in almost any river situation. If I were allowed to use only one kind of brace, this would be my choice.

Because the low brace is seldom practised, it may not feel "normal" or reliable. All it takes is repetition to build your confidence. You want the low brace to become your instinctive choice when balance is a concern because it is safer on the shoulders than the high brace. Let's review good form on flatwater.

Just as we did with the high brace, first practise a recovering low brace with your boat flat. Sit upright. With the paddle shaft held horizontally in front of your body, bring the shaft close to your navel by rolling your blade forward and down. With your elbows directly over your hands, rest the backside of the blade flat on the surface of the water out from your thigh. The higher the elbows, the more the shoulders move forward and over the shaft. This safe and strong position provides our greatest degree of stability.

To recover the paddle, slide the brace forward and inward with a slight twisting motion of the body. Then clear the blade from the water by rolling your knuckles back to slice the blade free.

Now, tilt your boat one or two degrees. Don't over-edge. The low brace encourages the paddler to control the degree of boat lean with the body. Looking helps. Remember that to drop your head toward, and pull up on, the lower knee simultaneously is the key to righting the boat. Following this dinking motion, recover your low brace.

The elbows (and wrists) control blade angle. Pure support is achieved with a flat blade that sits on the surface. For this to happen, the elbows need to be directly over the hands. Conversely, the boat moves best in response to a vertical blade in the water. Lowering the elbows automatically changes the blade angle. The advantage of the bevelled blade, one between these two extremes, is that it provides some degree of both support and movement.

Here's how you might adjust your blade on the river. If you drop into a hole or onto a pillow, have your elbows in the highest position for the most solid brace. Once your boat is stable, bevel the blade to ride the pillow around the rock, or to start moving around in the hole.

The low brace uses the back side of your paddle against the water, which means rolling your paddle and hands below your elbows.

Dropping your head toward the fall lets you completely upright your kayak with your lower body.

Dropping your head toward the fall is the only way to upright the kayak with your knees.

COMMON PROBLEMS WITH THE LOW BRACE

If this is such a solid and versatile brace, then why is it often the second choice of many learning kayakers?

If the low brace is used incorrectly, downstream flips can occur. Momentary leaning on a low brace can be okay only with the elbows in the highest position to maintain the flattest and most stable blade. If the elbows get lazy, the blade angle changes and the boater flips.

The second reason for a flip could be over-edging. Sometimes a kayaker edges too much in a hole or into a breaking wave, with the blade far downstream. This results in needing to rely on the blade for support. In this position the paddler can't free up the paddle to move around. Essentially, he has put down the kickstand and is now "stuck" in that position. If an attempt is made to back out with a bevelled blade with this much weight on it, the blade cannot support the over-edged boat and a downstream flip occurs.

A third type of flip occurs when the kayaker is moving backward in the hole. Feeling the solid support of the blade, he pushes the boat backward so aggressively that the upstream knee drops and bam! Window-shaded!

What to do? First, practise in small, friendly holes. Keep the brace in front of the body for stability and safety. Keep the blade in close to the boat to prevent over-edging. Maintain a firm minimal level of edge with the upstream knee. And be sure that the elbows stay up. If you could hear me barking encouragement from the eddy, I'd most likely be saying, "Elbows up! Lean forward!" (Mary)

4

STROKES

FORWARD STROKE • BACK STROKE • SWEEP STROKES
POWER STROKES • DRAWS • BUOYANCY ENERGY • PIVOT TURNS

"Find a good buddy to learn with. One of the greatest things about paddling is the adventure you'll share." (Kevin Varette)

FORWARD STROKE

Whitewater kayaks are designed to turn efficiently, so mastering a stroke that is supposed to make them go straight isn't going to be easy. When you're learning, you'll probably find that paddling in a straight line is next to impossible. If you're having trouble doing so, then you'll probably be happy to hear that you're not the only one. In fact, no one can paddle a whitewater kayak in a straight line and

everyone has difficulty just getting from A to B in the beginning. Even the best whitewater paddlers are turning back and forth slightly with each stroke. What happens is that as you get better, you start anticipating any corrections rather than reacting to the actions of your kayak. Having said this, we're going to be looking at what could be considered the ideal forward stroke. The reality is that each of your forward strokes will need to be modified slightly to accommodate any correction that is needed.

Make sure that the paddle is planted deeply in the water to get the utmost power from your stroke.

We're going to quickly look at three different aspects of the forward stroke. We'll look at what the paddle is doing, what the body is doing, and finally, what the boat is doing.

Starting with the paddle, the forward stroke starts at the toes and ends at the hip. To get the most forward pull out of each stroke, your paddle should be as vertical as possible and your blade should pull directly alongside your boat. If you're getting lots of

The forward stroke should finish at your hip.

splash at the beginning of your stroke, then you know your paddle isn't planted deeply enough in the water. Also, one of the most common errors is pulling the forward stroke past the hip. If your stroke passes your hip, your paddle will actually start pulling up against the water, and it will begin turning your boat. Of course this can be useful for making small corrections, but if they're not needed, then get your blade out of the water before it passes your hip and plant your next stroke at your toes.

Next, let's look at how the body works with the paddle. We'll start by looking at the top hand. The top hand should stay at around eye level throughout the stroke. Try to avoid punching forward too aggressively with this hand as you perform the stroke. The isolated effect of punching forward is to cause your lower blade to pull up against the water at the end of each stroke, which just creates more drag on your kayak. Think more about driving your upper shoulder forward and keeping that elbow down. This encourages torso rotation, which puts the power of your whole upper body behind your stroke. If you're effectively using torso rotation, your body should be wound up from the hips for each stroke you take. Once your body is wound up, don't hesitate before planting your stroke.

Your body is like an elastic band. If it's wound up, it will naturally want to unwind, and so the longer you take to get your next blade in the water, the more potential power (from the torso rotation) you'll lose. This is where the third Golden Rule comes into play. By keeping an active paddle in the water you'll maximize the power that comes from your torso rotation. As for your actual

Punching forward with the top hand doesn't provide your strokes with as much power, as the pivot point on your paddle is closer to your bottom hand. 2) Driving your shoulder forward with each stroke encourages torso rotation and gives each stroke more power as the pivot point will be closer to your top hand.

body position, we already mentioned that a moderately aggressive body position is ideal. This forward position helps keep your stern edges from inadvertently catching when you're in current.

With small playboats you'll also need to worry about having your bow dive underwater. To avoid this, you'll sometimes have no choice but to lean back for a moment. For instance, you may need to lean back when crossing eddy lines, or when paddling against the current as you do when ferrying. It's important to understand that there's no problem with leaning back, as long as you return to your neutral or moderately aggressive position as soon as possible.

Finally, your kayak's activity is an important factor in the effectiveness of your forward stroke. Ideally, your kayak would stay perfectly level as you paddle. Although this may be feasible when

paddling on flatwater, this is an unrealistic expectation when there are waves or currents to contend with, particularly in smaller playboats. You can make small modifications as you paddle to keep your bow from diving underwater. By tilting your boat a little and very briefly into each stroke, this will slice your stern slightly under water and keep your bow on top of the water.

A moderately aggressive forward lean is the ideal body position when forward paddling.

Tilting your boat slightly and very briefly into each stroke helps keep your bow on top of the water.

written just on the forward stroke! Try focusing on each component individually and don't get frustrated when your boat doesn't respond the way you want it to. Remember that whitewater kayaks aren't designed to go straight.

BACK STROKE

This forward paddling technique will come in really handy when ferrying, or when paddling through wave trains. Don't forget that since your forward strokes are most effective with a level boat and digging your stern in too much can make you unstable, you want to minimize the amount of tilt you use.

Although you might have figured that the forward stroke would be the easiest stroke to master, there are a remarkable number of things that you need to think about. In fact, entire books have been

Most paddlers will develop a forward stroke that is powerful enough to get them where they need to go, but very few paddlers ever reach that same level of comfort with their back stroke.

Taking the time to practise your back paddling will go a long way toward improving your overall skills. Not only will the practice make your stroke more effective, you'll have an increased awareness when you find yourself backward on the river. Working on the back stroke is also a great way to help prevent shoulder injuries. For anatomical reasons, shoulder dislocations are anterior (forward) over 90% of the time. The back stroke strengthens important front

Keeping your weight forward and tilting your boat slightly into each stroke helps keep the stern out of the water as you back paddle.

shoulder muscles that the forward stroke doesn't. This may not stop a dislocation from happening, but it can certainly help prevent it. So let's take a look at a few things to keep in mind when practising backward paddling.

First of all, you need to get used to watching where you're going when practising. You might laugh at these little words of wisdom, but you'd be amazed at how often paddlers get caught up with the simple task of paddling in a straight line and end up backing right into something or someone!

Choose one shoulder to look over, and do so every few strokes. You'll find it's easiest to look over that shoulder as you reach to take a stroke on that same side, since your body will be partly turned in that direction. If you know that you're not going to run into anything, you can use landmarks in front of you to help keep you going straight. For example, you could choose a tree in the distance and be fairly certain that if you keep that tree in the same position relative to the direction in which your bow is pointing, then you

should be on track. However, it's still important to practise looking over your shoulder, since this is something you'll need to be able to do comfortably later on.

As whitewater kayaks have shrunk and been designed with slicier edges, back paddling with your body in a moderately aggressive position has become all that much more important. In this position, you have the most control over your kayak, and, more importantly, it helps keep your stern edges from catching water. But there will be times when paddling in this aggressive position won't be enough to keep your stern edges from diving underwater, particularly when paddling against the current, crossing through an eddy line, or using a small playboat. In these cases, you'll need to use the same boat tilt method that we discussed for the forward stroke.

By tilting your boat a little and very briefly into each of your strokes, you can slice your bow slightly under water, which keeps your stern on top of the water. The amount you'll actually tilt your boat and pull your bow underwater will depend on

The back stroke starts just behind the hip and ends at the toes. With your top hand between shoulder and eye level, you'll get the most push from your stroke.

the situation, but do remember that your back stroke will be most efficient when your boat is kept flat to the water, so don't overuse this boat tilt technique.

Now let's look at the dynamics of the back stroke itself. Your stroke will begin just behind your hip and end at your toes. At first you'll probably find that your top hand is quite low during your strokes because of all the corrections you're making to keep yourself moving in the right direction. Although there's nothing wrong with this, it needs to be understood that the ideal back stroke has your top hand between shoulder and eye level, where you'll get the most push from your stroke.

Another way to make your back stroke more effective is to apply the second Golden Rule and use the power of your torso rotation to your advantage. As you should already know, the way you get the power of torso rotation into your strokes is by winding up your upper body. Think about turning your chest to face the knee on the stroking side of the kayak as you plant each stroke. Now as you push on your back stroke, think about driving your back shoulder forward. You'll be amazed at how much longer you can paddle and how much more power you'll get by sharing the workload with your torso muscles.

SWEEP STROKES

The sweep is likely the most common paddle stroke you'll use to turn your boat, whether you are initiating a change in direction or correcting your current one. Whereas propelling strokes follow a path very close to the boat with a vertical paddle, sweep strokes require you to move the blade out and away from the boat with a relatively flat paddle. As you reach further out to the side, you gain more leverage for your turn. Sweeps can be forward (using the power face) or reverse (using the non-power face); we'll have a look at them independently.

FORWARD SWEEP

The forward sweep uses a combination of torso power and pulling on the power face to turn the boat. One of the most commonly used strokes, it's complemented by various techniques to achieve different kinds of turns, but for now we'll just look at the sweep itself.

Start the sweep by rotating your torso and head in the direction you want to turn. You should feel this stretch in your lower back, as your outside hip is pulled forward and your inside hip is pulled back. Now, on the side opposite to that which you are facing, place the blade completely in the water at the front of the boat, as if you were taking a forward stroke. The difference is that you'll keep the top hand nice and low with the elbow bent. This hand should remain between chest and chin height to orient the paddle horizontally rather than vertically. Get comfortable with this set up position; remember, you're looking where you're going and not down at your active blade.

For a complete forward sweep, your blade will follow a wide arc that starts at the bow, extends out to the side, and pulls in at your stern. Throughout the stroke (or at least until near its end), your top arm is low and bent, while your bottom arm is straight. To maximize power, when you pull on the blade, try to pull your legs around with your stomach muscles at the same time. This will become more and more important as you progress into advanced techniques.

Once your sweep stroke has reached the three-quarters of the way mark, your tactics will change for what we call the recovery phase, or last part, of the sweep.

TURNING AND TORSO ROTATION

Before getting into the techniques of turning, it's important to emphasize one key element of all turns (and you've heard it before!): torso rotation. Of course, torso rotation requires the separation of upper and lower body, so we'll proceed with the assumption that this is understood. One way to think of your upper body is as a steering wheel—you turn it to make the boat go in the direction you've chosen as aggressively as you want. Another is to imagine two arrows pointing straight out from your shoulders. For proper rotation, both arrows should be pointed in the direction you want the boat to go. Be wary of this analogy however, because rotation should happen at the hips to involve the lower torso muscles (not just the shoulders).

Without rotating your torso, you forego all of the power available from it—like trying to fling a rubber band without first stretching it. You also inevitably let the boat turn ahead of you, which leaves you recovering after the turn instead of ready for whatever is next. Finally, not using torso rotation could put your shoulder at risk.

When your hands are in front of your shoulders, you're generally in a safe position. Rotating your whole upper body allows you to maintain this "box" throughout a turn. However, extending your arm without rotating the torso will put it outside of the box and very vulnerable. In the wrong position, it doesn't take much force to pop a joint like the shoulder.

Think of your upper body as a steering wheel – you turn it in the direction that you want to go.

The sweep begins at the toes, with the body wound up and facing in the direction you'd like to turn.

Sweep as wide an arc as possible to get the most turning power.

Pull your arm in towards your body as your sweep nears its end.

Remove the paddle from the water before the blade gets pinned against the stern of your kayak.

Your goal is to avoid having your paddle get pinned against your kayak, or putting your shoulder in a position of risk. To do these things, you'll pull your back arm in towards your body at the end of the stroke and remove your paddle from the water.

To just change or correct the direction of the boat slightly instead of doing a complete turn, you can use a partial sweep. Do this by starting with your blade anywhere along the arc and finishing at the stern, but still rotate! (See "Stern Draw" for more information on correcting direction.)

REVERSE SWEEP

The reverse sweep is very similar to the forward sweep, except that it uses the back side of the blade and follows the opposite path. It's used frequently, especially when playboating. It can be a very powerful stroke, as the blade is often placed against the flow of the water to harness its force.

To set up for the back sweep, rotate your torso and look where you want to go. With your top arm bent and low again,

Initiate the sweep with your blade completely in the water at the stern of your kayak, and with your body aggressively leading the way.

Sweep as wide an arc as possible.

Continue leading the way as you sweep to your toes.

place the blade completely in the water back at the stern. Remember, the safest and most powerful way to do this is by twisting at the hips, not leaning or reaching back. If you're set up correctly, your paddle shaft should be almost parallel to your boat, with both of your hands on the inside of the turn. The blade will follow a wide arc: starting at the stern, pushing out to the side and finishing at the bow. The lower arm is extended and the top arm remains bent throughout the turn. As you push on the blade, focus on using those stomach muscles to help pull the boat around. Again, you can use a partial back sweep to change direction slightly or correct your angle by rotating and placing the blade anywhere along the arc.

POWER STROKES

Now that you understand the concepts of spin momentum and carving, it's time to start talking about how to control it and make it work for you. The first thing we can do is to use edging to give the boat some capacity to stay on line. As compared to a flat hull, which planes across the surface, an edge literally digs into the water. The channel that it carves out acts as a track for the boat to stay on. The effect this has on controlling spin momentum is best illustrated in the Power Stroke exercise.

Start by getting some forward speed and initiating spin momentum in one direction with a light sweep. Now, instead of letting the boat stay flat and spin to a halt, lift the outside knee to drop the edge on the inside of the turn. Look in the direction you're turning and start taking completely vertical forward strokes on the inside of the turn. These strokes should be so vertical that your top hand is crossed right over the boat and the blade is almost passing underneath the kayak. Your goal is to complete a circle, having taken only these powerful forward strokes and no turning strokes.

If you're having trouble, make sure that you're looking to the middle of the circle, that your strokes are vertical (anything less than vertical will act to turn the boat in the other direction), and that you keep your speed up. Remember that the key to balancing on edge is upper and lower body separation. Your paddle is not offering much bracing support in this powerful position, so you'll need to keep your centre of gravity over the boat. Committing to this exercise will likely

result in a few flips! It may be frustrating at first, but keep practising on both sides until you get it. Once you do, try adding as much power as you can to each stroke and tilting the boat more aggressively on edge. There are a couple of ways you can add power to your power stroke. Most obviously, you can pull harder on your paddle, but to get the most power from your power stroke, you'll need to get your whole body into the act.

Try focusing on thrusting your hips past the paddle and pushing forward with your toes. This has the effect of putting you into a leaning back position. This isn't a problem, as long as you recognize that this isn't where you want to stay. You need to get back upright right away and reach forward for the next stroke. This hip thrust technique will come in incredibly handy down the road when you start considering

Power strokes are vertical forward strokes that are used to propel you forward without altering your kayaks spin momentum.

river running skills such as eddy turns, or even for more advanced skills such as running waterfalls.

One of the best ways to add power to your power stroke is to thrust your hips past your paddle and push forward with your toes. This hip thrust is a very common advanced river running technique.

DRAWS

Draws are dynamic strokes that either pull water towards or push water away from the side of the boat at any point along its length for a variety of effects. That's a mouthful! They don't propel the boat forward or backward, but are often used while moving or in combination with other strokes. Draws can serve as a keel to keep

the boat on its track, as a rudder to steer a moving boat temporarily, as a powerful pivoting stroke, and for many other useful functions. Becoming proficient with all types of draws is a significant and vital part of your learning process.

BASIC DRAWS

The first things to get comfortable with are the basic positions for draws, the lateral forces involved, and the art of feathering your blade. You can begin by using a draw while stationary to shuffle the boat sideways. This can be achieved with a T-stroke draw or a sculling draw.

T-Stroke

For the T-stroke, start by rotating your upper body at the hips towards the side that your draw stroke will be on (pick either one). Looking in the same direction, plant your blade out beside you approximately a foot or two away from the boat with the power face towards you. Position the paddle as vertically as possible. The more you can twist at the hips, the easier this will be to achieve. The boat should remain flat to avoid catching an edge. With the blade completely under water, pull with your lower hand in towards the boat. This should make the boat shift sideways towards the blade. Before the paddle hits the boat, stop pulling and curl your wrist forward 90 degrees, until you can slice (or "feather") the blade back to its starting position. Repeat this several times until you can move the boat sideways in both

The T-stroke involves pulling water directly toward your hip, and then slicing the blade back out to repeat the motions. Notice how aggressively the upper body is turned towards the draw.

power face. To open the power face is to expose more of it to the bow; to close it is to expose more of it to the stern. This requires you to rotate your wrists forward and backward with the blade in the water, which you'll become more proficient at with time. To scull, start with the blade on the surface and feather it back and forth between a slight open face and a slight closed face while working on a path about the length of your cockpit. To maintain a climbing angle on your blade (which allows you to apply pressure on the blade without its sinking or pulling it into the kayak), the leading edge of the blade needs to be raised. This means opening the power face while pushing to the bow and closing it while sliding it to the stern. Think about buttering toast with only the power

directions. To move directly sideways, your draw must be centred and the path of your stroke should be forming a "T" with the boat. If it's not, you'll find yourself pulling either the bow or stern around in a circle (strokes that we'll look at below).

Sculling

The sculling draw is set up in the same way as the T-stroke. However, once you're wound up and the blade is planted out to the side, practise opening and closing your

Sculling involves applying constant pressure with the power face of your paddle, which you can only do by maintaining a climbing angle with your blade.

face of your paddle. As you're doing this, put more of the blade under water and pull in lightly toward you to start moving the boat sideways. Try to keep the blade at least a foot or two away from the boat by balancing how much you open or close the face with how hard you pull. The most effective draw has your paddle in an almost vertical position. To do this, you'll need to develop the balance to reach comfortably across your kayak with your top hand. Again, get comfortable with this on both sides—it can come in handy for manoeuvring the boat and is excellent practise for paddle dexterity.

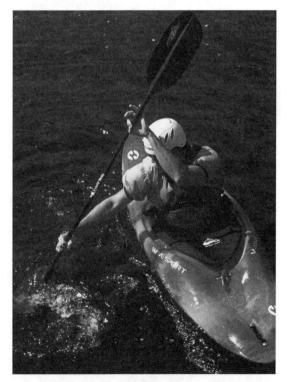

The most effective draw has your paddle in an almost vertical position. This requires balance as you'll need to reach completely across your kayak with your top hand.

THE GLIDING DRAW

Now that you're competently drawing your kayak laterally, we're going to take a look at a slight variation of the draw stroke that will let you carve turns when you've got forward momentum. The gliding draw does this by acting like the skeg on a sailboat. It lets your kayak carve a smooth turn without spinning out and losing valuable forward momentum. Just as with downhill skiing or snowboarding, the key to carving a kayak is getting your boat on edge, and preventing your back end from sliding out. Practise carving on flatwater first by building up some forward speed then establishing spin momentum with a small sweep. Before your kayak has a

Following a power stroke, the gliding draw gets planted and allows the kayak to carve a smooth turn.

The gliding draw gets planted just behind the hip and about two feet out to the side of your kayak, with your upper body rotated to face it.

chance to spin out, tilt it on edge and take a power stroke to give yourself a final boost and to keep your kayak carving. Using the same paddle blade, you'll then reach and plant a draw out to the side of your kayak, on the inside of your turn. Since the goal is to keep all your forward momentum, it should make sense that this draw stroke gets planted with the blade parallel to the direction of your kayak, so as to cause minimal resistance. To get the most power out of your draw, your paddle shaft should be held as vertically as possible and your chest should be rotated to face it. In order to keep a smoothly carving turn, plant your draw somewhere just behind your hip, but expect to need small adjustments. If your stern slides out, then your draw is too far forward. If your kayak starts turning in the opposite direction, then your draw is too far back.

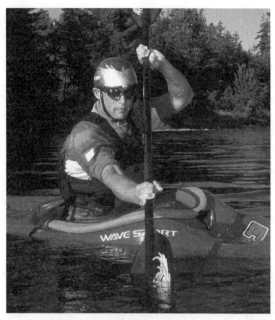

A T-stroke up at your feet will turn your kayak towards your paddle.

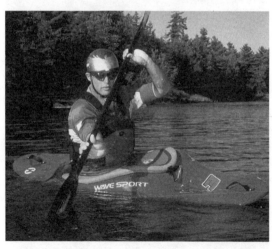

An open-faced draw lets you catch more water and draw the bow around powerfully.

BOW DRAWS

As you're discovering, a draw can be placed anywhere along the length of your boat—either statically, by keeping it in one place, or dynamically, by sliding it forward or backward. At each position alongside the boat, the draw stroke will have a different effect. One of the most efficient ways to change the direction of your boat is to move your draw forward where it will act to pull the bow around. Try this in your stationary position first by doing the T-stroke draw with the blade up near your feet, as opposed to beside your hip. You will not have to rotate as far to the side, but your paddle should still be vertical and the blade completely submerged in the water. You should be able to spin the boat in controlled circles in both directions with repeated T-stroke bow draws.

The next step is to get comfortable with the bow draw while your boat is moving forward. Start with a little forward speed in a straight line and then plant the bow draw and cock your wrists slightly outwards to open the face of the paddle. You'll find that the boat turns towards your paddle without your having to pull it in. Because of your forward speed, placing an open-faced bow draw catches "incoming" water and harnesses its power to act on the boat. The forces at play here are very much the same as those you'll encounter in moving water. This leads us into taking a closer look at two distinct forms of bow draws that you'll use on the river: the open-faced bow draw and the closed-faced bow draw. It is important to note at this time that bow draws are usually accompanied by a front or back sweep that initiates your spin momentum.

The open-faced bow draw, or duffek, is the most powerful means of turning your kayak when you have forward speed. Notice how aggressively the head and body lead the way. This lets you draw on the power of torso rotation, while keeping your hands in front of your body, and therefore your shoulders safe.

The open-faced bow draw is also commonly referred to as the "Duffek" stroke (named after a Czechoslovakian slalom paddler), and is the most powerful means of turning your kayak when you have forward speed. Since whitewater kayaks are designed to turn very efficiently to begin with, you'll only need to use this stroke in the most aggressive turning situations and when maintaining forward speed is not a real concern, since the stroke acts as a brake. You can plant this bow draw anywhere along the length of your kayak from the very front to directly out to the side of your body. The further out to your side that you plant the stroke, and the more you open the power face, the more powerful your draw will be. By reaching directly out to your side and opening your power face right up, you can catch an incredible amount of water and spin your kayak around very effectively. To harness all this power and keep your shoulders safe at the same time, you'll need to rotate your head and upper body to face your draw. This effectively winds up your body, keeping your hands in front of you in the power position that we spoke about in the "Shoulder Safety" segment.

If you don't need to make an ultra-aggressive turn and would like to conserve some of your forward momentum, then the closed-faced bow draw is your best choice. The closed-faced bow draw involves using a draw that doesn't catch water. Instead of being opened to your bow, the power face of your paddle will actually face your body throughout the stroke. Starting with a gliding draw, your paddle will be planted just behind your hip and a foot or two out to the side with the blade parallel to the length of your kayak so that it

The close faced bow draw starts from a gliding draw, which slices forward and pulls towards the body.

Make sure that the power face continues to face your body as you slide the draw forward to your toes. This prevents it from catching the incoming water.

The closed faced draw ends at your toes, with your paddle in position for a powerful forward stroke.

THE C-STROKE

One of the best ways to practise your draws uses the Power Stroke drill we just looked at. This time, though, curl your wrists forward when your forward stroke has reached your hip, and slice your paddle blade out to your side and into a gliding draw. After gliding for a moment, continue with a closed-faced bow draw, which involves slicing your draw forward and pulling it to your toes while keeping the power face facing your upper body so as not to catch incoming water. Once your draw reaches your toes, you're back at step one and ready for another "power" forward stroke. This circular motion that keeps your paddle active in the water is referred to as the C-stroke. As well as being a great drill to practise, you'll also frequently use the C-Stroke in whitewater to maintain control of your kayak throughout a turn.

will slice effortlessly through the water. Your head and upper body should of course be turned to face your paddle, which keeps your shoulders safe. Now slice your draw forward by unwinding your upper body, and begin pulling in on your draw. As you do so, your boat will begin to turn towards your paddle. Make sure that the power face continues to face your body. If it does, then your paddle blade should actually become "closed" to the incoming current as you continue to pull on your draw and slice your paddle forward. This closed-faced draw doesn't act as a brake because it doesn't "catch" incoming water. In fact, it can actually provide your boat with a small amount of added forward momentum.

The stern draw involves pulling the stern towards your paddle and requires that you reach right across your boat with the front arm.

STERN DRAW AND PRY

The Stern Draw

You're now becoming an expert on draws, and have likely already figured out that the stern draw is performed at the stern and acts to pull it around. In effect, this is the same as the last portion of a forward sweep. There are a couple differences between it and the other draws, however.

First of all, in a stern draw, your paddle angle will have to drop below vertical so you can reach back with your lower hand and get the blade to the stern. Your upper body will actually be turned away from the stroke, so you are leading the boat in the direction you'll be making it turn. This has the potential to put your shoulder in an awkward position, so to compensate for this, you'll finish your stern draw by pulling your back arm in with your elbow bent, and punching across your kayak with your front arm. Remember to remove your paddle from the water before it hits your stern to avoid having it get pinned against your boat. Practise this by turning your stationary boat in circles using the T-stroke stern draw on both sides. This is one of the most efficient ways of making small adjustments to your direction, because it turns the boat without taking away your forward momentum. It's only one function of the stern draw, however.

The Stern Pry

The stern pry is essentially the first part of a back sweep and is used primarily as your basic rudder when surfing. To turn your boat with the stern pry, you'll simply push away from the stern, applying force on the water with the back side of the blade. Make sure that your whole upper body is turned towards your paddle when prying your stern. By doing so, you're leading with your head and body and keeping your shoulders in the safest position.

The stern pry is initiated with the body wound up and uses the back side of the paddle to push the stern away.

BUOYANCY ENERGY

Buoyancy energy refers to your kayak's desire to be on the surface of the water due to all the air that is trapped inside. When one end of your kayak is underwater, it will have a lot of buoyancy energy and will want to take the quickest path back to the surface. Using your edges, you can dictate in which direction this end will return to the surface. This energy can be a very powerful tool, but if misdirected it can also work against you. You'll need to learn to harness the power of buoyancy energy for any playboating move that requires having an end of your kayak underwater (which is most of them!). It will also come in handy in a variety of ways while river running. We're going to start by looking at how buoyancy energy can be used to optimize one of the fundamental paddling strokes, the sweep stroke. A sweep stroke that takes advantage of buoyancy energy is referred to as a "pivot turn."

ALTERNATING STERN DRAW AND PRY DRILL

In moving situations, by alternating between a stern draw and a stern pry, you can create a very effective rudder to steer the boat with. To practise in flatwater, start with some forward speed and then use a single paddle blade and alternate between a stern draw and a stern pry to make your boat zigzag a few times before losing speed. Focus on getting power not just from your arms, but from your entire torso, by always winding it up in the direction the boat will be turning and by actively pulling your legs around with your stomach muscles.

After driving the bow underwater, Kevin controls its return to the surface by edging his boat.

PIVOT TURNS

One of the most important features of kayaks is that they have less volume at their ends than at their centre, and pivot turns are the fundamental reason for this. They're the most powerful and effective means of turning the kayak in nearly all situations, whether river running or playboating. They also form a crucial element of the foundation you'll need to keep progressing. A pivot turn refers to a directional change in which one end of the boat is submerged in order to elevate the other. This facilitates the turn by reducing the amount of resistance or "drag" on one end, and taking advantage of buoyancy energy that is created by submerging the other end (which we'll discuss below). Whereas in a flat spin (like the sweep turns we practised earlier) the boat rotates around its centre, in a pivot turn the boat pivots around a point closer to the bow or stern. The more elevated one end is, the further down the opposite end the pivot point will be.

This technique combines four skills we have discussed so far: balance, edging, recruiting power from the torso, and a choice of turning strokes (sweeps or draws). Go over each of these again before proceeding, and make sure you understand them thoroughly. There's a lot happening at once during a pivot turn and there are many ways to break it down, but we'll try to keep it simple throughout by just separating the initiation of the turn from its completion.

THE STERN PIVOT

We'll start with the stern pivot because it's the easier of the two. We'll also use the forward sweep stroke to power the turn for now. The stern pivot involves slicing the stern underwater to elevate, "release" or "free" the bow, and in doing so, you should be able to turn a full 360-degrees with just your single initiating sweep stroke. Begin by setting up for a forward sweep with the boat stationary. Remember to rotate your upper body and look in the direction you're going to turn. Before you start the sweep stroke, you need to edge the boat by lifting the knee on the side opposite to that which your stroke is on. With this tilt, the stern is set to slice underneath the water when your sweep begins. Finally, you'll want to thrust your weight backward just as you start pulling on the blade to help sink the stern. This happens right at the beginning; and then you should literally bounce back into the forward position. Now we've covered all of the elements needed to initiate the stern pivot.

Completing this turn will involve a few more important factors. First of all, the sweep stroke is going to happen in a slightly different "plane" than it doesn't when the boat is flat. Although it does not change in relation to the boat, the sweep is going to make its way deeper into the water. One way to grasp this concept is by doing a quick exercise. Sitting still, let your paddle rest across your cockpit rim in front of you. In this position the paddle and boat are both flat, and the blade is above the surface of the water. Visualize the paddle's path were you to sweep in this position—it would be on a plane parallel to a line drawn between the two edges of the boat. This is the plane on which a flat spin happens. Now tilt the boat on edge with the paddle still resting on the cockpit rim. Both the boat and paddle are tilted with one blade underwater. Visualize the path that the paddle would take in this position if it were to sweep on a plane parallel to the boat's tilt. It would happen deeper in the water, but it's the same sweep stroke that we learned. A basic rule is that

The stern pivot turn involves slicing the stern of your kayak underwater to elevate the bow. This gets down by edging your boat and throwing your weight backward as you take a powerful sweep stroke.

when using a sweep stroke to help submerge one end, it happens deep in the water. So for the sweep in this stern pivot, you need to pull downward as well as out to the side with your blade.

Now that you've pulled the stern under, you need to make a quick adjustment of the edge to sustain the momentum of your spin. If you were to keep the initial tilt on the boat after you reached the end of your sweep stroke—when there is no longer any force pulling the stern downward—it would immediately begin to resurface in the direction it came from. We refer to this (a lot!) as "hitting the wall." It happens because you've created a significant amount of "buoyancy energy" by submerging plastic and air. This energy wants to force the stern back up to the surface following the easiest available path. With your boat on its current tilt, that path is straight back up in the direction that it came. The way to prevent hitting the wall is by levelling the boat out just before you reach the end of your initiating stroke (the sweep in this case). To do this, think about lifting the knee that is on the same side as your sweep stroke until the boat is flat again. If you do this quickly and correctly, your spin momentum will not have been interfered with and the stern will gradually corkscrew back up to the surface in the direction of your turn. You will have taken advantage of the buoyancy energy you created to help you complete the spin! Be

careful not to overdo the edge transition by tilting the boat completely on the opposite edge. This will send the stern straight up to the surface and kill the spin as well.

A final tip that will help you succeed at this exercise and will be crucial in whitewater is to "rewind" your torso once the initiating sweep stroke is complete, and to always look ahead to where you're going. By the time the blade comes out of the water at the end of your stroke, the boat will be spinning ahead of you. Quickly rotate your body so it's leading the boat again. This will help pull the boat through the rest of its turn and prepare you for whatever comes next. Practise this drill in flatwater on both sides with the goal of spinning a full 360 degrees using only one stroke. As you improve, see how vertical you can get the boat while staying balanced and in control.

Finish your stern pivot turn with your body rewound, and leading the way once again.

VARIATIONS OF THE STERN PIVOT

The stern pivot doesn't only work with the forward sweep. This technique can be practised and used with the reverse sweep

By levelling the boat out before your stroke has finished, you'll avoid hitting the wall and will continue to spin around.

and bow draw as well. The concept is the same; the only thing that changes is the stroke you're using to help initiate spin momentum and pull the stern under. Each of them can be used in a variety of situations. Practising all three will help you master the components of the stern pivot and prepare you for more advanced moves.

For a stern pivot turn with a reverse sweep, you'll use the same stern pivot technique we discussed earlier, but combine it with a back sweep. The important difference with this back sweep is that it must be started with the blade deep in the water so you can push up and out on it throughout the stroke. To get the complete 360-degree turn, you'll have to wind up your upper body very aggressively, reaching back past your stern to start the sweep stroke. This time, lift the edge on the same side as your stroke, however, so that the opposite edge is set to slice downward when you begin. Again, thrust your weight back when you initiate the sweep to help sink the stern. Return your body to the forward position and level the boat off before the stroke is

finished to avoid hitting the wall. Finally, rewind your body once the blade leaves the water to help pull the boat around and to prepare yourself for whatever is next.

The bow draw is used primarily to keep a pivot turn going after a forward or back sweep has initiated the turn. Immediately following the initiation stroke, you'll plant the bow draw on the inside of your spin and pull aggressively to your knees. The more vertical your paddle shaft is, the more powerful the stroke will be. It also helps to open your power face to catch more water. Before your bow draw hits your kayak, release the water by cocking your wrists inward, and then feathering the blade back out to the side of your kayak where you can open your draw, catch water, and repeat the process. Be sure to keep your body wound up throughout the turn, which helps you use the power of torso rotation and maintain a safe shoulder position.

the bow draw is often used to keep a pivot turn going after it has been initiated.

THE BOW PIVOT

A bow pivot turn follows the same routine as the stern pivot turn, only this time you'll

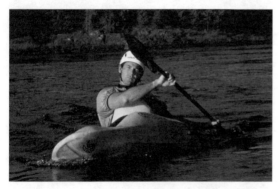

The stern pivot turn can also be accomplished using a reverse sweep as the initiating stroke.

pull your bow underwater. This is a trickier skill to master because a kayak's bow is always larger in volume than the stern, which means you'll have more buoyancy to submerge, and more energy to control, once it's underwater. You'll also need to use a back sweep to initiate the turn, which is less powerful than the forward sweep that primarily gets used for the stern pivot turn. To compensate for these obstacles, you'll need to be less aggressive with your edging and will need to level off your kayak earlier to avoid hitting the wall.

Now let's look at the bow pivot turn in more detail. To submerge your bow, you'll need to do a couple of things as you take your back sweep. You need to tilt your kayak into the stroke and throw your weight aggressively forward. As soon as your bow enters the water you need to begin levelling off your boat tilt in order to avoid hitting the wall. When practising the bow pivot turn, it's difficult to keep your head and body wound up because they naturally unwind as you push on your back sweep. There's no problem with this as long as you "rewind" your torso once the initiating sweep stroke is complete. This will help pull the boat through the rest of its turn and prepare you for whatever comes next. Like the stern pivot turn, practise this drill in flatwater on both sides with the goal of spinning a full 360 degrees using only one stroke. As your technique improves, apply more power and see how vertical you can get your boat while spinning your boat the full 360 degrees.

The bow pivot turn.

5

ROLLING A KAYAK

THE HIP SNAP • THE ROLL - AN OVERVIEW • THE STANDARD ROLL
THE HAND ROLL • THE BACK DECK ROLL • ROLLING IN MOVING WATER
ROLLING IN A HOLE • ADVANCED ROLLING

"All experts were once beginners!" (Tyler Curtis)

Rolling is one of the most important skills for any whitewater kayaker to master. Once you can reliably roll in whitewater, your confidence will soar, and your paddling will dramatically improve. This doesn't mean that you shouldn't expect to swim every once in a while. Sometimes you won't have a choice, but swimming should be one of your last resorts. Aside from being tiring, frightening, and humbling, you're much more vulnerable to hazards when swimming. So, next time you miss a roll, set up and try it again. When

the time does come to swim, make sure you haven't waited until you're completely out of air and exhausted. You're still going to need enough energy to get to shore.

There are three forms of the kayak roll. There's the standard roll, the backdeck roll, and the hand roll. We're going to take a look at each of these techniques independently, starting with the standard roll. First, we'll start by looking at a common element that provides the foundation for all types of rolls.

THE HIP SNAP

The hip snap (otherwise known as the hip flick) refers to the action of rotating your hips to upright your kayak. The hip snap is without a doubt the single most important technique to master in order to have success with your roll.

The idea behind the hip snap is simple. By staying loose at your midline (separating your upper and lower body movements), you can use your knee to roll your hips and your kayak upright while your body remains in the water. In order to do this effectively, you'll need some form of support for your upper body. For the standard rolls and the backdeck roll, your paddle provides this support. For the hand roll, your hands provide the support. Here's a great way of practising your hip snap.

THE ROLL – AN OVERVIEW

The idea behind the roll is quite simple. To roll a kayak upright, you're going to extend your body out to the side and get yourself as close to the surface of the water as possible. From this position, you need some support so that you can hip snap your kayak upright while keeping your head and body close to the water surface level. When practising your hip snap, the support you needed for this came from a friend's kayak, or from the side of a pool or dock. This support will now come from your paddle (or your hands in the case of the hand roll).

Clearly, you won't get as much purchase from your paddle as you did from the kayak or the pool side, but having practised your hip snap tirelessly, you should be comfortable with the fact that your hips don't need very much support to rotate the boat upright. Once your hips have rotated the boat as upright as possible (which will be felt by your cockpit rim hitting you in the side), your body will need to move over top of your kayak and into a stable position.

This recovery takes us back to Mary's bracing segment and the importance of the head "dink." In Mary's segment we looked at how the head, upper body, and lower body work together when recovering with a brace. You learned that by lifting your head, you pull on your top knee, which will effectively pull your kayak back upside down. By dropping your head to the water, you allow your bottom knee to continue to pull your kayak upright while at the same time keeping your centre of gravity as low as possible as your body moves over your kayak.

HIP SNAP PRACTICE

This drill involves practising the hip snap technique while holding onto something for support. It can be done alone or with the help of a friend. Alone, you can use the side of a pool or dock. With a friend, you can use an end of his or her kayak. The idea is to hold onto whatever aid you have available, and then to lean right over on your side and lay your cheek on your hands. Relax your hips as much as possible and pull your top knee over so that the kayak collapses on top of you. You'll know that your hips are loose enough and that your kayak has flipped over all the way when you feel its cockpit rim come into contact with your side.

Now it's time to right the boat again. Keeping your cheek on your hands, pull the trailing knee (the one that's underwater) up toward your body and roll your hips and kayak to an almost upright position while minimizing the amount you push with your hands. For this drill, you're going to maintain your grip and repeat these steps, so once you feel the lower cockpit rim come into contact with your side, that's as far as you're going to right the boat, and it's time to start over. Ideally this drill is done off the bow of a friend's kayak, as the bow will sink if you push off too heavily with your arms. You should be able to do this drill while keeping the deck of your friend's kayak dry.

When you get comfortable with your hip snap on one side, practise it on the other. Having an effective hip snap on both sides will come in handy for kayak rescues, and it will provide you with an even better understanding of the technique.

The hip snap will have the biggest effect on the success or failure of your roll. The key to the hip snap is keeping your head down and relying on your knees to upright the kayak. When practising this, try to put as little pressure on your hands as possible.

THE STANDARD ROLL

The standard roll is the most commonly used roll, although there are a number of different forms of it. The most familiar of these are the C-to-C and sweeping rolls. There is an endless debate as to which roll is best to learn, which we're not going to get into, but what we can tell you is that a sweeping roll is the more effective one of the two, and although you may prefer to use the C-to-C in the beginning, over time your roll should evolve into a sweeping style. The sweeping roll is quicker, more fluid, and requires less setting up.

We're now going to break down the roll into three distinct parts and look at both types of rolls at the same time. We'll start with the set up, followed by the catch, and we'll finish with the recovery.

THE SETUP

The C-to-C and sweeping rolls both start from the same set up position. Regardless of how you flip over, your first order of business is to get into this position. It's best to start on flat water, getting into the set-up

The set-up position involves placing your paddle alongside your kayak with the forward blade flat to the water surface and power face up.

position before flipping over. The set-up position has your paddle placed alongside your kayak with the forward blade flat to the water's surface and power face up. Which side of the kayak you set up on is generally determined by which is your control hand (the control hand being that which stays glued to your paddle). Most people prefer to set the paddle up with their control hand closest to the bow. As most paddlers use right-hand control paddles, the paddle is most often placed on the left side of the kayak with the right hand closest to the bow.

Tuck your head and body forward and try to push the paddle right into the water

1) With your body directly underneath the kayak, your hip snap will not be able to fully upright your kayak.
2) Setting up with your body extended out to the side gives your hips a much wider range of motion and allows you to roll the kayak almost completely upright.

When setting up underwater, the further out to the side of the kayak you can get your body,
The more easily your hip snap will be able to right your kayak.

(still flat and parallel to the boat). There are a couple of good reasons for starting with this set up position. For one, tucking forward provides you with the most protection while under water, as your helmet and life jacket are between you and any looming rocks. Secondly, being upside down can be very disorienting, so the set-up position is a consistent starting point from which you can always get your bearings.

There are a couple of cues to be aware of when setting up under water. Your forearms should press against the side of your kayak and your hands should be in the air. You should also be extending your body out to the side so that your head is as close to the surface as possible. The further out to the side you can get your body, the more easily your hip snap will be able to right your kayak.

THE CATCH

The catch refers to the part of the roll where you grab water with your blade to support your upper body while you hip snap your kayak upright. It must be clearly understood that you're not grabbing water to pull yourself upright. Your paddle won't supply enough support to do this, and it'll put an undue amount of stress on your body. Remember how we focused on minimizing the use of our arms when practising the hip snap. If you were successful in doing this, then you have felt how little pressure is needed from your paddle to roll the boat upright with your trailing knee.

The catch is also where the sweeping and C-to-C rolls differ. First of all, it must be understood that you'll get the most support/leverage from your blade when it's out at ninety degrees (perpendicular) to your kayak. The C-to-C roll starts by swinging your control hand out to ninety degrees while your other forearm acts as a pivot that keeps the paddle over the bottom of your upturned kayak. With your paddle blade out at ninety degrees and as close to the surface of the water as possible, you can pull downwards on your paddle and "catch" water in a position that provides you with the most leverage.

Your paddle actually goes through very similar motions for the sweeping roll, although it needs to swing out to ninety degrees in a slightly wider arc. The difference is that as it does so, you apply downward pressure on the blade and get the support you need to start rolling your kayak.

One of your biggest challenges is keeping your blade near the surface of the water as you sweep and pull downwards on it. The only way to do so is by maintaining a slight climbing angle on the paddle blade. This means keeping the leading edge of the blade slightly higher so that it wants to "climb" to the surface. You don't need very much climbing angle on your paddle, because you won't be applying too much

downward pressure on it, right? It's also important to understand that your paddle won't provide as much support at the beginning of its travels (just as a brace planted at the bow of your kayak wouldn't give you much bracing power), so don't try to snap your hips too aggressively too early.

Without having hip snapped yet, you'll find that just the initial pressure you apply

1) A climbing angle keeps your blade near the surface of the water.
2) If your leading edge is lower than the trailing edge of the blade, it will dive underwater.

The pressure you apply on your paddle at the beginning of the sweep will draw your body closer to the water surface and start your kayak rolling before you've initiated your hip snap.

on your paddle will draw your head and body slightly closer to the surface, which starts your kayak's rolling motion. This action alone can roll your kayak upright a good twenty degrees before even starting your hip snap, which gives your roll a good head start. As your paddle sweeps further out, you'll gain more and more leverage, and you can begin snapping your hips to right the boat. Because this sweep gives you an extended period of time with support, you can roll your hips in a

smoother, slightly less "jerky" motion than is required for the C-to-C roll.

There are a few reasons why we consider the sweeping roll more effective in general, although both styles will do the trick. The roll starts sooner, the paddle likely won't end up as deep in the water, and the hip snap can be more fluid and less abrupt as you get a longer-lasting support (brace) from your paddle. What makes it slightly more difficult is the finer paddle control that's required to achieve

COMMON PROBLEMS WITH THE CATCH

There are a couple of common problems that pop up during the "catch" phase of the roll. At times, your paddle might get knocked around in your hand, or you may just lose grip with one hand. This turn of events can be disastrous for your roll, as your hand position is what dictates your blade angle. Poor hand positioning on the paddle often results in knifing, which means the blade is angled so that it slices through the water when it's pulled upon. If you feel no support or resistance when you pull on your paddle, you need to double-check your blade angle. The best way to do this is to slide your control hand over to the blade and feel for its position relative to the surface of the water. Remember it should be flat to the water's surface.

You might also want to place an index on the control handgrip of your paddle. This index can be a small strip of foam or wood that is taped to your paddle shaft so that it fits under the fingers of your control hand. Over time, you'll be able to recognize when your hand positioning is off just by the feel of the index. Many paddles now have built-in indexes or oval shafts, which serve the same purpose.

A common error for paddlers trying the sweeping roll is the underwater forward stroke. The underwater forward stroke is a phenomenon common to paddlers who rely too heavily on their paddle for support. In doing so, they need to use a very steep climbing angle on their sweeping blade to prevent it from getting pulled down too deeply. The pressure that is felt from this extreme climbing angle encourages the paddler to pull even harder. In turn, the sweep becomes a forward stroke, and the paddle never actually sweeps out to the point of maximum leverage.

Although paddlers can occasionally force the boat upright like this, it's not a reliable method of rolling. If you find yourself pulling harder than you think you need to, or if your roll kicks up a lot of splash, then you may be taking more of an underwater forward stroke than need be.

steady downward pressure without having your blade dive deep underwater. Also, when doing the sweeping roll, you must resist the urge to use the blade's support to pull your body up.

A last issue to consider during the catch phase of the roll is how the body is involved. As you should already know from the first golden rule, all kayaking skills require the use of your arms and upper body separate from, but in conjunction with, your lower body. By relying on your arms alone, you lose an incredible amount of power and can potentially put your shoulders at risk. In the "Shoulder Safety" segment, we learned that keeping your hands in front of your body is instrumental in protecting your shoulders. You need to apply this rule to your roll.

One of the best ways to keep your hands in front of your body is to watch your active blade through its C-to-C or sweeping motions. If you don't like to open your eyes

underwater, then just imagine that you're watching the blade! Turning your head in time with your active blade will naturally turn your upper body at the same rate. This gets the power of torso rotation involved with your movements and keeps your shoulders safe.

THE RECOVERY

The recovery is the final stage of your roll. If you've set up properly and initiated the roll well with a powerful hip snap, then it's a relatively straightforward step. Having said that, a poor recovery is also one of the biggest reasons for a failed roll, and it all has to do with teaching yourself not to prematurely raise your head out of the water. As you've already seen in the hip snap segment and in Mary DeRiemer's bracing segment, lifting your head causes you to pull

By keeping your eyes on your paddle blade, your upper body will naturally turn during the roll, which keeps your shoulders safe and sets up your recovery.

The hands stay in front of the body and the eyes watch the paddle blade sweeping through the water.

on your top knee, which effectively cranks your kayak back upside down. By dropping your head to the water, you allow your bottom knee to continue to pull your kayak upright while at the same time keeping your centre of gravity as low as possible.

If you don't believe it, then try Mary's drill right now. Sit on the floor as though you were in your kayak. Tilt your "boat" on edge by lifting one cheek off the floor. Balance yourself by keeping your hands in the air below and in front of your shoulders on either side of your body. Notice that your spine curves toward the high hip/knee in an effort to counterbalance. When the river puts you in this position, the instinctive response is to keep the head as far above the water as possible. This, however, only serves to pull up harder on the knee that's already too high for balance. This negative spiral continues until, despite all efforts with the paddle, your head succeeds in pulling your boat far enough off balance that it causes you to flip over. The river provided the

initial instability; your head put the finishing touch on your flip!

If all has gone well, then you should recover from your roll with your head turned to face your active paddle blade (which keeps your shoulders safe and promotes torso rotation), and with your head also being the last part of your body to return to its position over the kayak. The boat comes up, and then the body, and finally the head. You're now in a stable position and ready to go.

The key to a successful roll is keeping your head in the water until the very end.

The roll is finished with the head and body turned to face the active paddle blade, which keeps the shoulders safe.

ROLLING TIP AND TRICKS

Use nose plugs! There are few things as unpleasant and panic-inducing as the rush of river or pool water up the nose. Aside from being distracting, you'll also blow air from your nose in an attempt to stop the flow of water, which ultimately means leaves you out of breath and will cause you to rush your roll.

Try a diving mask or goggles! Although we don't open our eyes underwater, it can be very helpful for some people to see what they're doing down there. With goggles, you can clearly see if your paddle is near the surface or if it is diving and can make the required corrections.

THE HAND ROLL

The hand roll is a roll done without the help of a paddle: a move that requires an effective hip snap and careful timing. The hand roll is a great move to master for a number of reasons. Most importantly, it's a confidence booster, and if you haven't figured it out by now, whitewater kayaking is as much about confidence as it is about skill.

We're going to look at the hand roll with the assumption that you already have a roll. We've broken the roll down into three unique parts: the set-up, the initiation, and the finish/recovery.

The idea behind the set-up of the hand roll is the same as that for a standard roll. You need to get your body out as far to the side of the kayak and as close to the surface as possible to maximize the potential of your hip snap. Though the concept is the same, the position of your body (preferred by most) is quite different. This position has you leaning out to the side with your head and chest facing downward instead of up towards the sky. Your arms should be up and in front of your face. Most paddlers are stronger rolling up on their right side, which means leaning out to the left with our left arm being closest to the bow of the boat.

The hand roll can be initiated in one of two ways: by pushing down with both hands at the same time, or by using a double-pump technique. We're going to look at this technique, which involves using one arm at a time in a two-step motion that resembles the climbing of a ladder.

The reason we find this double pump technique most effective is that it gives your hips more time to roll the boat underneath your body than a single, double-handed slap against the water. It also helps force you to keep your head down throughout the roll and provides a clear landmark for timing when the body should swing up on top of the kayak.

The first step involves pushing down on the water with the left hand, which provides the purchase necessary for your hips to start the boat snapping upright. As soon as this hand begins losing its effectiveness, reach out and push

The setup involves leaning out to the side with your chest facing downward.

The double pump technique involves pushing down on the water with one arm after the other.

As the second arm pushes downward, the head and body swing over top the kayak.

Keep your body as low to the kayak as possible as you bring it back over the kayak.

downward with your right hand and continue to rotate the boat upright with your hips. Of course it goes without saying that your head must stay down throughout this process. As you begin sweeping downward with your second hand, you've reached the recovery phase of the roll and it's time to swing your body back over top of the kayak.

There's some debate as to whether the hand roll and recovery are best done leaning back or forward. We've presented the forward-leaning version, but our recommendation is that you simply use the technique that works most reliably for you. Whichever you choose, keep your body as close to the boat as possible and leave the head for last!

Once you've nailed your hand roll, try some eddy turns and quick S-turns on a clean eddy line, or surfing and spinning in small holes without your paddle. This will

A closer look at the double pump technique: The left arm pushes down first, followed immediately by the right arm.

Through my first few years of paddling I would sometimes let go of my paddle underwater and hand roll myself up. I did this because it was quicker to set-up underwater without the paddle and I knew I could get up just as reliably using my hand roll. Of course this left me without paddle in the middle of a rapid, but that was of secondary concern at the time. I got by like this in class 2/3 whitewater, but I knew this approach wasn't going to work as the whitewater I paddled became more adventuresome. Without knowing it at the time, this caused me to develop my back deck roll technique, which continues to be the rolling technique I use 99% of the time… but that's another story.

(Ken Whiting)

help you become more aware of your body's position over your kayak and of how to let the river do more of the work, which will ultimately open the door to the moves you've only dreamed about.

THE BACK DECK ROLL

The back deck roll evolved from the need to roll as quickly as possible, which it facilitates by skipping the set up step that other rolls require. It's not uncommon to hear people comment that although it's a quick roll, it's a dangerous one that leaves a paddler's face exposed, and puts the shoulder at risk. It's true that your face isn't as well protected, but you spend a LOT less time underwater, and your head stays much closer to the surface throughout the roll. Also, for much of the time you're under water, your arms are actually in front of your face. With regard to shoulder safety, there's the potential for the shoulder to be put in an awkward position, but if you keep your hands in front of your body and don't overextend your arms, this roll won't pose any more risk to your shoulder than the standard C-to-C or sweeping rolls. So when should you use the back deck roll? We use it virtually all the time, and once you master it, it just might become your standard roll as well.

The key to the back deck roll is committing yourself to flipping once you've passed the point of no return (the point at which no brace will save you

efficiently or safely). This commitment involves throwing yourself on the back deck of your kayak and leading the way with your paddle and body. If you can do these two things before you've completely turned upside down, then you can start the process of rolling yourself upright before your kayak has even finished flipping over!

Because of the right-handed offset on most kayak paddles, it's easiest to perform the back deck roll flipping to the left, with your right blade doing the work. Start with your paddle held comfortably in front of your chest, with elbows hanging down and wrists cocked back so that your right paddle blade is facing directly down. You've now formed a rectangle with your arms, paddle and chest. This rectangle should stay relatively intact throughout the roll. Now lean back and aggressively turn your head and upper body to the left. As

The back deck roll requires that you lean back and turn your head and body aggressively in the direction that you are rolling.

Get your right blade in the water as soon as possible. This right blade provides the purchase from which your hips can roll the kayak.

weird as this sounds (or maybe not for some), think about trying to kiss the stern of your kayak! This keeps your head turned and your neck cocked back. With your head and body aggressively leading the way and your kayak committed to flipping, plant the power face of your left paddle blade at the stern of your boat. As you continue to flip, keep turning your body and get your right blade in the water as quickly as possible. This right blade will be providing the support/brace needed to roll the kayak.

You should now be lying on the back deck of your boat, which should be almost completely upside down. Continuing to lead the way with your head and body, push your right blade out in a wide arc over your head, and then out to the side and all the way to your toes. If your wrists remain cocked back as they should be, then your right blade will be on a sculling angle that keeps it near the surface and provides the brace your hips need to roll the kayak upright.

Still keeping that rectangle between your arms, chest, and paddle intact, your body

will need to swing forward through the last part of the roll. When your right blade finally reaches your toes, your boat should be completely upright and your body should be

The right blade swings a wide arc over your head, out to the side, and then to the toes. With a climbing angle on this blade, you will get steady downward pressure from which your hips can roll the kayak upright.

in an aggressive position, ready for the next stroke. This may take a while to master, but with enough aggression, commitment and practise, it will eventually click and open the door to new possibilities for your roll.

ROLLING IN MOVING WATER

Rolling in moving water can be more difficult in some instances, but current can also help your roll out at times. The biggest problems paddlers have with rolling in moving water are the mental hurdles rather than the physical ones. There's no doubt that being held underwater with your legs sealed into a big plastic boat can be somewhat disconcerting, even without the sound of whitewater roaring in your ears.

If you're having trouble rolling in moving water, then the best thing to do is to find a nice, mellow, deep section of current to flip and roll repeatedly in. As you get more and more comfortable, move into a faster current and practise there. Take your time and build your confidence slowly. On the physical side, there are two things that can cause problems with your roll. By trying to roll up on the upstream side, current has the tendency to force your active blade underwater more quickly. This doesn't mean that it's impossible to roll; it just means that you will get relatively less brace from your paddle and will have to have a quick and effective hip snap.

Waves are another potential source of problems for rollers. Large waves, or, in particular, breaking waves, can push the boat around and make it more difficult to get your paddle set up on the surface of the water. To minimize the effects of the current or waves, the ideal scenario is to set up and roll on the downstream side of your kayak. On the downstream side, you are pulling against the current, which can even provide added bracing power (not that you really need it!). As we already mentioned, with good technique you can usually get away with rolling on the upstream side of the kayak, but this is where an offside roll comes in handy.

ROLLING IN A HOLE

Rolling in a hole can be one of the easiest things to do, or it can be virtually impossible. It all depends on which side of the boat you're trying to roll up on. If you're trying to roll up on the upstream side of the boat, give up! You're not going to get anywhere. On the other hand, if you are setting up on the downstream side, then there's a good chance you'll be upright before you know it. The reason is that the green water rushing under the foam pile can hit the power face of your paddle and literally push you upright with minimal hip snap involved.

You might even have seen someone unintentionally do a full revolution in a hole (otherwise referred to as "window shading"). This happens when a paddler is rolled upright more quickly than was expected, with the help of the hole. In the true window shade, the stunned paddler then catches her upstream edge and gets flipped right back upside down! This may shed some light on why some people also refer to holes as "rollers"!

When upside down in a hole, your only option is to roll on the downstream side. There, the greenwater will actually give your roll a boost, and you'll likely find yourself upright more quickly than expected.

ADVANCED ROLLING

When you watch good paddlers roll, you might be surprised at how quickly they resurface. It's almost as if they didn't bother setting up. Well that's because they often don't go through the complete set up routine. As long as you get your paddle in a position to grab water, and get your body in a position that will allow your hips to roll the kayak upright, then you can roll in all sorts of different positions. Only practice will teach you what you can and can't get away with, so get out there and start rolling!

Piece of North America

Water

F. MASON

6

THE ANATOMY OF WHITEWATER

RIVER DYNAMICS • RIVER CLASSIFICATION
RIVER FEATURES • HAZARDS

"Find a good buddy to learn with. One of the greatest things about paddling is the adventure you'll share." (Kevin Varette)

RIVER DYNAMICS

One of the most fascinating and challenging aspects of whitewater kayaking is learning about nature's most powerful medium. The river is a complex, dynamic environment with enough energy to offer you a lifetime of enjoyment. The more you understand it, the more equipped you are to work with it and harness its power. Volumes have been written on hydrodynamics, but we'll just

focus on the aspects of current and specific river features that affect you as a kayaker.

FLOW

For this rudimentary discussion, flow refers to how the water is moving, particularly at or near the surface, where it affects us. There are three basic types of flow that interest us: laminar, helical and turbulent. It's important to understand at least the fundamentals of each so you know why the water is affecting your boat the way it is. As your paddling career evolves, the lens through which you see rivers will be modified to distinguish these flows. This capacity to understand flow will gain importance as you progress, helping you to make key decisions either while descending a river or playing on a feature. Learning about flow is the first step in developing an intuitive capacity for anticipating its effects on your boat.

Laminar flow refers to the streamline motion of water as it moves along a consistent path. This is what we generally know as the "current" of a river. It's caused by the gradient of the riverbed, and is affected by the width, depth, and course of the river. Its most common form is the basic downstream flow that, on its own, has the simple and predictable effect of turning and/or carrying your boat downriver.

Helical flow is the circular, spiralling, or tumbling motion of water that results from one force acting on it in one direction while another force acts on it in an opposing direction. To simplify this concept, imagine the forces being applied by your two hands on someone's arms if you were to spin her around as if to make her dizzy. As we'll see, this type of flow can affect us in a variety of ways— giving us both grief and serious enjoyment!

Turbulent flow is more irregular and less predictable than laminar or helical flow. Whitewater is pretty turbulent in general, but this term specifically refers to

disturbances in the water that usually last for an instant, or not much longer. They might be repetitive, but are slightly different each time they happen. For this reason, their effects on your boat vary.

VOLUME

When paddlers speak of different rivers, one of the major descriptors is whether they are high, medium or low volume. They're essentially talking about how much water there is in a river. Volume is measured by how much water passes by a given spot in a given time. Its units are either cubic feet per second (cfs) or cubic metres per second (cms). Volumes range from as low as 100 cfs (a small creek) to over 100,000 cfs (a large river). A high-volume river is typically characterized by faster flows, deeper rapids, and bigger waves. A low-volume river would

Volume is expressed in cubic feet per second (cfs), or cubic meters per second (cms), and refers to the amount of water that passes a point over a second in time.

generally have slower flows, shallower rapids with more obstacles, and smaller waves. The actual volume will give you some indication of a river's character, but it needs to be combined with information about its width and gradient before you know much about it. For example, two rivers may have the same volume, but one could be wide, slow, and shallow with small waves, while the other could be a narrow canyon with fast flows and huge waves. Volume is just one piece of information available about a river's character.

GRADIENT

In simple terms, the gradient is the amount that a river drops vertically over a given distance. It gives the average for a section and is most often measured in feet per mile (ft/mile). Rivers that are regularly paddled range in gradient from flat to over 600 ft/mile. In general, steeper rivers are more challenging, but gradient is not a sufficient indicator of difficulty on its own. For instance, a section may have a gradient of 100 ft/mile and be either an easy low-volume run or a juicy high-volume challenge. The same gradient may describe a section of river that is relatively flat with a couple big drops. Once you know the volume and gradient of a river, it's time to start collecting more specific information about the rapids.

DIRECTIONS

Like any sport, kayaking has its own lingo (actually, one that it shares for the most part

Vertical distance = 20 feet

OOPS...I SHOULD OF USED A CALCULATOR TO FIGURE OUT THE GRADIENT.

Horizontal distance = 10 feet
Gradient=10,560 feet per mile

with all other forms of whitewater recreation). We've already covered some of this lingo in the discussion of river dynamics above. Another essential component of it consists of directional vocabulary used on the river. The following are most commonly used by paddlers to refer to different directions:

Upstream/Downstream: Pretty straightforward —upstream is where the flow is coming from and downstream is where it's going. In other words, the net flow of water is from upstream to downstream. This does not change!

River Right/Left: These directions refer to the corresponding side of the river when looking downstream. They are the most frequently used indicators.

Surfer's Right/Left: These directions refer to the corresponding side of the river when looking upstream. They are used mainly by playboaters, who spend much of their time oriented upstream while surfing.

12 O'clock: Directions on the clock can be very handy in visualizing different angles you might want to set up with respect to the current. If your bow is pointed at 12

"Surfer's right" and "river right" refer to two very different sides of the river.

o'clock, it's pointing directly upstream. At 3 o'clock, your bow is pointing to river left (surfer's right) and at 9 o'clock, it's pointing to surfer's left (river right).

TYPES OF RIVERS

One of the best things about paddling is the variety of experiences it has to offer. From today's urban river parks to jungle creeks, from enormous cascading waterways to remote granite canyons carved deep into the mountains, there are so many different settings to experience. As we discussed above, there are big water or high-volume runs right down to low-volume steep creeks. Rivers also vary in their continuity. Some have continuous rapids that are sustained for long distances in tight canyons, while others are "drop and pool," meaning they have distinct rapids separated by calm sections. Some rivers are fed by glacial or snow melt from the mountains, and have really cold water even on the warmest summer days. Others are fed by wide expanses of farmland

and rolling hills, with water that has lots of time to warm up each season. Still others are controlled by hydroelectric dams and only flow on certain days of the week with water temperatures that are determined by whether the hydro company releases from the bottom of their reservoir or the surface. You never know where you might end up paddling!

RIVER CLASSIFICATION

Whitewater is rated on a scale of increasing difficulty from Class 1 to Class 6. This classification system provides a useful guide to the technical difficulty of a river, but there are so many other variables that can have a huge impact on the difficulty or danger of a river. Is it continuous in nature or drop and pool? Is the water warm or freezing in temperature? How remote is the run and how far away is help? Can you walk out if need be, or is it in a canyon? Is portaging an option for all rapids, or are you committed to running everything? As you can see, there can be massive

A large-volume river can feel like an ocean, while creeks can sometimes feel like natural waterslides.

differences between two rivers of the same class. For this reason, it's your responsibility to find out more about any river you're considering paddling. For many areas, there are guidebooks with detailed descriptions and images of the rivers, and more of these are available each year. It's always a good idea to pick one of these up. You can also ask questions on On-line chatboards or stop in at the local retailer for information. You can never be too well informed.

The classification system is still very useful for giving a river a general level of difficulty. It must be accepted that this system is in no way an exact science, and that it's open to interpretation. Here are some general guidelines for the whitewater classification system.

Class 1 (Easy): Fast-moving current with small waves and few obstructions that are easily avoided. Low-risk. Easy self-rescue.

Class 2 (Novice): Straightforward rapids with wide-open channels that are evident without scouting. Occasional manoeuvring is required. Trained paddlers will easily avoid any rocks or medium-sized waves. Swimmers are seldom injured.

Class 3 (Intermediate): Rapids with moderate, irregular waves, strong eddies and currents. Complex manoeuvres and good boat control are required. Major hazards are easily avoided. Scouting is recommended for inexperienced paddlers. Self-rescue is usually easy and injuries to swimmers are rare.

Class 4 (Advanced): Powerful, turbulent, and predictable rapids with large, unavoidable waves and holes or constricted passages. Fast and reliable eddy turns and precise boat handling are needed to navigate safely through. Scouting is necessary, and rapids may require "must-make" moves above dangerous hazards. Strong roll is highly recommended, as there is a moderate to high risk of injury to swimmers. Self-rescue is difficult, so skilled group assistance is often needed.

Class 5 (Expert): Extremely long, obstructed, or violent rapids with exposure to substantial risk. Expect large, unavoidable waves and holes, or steep, congested chutes. Eddies may be small, turbulent, difficult to reach, or non-existent. Reliable roll, proper equipment, extensive experience, high level of fitness and practiced rescue skills essential for survival. Scouting highly recommended, but may be difficult. Swims are very dangerous and rescues are difficult.

Class 6 (Extreme): These runs exemplify the boundaries of difficulty, unpredictability and danger, and have almost never been attempted, if ever. The consequences of errors are very severe and rescue may be impossible. Only expert teams with ideal conditions and extensive safety systems should ever consider these rapids.

RIVER FEATURES

As a paddler, you'll inevitably find yourself one day among a group of bystanders pulled over along a scenic road to look down from a bridge at a beautiful river or creek. Just as a mountaineer sees a knife-edge ridgeline, or a windsurfer sees a white-capped lake on a blustery day, you won't be seeing what those around you are

seeing. You'll observe a wonderful system of dynamic components, each one acting in its own unique way. As you progress, you'll dissect this scene, analyzing each feature, deciding which ones are worth further contemplation. You'll finish by coming up with a plan of action, whether imaginary (because you are with your grandma on a Sunday afternoon and have no gear) or not. You're going in!

The more you know about river features, the better equipped you are to have fun and be safe on the river. We'll cover some basics here, and they're important to understand, but we're limited to merely expanding your awareness with text. The knowledge becomes truly ingrained only with experience, and then you can use your intuition to anticipate the river's next move.

EDDIES

An eddy is a pocket of water directly downstream from some form of obstruction, for example, a rock or a part of the river bank that juts out. The deflection of water by the obstruction creates a relatively calm area below—a paddler's parking spot. The concept is quite simple. When water is deflected, it's pushed away from one area and towards another, creating a differential in the amount of water between the two areas. Because of gravity, the river naturally wants to equalize this differential by flattening itself out. To achieve this, the water circles back into the area that it was originally deflected away from. The result is an eddy on the downstream side of the obstruction. This flow creates an upstream current (from bottom to top) in the eddy that can vary in strength from being almost unnoticeable to very powerful. In big enough eddies on high-volume rivers, you can actually have Class 3 whitewater, or an eddy within an eddy! Very small eddies, just big enough to accommodate a kayak, are commonly called "micro-eddies."

EDDY LINES

The eddy line forms where the upstream-flowing water of the eddy (the eddy current) meets the downstream-flowing water of the river (the main current). This meeting of opposing currents creates a helical (whirlpool-like) flow that can be really fun or really bothersome, depending on the situation. The eddy line is narrowest and most crisply defined at the top of the eddy; it dissipates toward the bottom of the eddy. Reading eddy lines is a crucial skill to develop.

DOWNSTREAM "V"

The downstream "v" is a general term used to describe the path of least resistance through a rapid. This is the point where the water is naturally being directed and therefore deepest; it's most commonly the place that kayakers choose to be. For example, when there are two boulders across from each other, the water is

River Anatomy

deflected diagonally away from the obstructions, creating this v-shaped path between them.

REACTIONARIES

As water flows into obstructions, it reacts by deflecting off to one or both sides. This causes a reactionary (or "diagonal," or "lateral") wave that is angled downstream and away from the obstruction. Reactionaries, especially big ones, act to push a kayak in the direction they are reacting. A downstream 'v' is generally formed by two converging diagonals.

PILLOWS

On larger boulders, before reacting off to the side, the water can be pushed back upstream. This forms a unique breaking wave or pillow just above the boulder. It's so named because it cushions the blow! This pillow can be a weird and wonderful place to surf or can provide a facilitated detour of the rock. Significant pillows are generally a big-water occurrence

SEAM LINES

At the point where the two channels of a river that has been split come back together, or at the confluence of two rivers, a seam line is formed. Because the currents are not directly opposing, there is less of a helical (whirlpool-like) flow than on an

eddy line, but the two are otherwise quite similar. When the currents meet, they collide and move primarily in the only direction they can—downward. This is why it's a common sight to see someone who is swimming in a river get sucked down periodically if they encounter a seam line. It's also why seam lines can be fun play spots. The seam line dissipates slightly downstream of the point of confluence.

HYDRAULICS

Also known as "holes," "stoppers," or "reversals," hydraulics are formed when the water flows over an obstacle at a steep enough gradient to cause a recirculating flow downstream. As the water drops over the ledge or rock, it creates a depression or "trough." Because of the river's natural tendency to flatten out, water flows back upstream to fill up the trough. Tumbling over the drop and then recirculating causes the water to become aerated, so hydraulics are always white and bubbly. Where this aerated recycling water meets the incoming dark or "hard" water is called the "seam" of the hole. Holes come in a huge variety of shapes and sizes, depending on the gradient of the drop, the volume and depth of water, and nearby obstructions. In general, holes formed by steeper drops have a longer recirculating component ("recirc" or "backwash") and a stronger capacity to hold a kayak (see "Pourover" segment).

A hydraulic is one of the most intimidating yet important river features to get comfortable with. You spend much of your time on the river avoiding them, punching through them, or playing in them. The better you know the anatomy of a hole, the more equipped you'll be to do all of these. One important concept is that the hole is a surface feature, which means that the water below it is still flowing downstream (except for some vertical drops that reach the bottom before recirculating—you generally stay away

Hole Anatomy

from these!). So if you were to reach underneath the aerated backwash, you would feel the current pushing downstream. Try throwing a piece of wood into a hole. It will usually bounce around for a minute, and then get one bounce that sinks it enough to catch this current below. A second later it will emerge downstream. This is also one way for a person to get out of a sticky spot (see the "Safety and Rescue" segment).

Most natural holes will have weak spots on the sides and/or in the middle, depending on their shape, location and the proximity of obstructions that might affect the flow. We refer to the sides of holes as "corners" and to a weak spot in the middle (where the recirculating flow is broken) as a "tongue." These both present potential exit points when you want to get out of a hole; and are also very useful for playboating. The lack of natural weak spots is one of the things that make man-made hydraulics like dams and weirs so dangerous.

POUROVERS

Watch out for these! Pourovers are formed when water flows over a vertical, or nearly vertical, drop. The water pours over the ledge and straight down, making a deep depression in the river. This causes more water to recirculate from farther down. Pourovers often don't have tongues, so on top of being strong recirculators, they're usually pretty hard to get out of. Some pourovers are fun to play in, but more

1) Pourovers are formed when water flows over vertical, or nearly vertical, drops. Pourovers usually represent the nastiest form of holes for kayakers.
2) Long, shallow sloping holes are more easily navigated and can be swum through more easily, as most of the water is flowing under the hole.

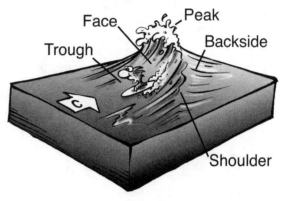

Wave Anatomy

often than not, we like to avoid them or "boof" over them (see the "Boofing" segment).

WAVES

In general, waves are swells that result from a combination of increased flow and some physical feature of the riverbed. Waves are even more varied in their forms than hydraulics, and their causes tend to be a bit more mysterious (at least to paddlers!). They can be flat or steep, smooth or breaking, stationary or dynamic, predictable or explosive.

Regardless of their type, waves all have some common features. The "face" of the wave is the upstream side of the swell. The depression at the bottom of the face is the "trough." The very top of the face is the "peak" or "crest," which then drops off to the "backside." Mountaineers have peaks and valleys; paddlers have crests and troughs!

For now, we'll look at a few of the most common types of waves.

Rolling Waves

When water speeds up, it acquires energy, and a bumpy riverbed or narrowing of the channel can cause it to rise and fall slightly, like rolling hills. These rolling waves are not steep enough to have whitecaps (or to "break"), but they provide a gentle up-and-down ride that is great for starters. These are often found at the top or bottom of rapids, where the gradient is not very steep.

Standing Waves

When fast water is slowed down somehow (e.g., by a pool below a rapid, by submerged boulders, or by a narrowing of the channel),

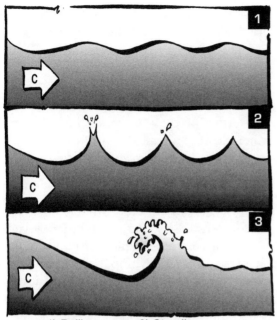

1) Rolling waves. 2) Standing waves. 3) Breaking wave.

the trough. This creates a feature similar to a hydraulic, because the water is tumbling upstream, often with enough force to stop and hold onto a kayak. The difference is that the breaking wave is not recirculating from downstream of its face, whereas hydraulics are recirculating from downstream. The effect is that they are usually not as sticky as a hole, though they can still give you a big, bouncy ride! Some large, unique waves form a curling or "tubing" break that is more reminiscent of some ocean waves. These can provide an awesome surf—or an equally awesome thrashing!

Exploding Waves

Exploding waves are formed when, in addition to the normal causes, fluctuating or unstable factors, such as surging side currents, make them continuously yet unpredictably build and crash. An exploding wave will start out as a smaller wave, and then swell until it finally becomes unstable and crashes (the explosion). It repeats this cycle over and over, but with only an ounce of predictability. Quite often, you'll watch one for a while, and just when you think you've got it figured out, its pattern totally changes! This is generally a big-volume phenomenon and can be one of the most exciting features on the river because it keeps you guessing.

For personal reasons, we can't broach this topic without briefly mentioning "Mundaca." Mundaca is a fantastic exploding

it gets pushed upward to form a stationary standing wave. These waves are in sets of at least three and have more defined faces and peaks than rolling waves. Depending on the volume of the river, these waves can be small or gigantic. One great thing about them is that no matter how big they get, standing waves are pure fun and present no hazard on their own.

Breaking Waves

When a wave is steep enough, water will begin to tumble down its face from the crest toward the trough and become aerated. On some waves, the break is very slight and remains up near the crest, while on others the break is all the way down to wave on the mighty Futaleufu River in Patagonia, Chile, our home away from home. We have witnessed this wave render hundreds of paddlers euphoric, in awe of the feature itself, and in awe of themselves for paddling right into it! This is the power of an exploding wave.

BOILS

Sometimes the effects of the riverbed are a little more mysterious and cause random, funny things to happen. The most recognizable is a boil, which gets its name from the bubbles in a pot of boiling water. A boil occurs when the current is forced directly upwards to the surface, often in unpredictable surges. One specific type of boil is found below a waterfall, where aerated water is finding its way back up to the surface after having plummeted toward the bottom. Boils are also found in constricted rapids or canyons, and randomly on large rivers. They usually last for only as long as it takes them to settle

out. The best way to get through them is discussed in the "Big Water" segment.

WHIRLPOOLS

The term whirlpool describes the action of water flowing in a downward spiral. It's caused by the collision of opposing flows, as with an eddy line. While small, the whirlpool is at most an unstable place for a paddler, but when the currents involved are powerful enough, the whirlpool can become a very entertaining or intimidating phenomenon. Big whirlpools can suck a person and even a kayak under water, which can be fun if done intentionally, but not so fun if it's a surprise!

A whirlpool.

HAZARDS

The bottom line is that although there are real objective hazards inherent in the whitewater environment, kayaking is as safe or as dangerous as you make it. It's important to learn from professionals, to be informed and aware of your surroundings,

A boil.

to make sensible decisions based on your skills and training, to communicate with those around you, to carry the right equipment for the situation, and to promote safety on the river. Knowing what features present hazards and how to identify them in rapids is an integral skill for staying safe. This knowledge is something you both learn and gain from experience. Never rush into situations you're unsure of. If you're careful and sensible, you can stay safe your entire life on the river.

SHALLOW WATER INJURIES AND FOOT ENTRAPMENTS

Shallow water is a basic hazard, but it's one of the most common causes of injury and broken equipment among paddlers. You can tell water is shallow either by being able to see the bottom, or by the little rippled waves that are caused when rocks are close to the surface. If you're unsure, try to get a better look or figure out a way to test the depth. If the water is shallow, take extra care not to flip or plant your blade deeply. Be especially careful if you notice that the rock on the banks looks sharp, as this is usually an indication of sharp rock in the river as well.

Flipping in shallow water exposes your entire upper body to trauma. To minimize the potential for damage when upside down, keep your body as shallow as possible by tucking it up to the boat, and roll as quickly as you can.

If you're swimming in shallow water, always resist the urge to stand up. A "foot entrapment" is when your foot becomes lodged in between rocks or anything else on the riverbed. Because the current won't cease, this can very quickly present a life-threatening situation, as you're being forced down by the current and getting increasingly tired. It's easily preventable by staying in the "bodysurfing position" in shallow water. In this position, you're flat on your back with your feet downstream, keeping your bum up, and using your arms to steer if necessary. This keeps you as shallow as possible, and lets you push off any obstructions with your feet. It's the recommended position for defensive swimming.

PINNING/BROACHING ROCKS

As you're running a rapid, especially a steep rapid, it's possible that your kayak may become pinned on a submerged or

Vertical pins are one of the biggest dangers on steep, shallow creeks.

exposed rock. In the case of a steep drop, the boat may become vertically pinned if the bow or stern gets lodged in the rock. This most often happens as a result of the shape of the rock, a crack in the rock, or a gap between two rocks. Regardless of which, there is just enough room for the end of the boat to become stuck.

Otherwise, your boat may be broached sideways against an obstruction. In both cases, the rock was in the path that you chose to run (or ended up running, if it was not intentional). Because of the force with which the river pushes against your boat, pins can be very dangerous situations. The main risks are that your boat may give way and bend, or that you cannot be rescued quickly enough.

Scouting a rapid from shore will always give you the best view of potentially hazardous spots. When you scout a rapid or waterfall, always look for signs of rocks just below or above the surface that may interfere with your run. When they're exposed, they're easier to detect, but when they're submerged, you have to resort to your ability to identify the signs. In general, the water will look "funny"; like it's not doing what it's supposed to. There may be strange ripples, or, halfway down a rapid, there may be a big "rooster-tail" spraying water up into the air, or a strange, rigid bump in the water. Below a waterfall, the water will usually plunge downward and then boil back up just downstream. If there's a rock at the bottom, there will be less or no boil activity and some splatting or spraying of the water. These and other abnormalities are indications that you should beware of potential pinning rocks.

UNDERCUT ROCKS

Undercuts are rocks that have been eroded by the flow of water over time. They're most dangerous when the river level is such that the erosion is right underneath the surface, forming somewhat of an underwater cave that is very hard to detect until it's too late.

The degree of hazard presented by undercuts depends on several things. If the rock is facing directly upstream, it's likely to be more dangerous than if it were angled downstream, because water is forcing you straight into it. This makes it more difficult to get out or to be rescued; and also it is more likely that logs and other items will be stuck in there that might complicate your situation. Larger rocks, a stronger current, and prevalence of wood in the river are other factors that increase the hazard posed by an undercut.

Detecting and avoiding undercuts can be challenging things to do. The first choice is to get local information about any major hazards. You also need to be aware of the characteristics of the river. Are the rocks eroded along the banks? Are they sharp shelves of sedimentary rock, or old, rounded granite walls? Are they

Undercut rocks should be avoided like the plague.

TREES ARE VICIOUS!

by Dave Scott

Don't get me wrong, I like trees and all, but they can, at times, be cruel and vicious. They lash out at you when you least expect it. It's important to maintain traditions like the annual family Christmas Tree Hunt, to keep the numbers down, and to keep them in control!

They move fast, too. Don't tell me that you've never had a tree suddenly pop out in front of you, whether while skiing, biking, kayaking, walking, or doing some other activity. Let's be honest, we've all had it happen. The roots just reach out and grab you. The roots weren't there before, but they sure grew suddenly from the ground and tried to trip you up. If the trees are feeling particularly unfriendly, after tripping you, you'll find a branch right at eye level to narrowly avoid. Only to fall down on your side on a root!

Trees: they supply us with leaves for raking; with sap for gluing your fingers together; with nesting branches, so birds can roost and leave their mark your newly washed car. Sure, they also supply us with wood, pulp for paper, shelter from the sun and the wind, and picturesque views for our memories, but they're just trying to buy us off. Nothing else can be on the one hand so useful, and on the other hand so vindictive, without having a greater conscience about them!

All this is to say that no, -2° C is not too cold to go kayaking. Also, 180 cubic meters per second (cms) on the Rouge River, which usually runs at 40 cms, is not too high a level at sub-zero temperatures. Fifteen to twenty-five km/h winds are not that much of a hindrance, and feel fine, if they're from behind you. Ten-foot waves where they are normally three feet high are no big deal. Ice-covered rocks, more slippery than you think, can be just plain old fun. But WATCH OUT!

Look down for a couple seconds to make sure there's no ice where you're about to step, and the branches will appear out of nowhere and attack. It takes a deliberate effort to find the tiny gap between the helmet and the eye. It's the sort of thing that doesn't "just happen." And then, once our footing has been regained, to sit there, blowing in the wind, bare of branches and looking so innocent? I don't buy it!

So there I was on Sunday. I could have been cold, but I wasn't. I could have been beaten up by the water, but I held my own. I could have fallen on the rocks, yet I remained steady. I could have been sunburned and windburned, yet I didn't turn cherry red.

But you get out of the boat ONE time to scout ONE rapid in the entire day, and a tree decides to make an example of you!

Go figure. All I can say now is that days like Sunday are made for being outdoors. And made all the better by good company, such as Pat, Yoan and Jean-Pierre.

Thanks, guys, but next time those trees better watch out!

smooth or jagged? Are there potholes or other peculiar features? Have you noticed wood jammed up against rocks or floating in eddies? These are all valuable pieces of information.

If you're unsure about a particular rock, compare what the water is doing when it flows into it with a rock you know is not undercut. In bigger water particularly, water flowing into a boulder will often create at least a moderate pillow or surge up against the rock. An undercut will often lack this pillow as water is allowed to continue flowing underneath it. You can check for boils or other signs of water emerging from the downstream side of the boulder, another sign of an undercut. Avoid any suspicious boulders or walls.

SIEVES/STRAINERS

Named after the device we use to keep pasta in and let water out, these nasty river features also let big things in (like kayaks or people), but let only water out. Sieves pose a significant hazard to paddlers and can be very difficult to detect.

A strainer lets water through, but stops bigger objects . . . like you!

Again, the first thing to do is ask locals if they know of any major hazards. Otherwise, be aware of the type of rock around you and any oddities. Are there a lot of cracks? These are the main causes of rock sieves, as water is allowed to flow through them, but anything bigger can get stuck. Ominous cracks in rocks, small channels between boulders, abnormalities in the flow above slabs of rock, and evidence of water emerging downstream of boulders are all potential signs of rock strainers. Needless to say, it's best to steer clear of these features.

LOG-JAMS

Where one log gets broached, subsequent logs flowing down the river can result in a pileup of wood that creates a specific kind of strainer. Water will flow through this log-jam, but anything bigger will get caught up in it. If you see a pile of logs, stay away!

BAD HOLES

Bad holes are holes that won't let go of your kayak easily. The worst holes will hold you even when you're swimming. As we discussed in the section on hydraulics, those with steep entries (like pourovers and waterfalls) typically have the strongest backwashes. Because the water is dropping so steeply into the trough, there's not much downstream momentum—even in the current below the backwash. Usually, if push comes to shove, swimming down into the current below the backwash is a way to escape.

The "smiling hole rule" says that if when looking downstream at a hole, it's shaped as a smile, with the corners of the hole being further downstream than the centre, then the hole will be safer than where the hole is in the shape of a frown, with the corners of the hole being more upstream than its centre.

When this current is not able to provide much help, the hole is considered more dangerous.

One of the scariest things about really steep holes is that they are almost impossible to see as you approach them—at most there may be a little hump or roller just above them formed by the ledge or boulder. These holes are one of the reasons why scouting any unknown water is important. Other bad holes are big, powerful ones that may not be as sticky, but have enough force to injure you, or are so violent that breathing can become an issue.

Although the steepness of the green water pouring into a hole plays the largest role in determining its severity, the "smiling" factor of a hole will also provide some insight. The "smiling hole rule" is simple. If when looking downstream at a hole it is shaped as a smile, with the corners of the hole being further downstream than the centre, then the hole will be safer than its ugly counterpart. The

"frowning" hole has corners that are further upstream than its centre, forming a frown when looking at it from upstream. A hole will always want to feed paddlers to the furthest point downstream. Therefore, in a smiling hole a kayaker will be fed to the corners where they can escape, whereas in a frowning hole paddlers will be fed into the centre of the hole where things can be a little bleaker.

Waterfalls can present their own unique hazards. The water flowing over the waterfall (the "curtain") can create a "double hole" (recirculating both ways) if it's landing away from the wall behind it, which has often been eroded away to form somewhat of a cave. It's possible in this case that a paddler may end up, either in or out of the boat, behind the curtain and in a very difficult rescue situation. You can usually tell if there's a cave behind the curtain when scouting.

Some waterfalls have been eroded on the backside, which is clearly not a good place to find yourself.

MAN-MADE WEIRS/DAMS

Aside from the fact that there may be all sorts of dangerous hidden materials and that you often are at the mercy of those controlling the water flow, man-made weirs and dams are inherently dangerous. Because the flow is generally carefully controlled and contained by barriers on both sides, the hydraulic formed ends up being free of any natural weak spots. The water entering the drop is smooth, the angle is usually steep and creates a dangerous backwash, and there are no natural corner or tongue formations. The majority of deaths on rivers are caused by people flirting with man-made dams and weirs, and then by untrained people trying to rescue them. If you choose to play here, no longer are you dealing with the laws of nature—so beware.

RIVER RUNNING

**THE RULES OF THE GAME • EDDY TURNS • FERRIES • S-TURNS
TURNING MIDSTREAM • BACKWARD AWARENESS • SCOUTING
HANDLING ROCKS • RIDING THROUGH WAVE TRAINS • MANAGING HOLES
LATERAL MOMENTUM • USING THE POWER OF THE RIVER • PORTAGING**

*"Every thread of current has something to teach those who are willing to learn.
Be humble, and above all, be curious!"* (Scott Docherty)

THE RULES OF THE GAME

For this "River Running" segment we're going to start by looking at eddy turns and ferries in their most basic and ideal forms. We're then going to look at other skills and techniques that will come in handy, including the scouting of a rapid and the picking of a line.

EDDY TURNS

Eddy turn refers to the action of moving from the main current into an eddy, or vice-versa. This is also commonly referred to as "peeling" in and out, or "eddying" in and out. Whether you're eddying in, or peeling out of an eddy, your goal is to break completely through the eddy line and to carve a smooth, arcing turn in which your kayak maintains its forward momentum.

To this point, we've looked at the individual components that are required to make a smooth eddy turn. It's now simply a matter of piecing these skills together with the right plan of action. This plan of action is determined by your end goal and by the power and variety of the currents that you're dealing with.

As you may have already learned, and as we'll discuss further in the "Picking a Line" segment, your success in running rapids relies heavily on your ability to look ahead and take actions that set you up for what is coming next. For simplicity's sake, let's assume that you're pulling out of an eddy into a mild current without obstacles. Your goal is to carve a smooth turn into the middle of the current and then head downstream. You now need to decide on how much speed, angle, and spin momentum is necessary to achieve this goal. Again, these decisions depend on

the strength of current that you're dealing with. As a general rule, you always want to cross eddy lines aggressively. The stronger the current, the more aggressive you'll want to be. This might seem like a simple enough rule, but the reality is that as currents get stronger, paddlers often become more timid. An aggressive approach is vital, though, as it ensures that you'll break right through the eddy line and into the main current. Breaking through the eddy line, as opposed to getting stuck on it, means avoiding one of the most unstable and unpredictable spots on the river. Seeing as we're considering relatively mild current for this example, you'll be taking a moderately aggressive approach.

Clearly, every situation will require a slightly different approach, but the basic eddy turn we're going to look at can be slightly modified to work in any circumstance. Your plan of action involves building up enough forward momentum to take you completely across the eddy line at about a 45 degree

One of my biggest revelations about whitewater paddling came very early on. It was during my first season of kayaking, while scouting McKoy's rapid on the Ottawa River. McKoy's was, and will always be, one of the most menacing and mentally challenging rapids for paddlers visiting the Ottawa River. As I looked at the rapid before me, I saw more than just a frightening mess of turbulent water. I saw distinct river features. At the same time I realized that running through McKoy's simply involved performing a fairly straightforward combination of eddy turns and ferries. Was that it? Could running whitewater really be that simple? Having practiced my eddy turns and ferries tirelessly, I decided to give it a shot and I slid into my kayak with new found confidence. Unfortunately I didn't really understand how fast the water was actually moving... and the waves were a lot bigger than I expected! In the end, I got thumped in the mighty Phil's Hole and rolled up wide eyed and red faced. When I reached the calm water below I had another major revelation... yes, a rapid could be broken down into some fairly basic eddy turns and ferry manoeuvers, but there were a whole bunch of other techniques that I needed to learn that would come in handy. One of the most important being the ability to pick a good line through a rapid! (Ken Whiting)

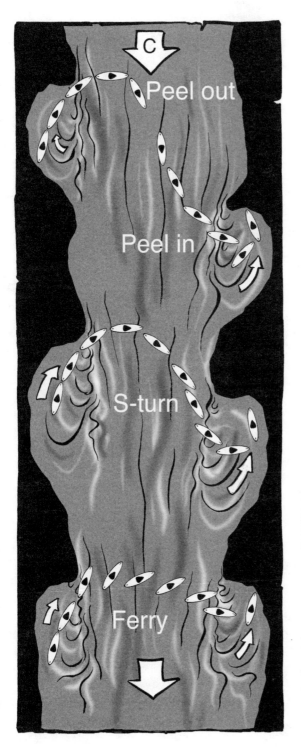

angle. As you break through the eddy line, you want your kayak to carve a smooth arc and end up facing downstream. This basic eddy turn starts with a good set-up position and the right angle, forward strokes to build forward momentum, a stern draw to establish the boat's carving direction (spin momentum), a power stroke to pull the boat completely across the eddy line, and a gliding draw to carve a smooth turn downstream. Let's look more closely at each of these steps.

A good set-up position gives you time to build adequate forward momentum that will take you across the eddy line at around a 45-degree angle. There are a couple of things to consider when deciding on your set-up position.

Firstly, it needs to be recognized that the inside of an eddy provides the calmest water and will result in the least amount of "drift" on your approach. Drift is the movement of your kayak by the current in a direction other than the one in which you wish to go. The outside of an eddy has the quickest current and will thus result in the most drift. Paddlers have a tendency to hang

When setting up your eddy turn, keep in mind that the inside of the eddy is the calmest, and the best place to begin your approach.

out on the outside of eddies, where they are closest to shore. This actually complicates their set-up as they will drift more on their approach and frequently find themselves having difficulty exiting at the point they have chosen with the desired angle.

A second issue to consider is that eddy lines are most defined and narrowest at their source (the top), which makes it the preferred area to cross, as there is less "funny water" and it's more predictable.

Having established a good set-up position and built up some forward speed, you then need to give your kayak a slight amount of turning momentum before you completely cross the eddy line. This turning momentum ensures that your kayak will carve in the right direction. Because whitewater kayaks are designed to turn so effectively, and since the main current will be helping to turn your boat downstream, you definitely won't need to use a full sweep stroke. Your goal is simply to start your kayak on its turning path, or to establish some turning momentum. This is most effectively done with a slight stern draw on the upstream side. With this turning momentum established, your focus is now on pulling yourself completely across the eddy line and into the main current, which is where the "power stroke" that we practised is so effective.

Recall that the power stroke is a vertical forward stroke designed to provide maximum forward propulsion with minimal impact on the kayak's turning momentum. We covered this stroke in detail earlier in this book and introduced a great drill for practising it on flatwater. When using it to cross an eddy line, your technique remains

1) A small stern draw on the upstream side of your kayak will establish turning momentum into the current. 2) A power stroke will then pull you and your kayak completely across the eddy line, and into the current, while allowing your kayak to carve a smooth turn downstream.

the same. You'll plant this power stroke across the eddy line in the main current and pull your boat and body aggressively forward. As you do this, you must be sure to have your boat tilted downstream. Holding a steady downstream tilt not only lets your kayak carve, but it prevents the main current from catching your upstream edge. The amount you tilt your kayak and the muscle you apply to your power stroke will depend on the speed of the water that you're entering. The faster the main current, the more aggressive your boat's tilt and the more powerful your stroke will need to be.

So you've now thrust yourself across the eddy line with your boat carving a smooth turn downstream. The final challenge is getting your kayak to continue carving this turn until you're facing directly downstream. You could continue to take power strokes while holding a steady tilt on your boat. This would allow you to continue carving your turn while maintaining your forward momentum, but it's not the most efficient and not always necessary.

Another option is to use the gliding draw that we covered in the "Strokes" segment of this book. The gliding draw is a fairly static draw stroke that gets planted firmly in the water to help your boat carve more effectively and maintain speed. The gliding draw gets planted about a foot behind your hip and between one and two feet out to the side of your boat with the blade parallel to the kayak, and with your body turned to face the paddle. This is a very committing stroke in its purest form, so you may want to start more conservatively by keeping your top hand over your kayak. As your balance improves and your confidence grows, you can push your top hand across the kayak to get your draw more vertical.

There you have the standard eddy turn technique. As mentioned before, this technique can be adapted to fit almost any situation. One of the most significant modifications that you can make involves turning your gliding draw into an active bow draw. Using the C-stroke technique we covered in the "Strokes" section, you can turn your boat downstream more quickly while maintaining constant control with an active blade in the water. You can also use an open-faced bow draw after breaking across the eddy line to turn your boat even more aggressively.

This open-faced bow draw is commonly referred to as the "Duffek" stroke. It allows you to grab a substantial amount of water to aggressively pull your bow around. By dropping your upstream edge slightly, you can also use your Duffek stroke for a slight stern pivot, which takes advantage of buoyancy energy to further help your turn. When would you use this stroke? A Duffek gets used when we need to move from an eddy into the main current and face downstream as quickly as possible.

We'll now take a quick look at pulling out of the main current into an eddy, otherwise known as "eddying out." You'll use the same technique that you used for

The gliding draw lets you control a smooth, carving eddy turn.

The "duffek" lets you grab a substantial amount of water, and pivot around very quickly.

peeling out of an eddy, although your set up is trickier because you have a large amount of "drift" to take into account. Your goal is to break through the eddy line as close to its source as possible, with your forward momentum breaking you through it on a 45 degree downstream angle.

To reach this goal, you need to account for the speed of the current that's taking you downstream. It's a simple notion that if you point your kayak directly at your destination, then the downstream drift will take you past your target; but most people have a challenging time mastering this kind

To peel into an eddy, you'll use the same technique that we discussed for peeling out of an eddy. The only difference is that you'll have more "drift" to take into account.

of anticipation. You need to aim upstream of your target enough that the drift and your forward momentum lead you directly to your target on the eddy line. An important tip is to keep your eyes on where you're going when catching an eddy. Don't get caught staring at the hood ornament of your kayak!

Of course practice is the only way to become truly proficient at reading whitewater and plotting a course to the next eddy, but there are a few key things you can keep in mind. It's essential to establish lateral momentum (momentum across the river) when catching an eddy, so that you can break right through the eddy line. This means that if you're planning to catch an eddy on the river right, you'll want to start away from that right-hand shore to give yourself a chance to build lateral momentum toward the eddy.

FERRIES

Ferrying is the act of moving from one side of the river to the other with minimal downstream drift. This is accomplished by paddling your kayak on an angle somewhere between directly upstream and perpendicular to the main current in the direction that you want to move. Although every situation will require a slightly different approach, we're going to look at a ferrying technique that can be adapted to fit any situation.

The idea behind the ferry is quite simple. To move across current you can't simply point your kayak to your fnal destination and paddle as if you were in flatwater, because the main current will pull you downstream. You need to angle your kayak upstream enough so that your strokes work to

A slightly off-vertical power stroke will pull you across the eddy line and into the current, and will establish your ferry angle. Make sure that you keep a steady downstream tilt on your kayak.

counterbalance this downstream pull. With experience, you'll learn what boat angle is most effective for the various situations that you come across. As a general rule, the more upstream angle you have (the closer you are to pointing directly upstream), the slower you'll move laterally and the more your paddle strokes will be working to keep you from drifting downstream. On the other hand, the less upstream angle that you have (the closer you are to pointing directly across the main current), the more quickly you'll move across the river and the less your strokes will be working to keep you from drifting downstream.

To start, you need to come up with an action plan, which is again determined by your end goal and by the power and character of the currents you're dealing with. To keep things simple, we'll consider ferrying from one eddy to another across fairly mild and wide current that has no significant obstacles to contend with. Your goal is to reach the eddy on the other side of the river. The success of your ferry will rely heavily on your set-up position and angle. You'll also need to break through the eddy line in control, maintain an effective ferry angle, hold a steady downstream tilt on your boat as you ferry and successfully break through the eddy line into your destination eddy. We'll now look a bit more closely at how you'll accomplish these things.

The most important part of your ferry is your entry into the main current. The key to ferrying is converting the upstream momentum you establish on your approach into lateral momentum as you cross the eddy line. This means that the less upstream angle you can get away with using, the better off

your ferry will be. If you have too much upstream angle, you'll fight the main current more than is necessary. For the scenario we're considering, your set-up and approach will be very similar to an eddy turn, although you might decide to approach with a little more upstream angle.

Starting near the middle of the eddy where you'll experience a minimal amount of drift, aim high on the eddy line (near its source) and build up some forward speed. As you cross the eddy line, establish a small amount of turning momentum towards the main current with a small stern draw on the upstream side. This turning momentum helps you break through the eddy line and convert your forward speed into lateral momentum.

Continuing just as you would with a peel-out, tilt your kayak on its downstream edge, and use a power stroke to pull yourself completely across the eddy line. This power stroke will also be responsible for establishing your ferry angle by preventing the main current from turning your boat downstream. This means that the power stroke you use for the ferry may not be quite as vertical as the power stroke you used for the eddy turn, because in the ferry you need this stroke to provide some turning power. Be careful that your power stroke doesn't provide too much turning power, as this would angle your kayak too far upstream or even back towards the eddy.

Now that you're in the main current with a good angle on your kayak, you're well on your way. At this point, your job is to maintain your ferry angle and your forward speed while holding a steady downstream tilt on your kayak that prevents your upstream edge from catching. The scenario we're considering involves a wide section of river, so you need to keep paddling your way across the current while balancing your boat on edge. As you do this, keep glancing at your target. Keeping track of your destination will let you know of any adjustments you need to make to your ferry angle along the way. If you find yourself moving upstream of the destination eddy, this means you have too much upstream

When crossing wide stretches of current, keep your boat tilted downstream and continue paddling your way across.

angle and you must ease it off a little. If you're drifting downstream of the eddy, this means you need to use a more aggressive upstream angle that fights the current more (turn the kayak more upstream).

As you get closer to your destination eddy, you have to make plans for punching through the eddy line and deep into the eddy. Do this using a version of the eddy turn technique that we covered earlier. To minimize your drift downstream, you'll ferry until you get fairly close to the eddy line. You'll then sweep your bow downstream and punch through the eddy line and into the eddy, pulling yourself completely across with a power stroke.

Recall that you want to break through the eddy line on a 45-degree downstream angle with forward speed. You also have to remember to switch your boat tilt as you cross the eddy line to carve into the eddy and prevent your outside edge from catching. The temptation is there to just ferry right into the eddy, which may work in some situations, but in others you may not have enough lateral momentum to break completely through the eddy line.

As you near your final destination, be sure to let your ferry angle go so that you can punch through the eddy line on the other side.

You'll then get stuck on the swirliest, most unstable water on the river, which becomes less and less of a good thing as the whitewater you paddle gets harder.

S-TURNS

An S-Turn is a ferrying technique used for crossing narrow current. This can be tricky, because you need to peel out of an eddy in a way that sets you up quickly for breaking into the eddy on the other side. Remember that for punching into the second eddy, you want to hit the eddy line with a 45-degree downstream angle.

This S-Turn is basically two linked eddy turns. Because your timing needs to be quite precise for the S-turn, keep a close eye on your destination eddy so that you can make any small corrections to your boat angle along the way. The gliding draw that you used for your basic eddy turn technique

comes in very handy for the S-Turn, as it lets you keep constant control over your boat's path and allows you to make small corrections. If you need to turn more quickly to establish the downstream angle needed to punch the destination eddy line, then you can slide your blade forward and use it as a bow draw temporarily. When you reach the destination eddy line, pull yourself completely through with a power stroke as you tilt your kayak onto its other edge and carve your way into the eddy.

TURNING MIDSTREAM

We've looked at how to carve in and out of eddies and how to ferry across the river; now it's time to consider how to make directional changes while in the main current.

There are two types of turns that you're likely to have to make: casual turns and aggressive turns. There really aren't many

An S-turn across a narrow stretch of current.

rules to consider for casual turns. Your basic sweep strokes will turn your boat quite effectively, especially if you combine a little edging with your sweeps to pivot the boat around. Near the peak of the waves is usually the best spot to turn, but is certainly not the only option. When you're at the peak of a wave, you have the best view of the rapid ahead, which obviously lets you make the most informed decision on how much to turn your kayak. As well, at the peak of the wave, a large part of your boat will be out of the water, making it much easier to turn. The reality is that any recent whitewater boat is designed to turn very well, so you don't need to restrict yourself to turning at the

An upstream pivot turn is usually the quickest way to pull your kayak onto the needed ferry angle. This is the same pivot turn that you learned on flatwater.

Using a sweep / duffek combination to aggressively change directions mid rapid.

peak of a wave. If you need to turn, you should be able to turn your boat very effectively at any point.

When you want to turn your boat more aggressively, your best option is the pivot turn. This is a skill that we've already looked at in depth and that you really need to master. Let's consider a situation where you are floating sideways pointing to river right, when you notice a massive hole in front of you that needs to be missed to the river left. You could just back ferry away from the hole, but let's say you saw it last minute and are too close to avoid it with a back ferry. Instead, you can use a stern pivot turn to pull your boat aggressively upstream and onto a ferry angle to the river left. The pivot turn that you'll use in this "combat" situation is no different than that which you use on flatwater. This means you'll aggressively lead with your head and body and pull the stern of your kayak underwater so that the bow can swing around effortlessly. To sink the stern, you need to tilt your kayak into your front sweep and throw your weight back slightly. The tricky part of this turn is making the right changes to your boat tilts. You need to maintain a downstream tilt on your kayak throughout the turn, or you'll catch your upstream edge. This means that once your sweep has pulled your bow past 12 o'clock, you need to have changed the tilt on your kayak.

You could also use a back sweep, or a Duffek stroke to initiate your pivot turn, or you could even use some combination of these strokes. For a review of the pivot turn, see the segment on this skill above. The key is developing your confidence and your edge control to a point where you can use a pivot

turn to make quick changes of direction in even the most chaotic whitewater.

BACKWARD AWARENESS

Developing your comfort level being backwards on a river will have a very positive impact on your paddling. When river running, you'll be able to confidently back ferry away from obstacles and will remain in control when spun backwards mid-rapid. Without having developed this backward awareness, you would probably find yourself panicking and struggling to regain control in these same situations. For the playboater, backward awareness is absolutely critical, since most moves involve spinning around—which means facing backward up to half of the time. If you are only controlled and comfortable when surfing facing upstream, then you'll be at the mercy of the river the rest of the time.

Backward awareness is crucial for playboaters, as most moves involve spinning around—which means facing backward 50% of the time.

There's only one way to develop your backward awareness: be backwards! Begin with practising your back paddling and your back sweeps. You can then move onto simple backward eddy turns and ferries. It will feel odd to start off, and you're almost guaranteed to flip a few times, but keep practising until you're comfortable crossing powerful eddy lines without having to think about which way to tilt your kayak and on which side to take your next stroke. The next step is to practice back surfing. Back surfing is an

incredibly powerful skill for the river runner as well as the playboater. Back surfing will let the river runner use waves to help their back ferries and even provides the opportunity to boat scout ahead while surfing. The fine edge control that you'll learn from successful backsurfing can help take your overall paddling to a whole new level.

SCOUTING

"If the fun to pain ratio isn't looking good, then why run it?" (Ken Whiting)

Scouting is the action of looking ahead at a rapid to identify any hazards and to decide on a route. You can scout either from our kayak ("boat scouting") or the riverbank. Of course, scouting from shore is generally the best means, as you can get a variety of different perspectives and a clearer view of the rapid as a whole. On the other hand, boat scouting is much quicker and warmer in some instances. Both of these forms of scouting are skills like any other, and take practice to develop. This practice does involve putting our ideas to the test, and invariably it will mean learning from both good and bad decisions.

When scouting there are four main things to consider: the approach, the rapid itself, the recovery area, and specific safety concerns. We'll start by looking at the rapid itself, as it will have a strong bearing on how you look at the approach and the recovery area. When looking at the rapid, seek out any possible hazards or places to avoid, and

The best way to develop your backward awareness is to practice eddy turns, ferries, and S-turns in reverse.

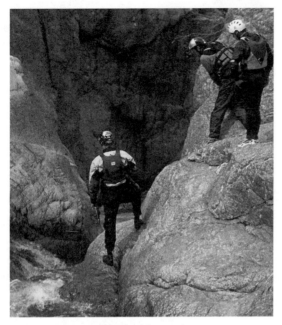

If in doubt, scout.

try to identify all the different lines that have potential. Given the required moves, the group you are with and your personal skill level, you should then be able to pick a line that you're comfortable with. Of course if you aren't comfortable with any lines at this point, then it's time to start portaging—no matter what anyone says!

With a line picked, turn your eyes upstream and have a look at the approach to the rapid, as it plays a pivotal role in the success of your run. Check out the speed and direction of the current flowing into the rapid—your starting point—and how each of these will affect the line that you've chosen. The next thing to look at is the recovery area. What's going on downstream of the rapid? Do you need to be anywhere in particular at the bottom, or is there a large recovery zone? What are the consequences

of swimming? These are of course very important things to consider and should have a real impact on your decisions.

The final thing to look at, but certainly not your least important consideration, is how you can run a rapid the most safely. You should be looking at the hazards and considering the worst-case scenarios. Where can you set up effective safety? For a more detailed discussion of safety and rescue considerations, see the "Safety and Rescue" section of this book.

When scouting from shore, try to gain as many different perspectives of a rapid as possible. It's amazing how different things can look from a slightly different location. For instance, by scouting from above and looking down upon a rapid, you'll get a great overview, but it is very difficult from this position to gauge the size of river features and the actual gradient of the river. Whenever possible, scout from water level as well as from above.

It's also important to choose useful landmarks that will be recognizable from your kayak. Landmarks are features that you can choose from shore to use as guides as you approach and descend a rapid. A landmark might be a particular wave, a rock, or even something unique on shore like a protruding branch. After choosing your landmarks, make note of how they look from the different scouting perspectives. When we walk back to our boats to run a rapid that we've just scouted, we'll stop frequently to relocate landmarks, and we'll crouch down to water level so that we know what to expect of the view from our boats.

BOAT SCOUTING

Boat scouting is best done from a calm eddy above a rapid that provides you with the option of getting out and portaging. Trust us when we say that there's nothing more terrifying and dangerous than finding yourself in an eddy that has you committed to running a rapid, yet not being able to see what lies ahead! The biggest problem with boat scouting is that your eye level is so low that it provides a very limited—and often obstructed—view of the rapid. Only with lots of experience can you effectively predict what lies ahead, and even then you'll be guessing, and are bound to be mistaken at times.

When boat scouting, you must consider the same issues that you would when scouting from shore. You'll look at the rapid from as many different angles as possible, which means scouting from as many different eddies as possible. You may even be able to ferry out to a hole or wave in midstream, from which you can sneak a quick look before returning back to your eddy or heading downstream. Continuous whitewater poses more of a

Boat scouting is quick, but provides you with a limited view of the rapid.

scouting challenge, because you can't see what lies below. You must stay in control at all times and have confidence in all the moves that you make. You can boat scout your way down a continuous rapid by hopping from eddy to eddy and re-evaluating the situation along the way. Just remember that you must always leave yourself an exit route. Remember, if you can't see what's coming up past the next eddy and it doesn't look like you can get out to portage from it, then get out of your boat and scout until you know the coast is clear. It only takes one overconfident eddy hop to make for an extremely long day.

PICKING LINES

"Don't be afraid to challenge yourself. Be sure to distinguish between fear that keeps you safe and fear that keeps you from a rewarding experience." (Anna Levesque)

If you've been paddling for any length of time, then there's a good chance that you'll have spent some time on the side of some road, picking lines through some of the nastiest whitewater imaginable! Even though you have no intention of ever running the rapids, you draw upon your knowledge of how you can use river features to your advantage and pick out the lines you'd take if you . . . Or you may have looked at a drop and said to yourself: "There's a good line there, and someday someone will take that line!" We both remember looking at a nearby massive two-stage waterfall on the Coulonge River in Quebec, seeing the potential and kind of thinking it might be doable, maybe.

Picking a line through a rapid is something that even non-paddlers can learn to do. The real challenge is in making good decisions about whether or not you're going to run the rapid.

The next summer, BJ Johnson and Willie Kern took the plunge and came out clean and smiling! The reason we bring this up is because the importance of this chapter has as much to do with discovering where our own personal lines are as it does with examining the actual rudiments of picking a line.

When picking a line through a rapid, it's important that you break things down into individual moves, all of which you are confident that you can make. You then need to look at how well these moves fall together as a sequence. It must be understood that your success in running

rapids relies greatly on your ability to look ahead and take actions that set you up for the future moves that are required. If you focus solely on getting through one feature at a time without real consideration for the next move, then you'll find yourself running rapids in a defensive, reactionary mode. This is a scary way to run rapids, as you're never really in charge of your situation, and things can quickly snowball out of your control, taking you from a reactive/defensive state to a survival mode.

With experience, we can all pick lines through rapids, but understanding our own

PRACTIC FOR PICKING LINES

Using a friendly rapid, try as many different lines as you can come up with to learn what you can and can't get away with. The knowledge you'll gain will be invaluable when you're running more adventurous rapids that are pushing your limits.

personal lines and limits is an ongoing exercise. You need to consider the reason you're on the water to begin with. You also need to be comfortable with the consequences of your decisions. Are you aware of and accepting the costs associated with missing a move and swimming through a rapid? How will your decisions impact the other paddlers in your group?

The bottom line is that picking a good line is something that you can learn to do very reliably, but making a good decision about whether or not to run a rapid is something entirely different. When picking a line, just remember to pick one that you're comfortable with, and not necessarily one that others think is easiest. We all have our own strengths and weaknesses, and this will affect how you perceive a rapid. Of course, this doesn't mean that advice from more experienced paddlers should be disregarded. A smart person will learn from his or her own mistakes, but the smarter person learns from other people's mistakes too! When deciding whether or not to run a rapid, you need to weigh a number of factors. Experience will help you make the right decisions, but even the most experienced paddlers need to continually ask themselves why they are there in the first place.

HANDLING ROCKS

People are often surprised to learn that rocks aren't always your enemies on the river. Rocks can provide valuable, calm eddies amidst the chaos of a rapid. Rocks also slow down the flow of the main current, create

weak spots that allow you to escape from holes, and provide ramps or jumps that you can use to clear nasty pourovers. Of course, rocks can also be pretty painful in a lot of different ways if hit unintentionally, so they must be treated with caution.

In this segment, we're going to look at some of the basic rules for dealing with rocks. We'll take a closer look at how to use rocks to your advantage in both the "Creekboating" and "Big Water" segments.

When approaching a rock, you have a couple of options. The best options are to pivot turn, ferry, or back ferry away from it; but if it can't be avoided, you need to take actions that once again fight your natural instincts. The natural response to colliding with a rock is to turn sideways and lean away from it, which puts your kayak between yourself and the rock. Unfortunately, this action will have some very undesirable results, as leaning away from the rock means leaning upstream. As soon as your kayak hits the rock or the pillow of water bouncing off the rock, current will pile up on your upstream edge and flip you mercilessly. You'll now find yourself upside down against a rock, in what is a very difficult position to roll. So what should you have done?

When drifting into a rock that can't be avoided, you need to keep your boat tilted downstream to prevent your upstream edge from catching the main current. In lighter current, or when dealing with lower-angle, rounded rocks, this might simply mean holding an edge and bouncing into the rock or its pillow at the ready with a brace. You might even get broached and have to push yourself

Rocks can provide great ramps for clearing holes.

laterally off the rock with your downstream hand. In faster current, or when the rock is more vertical, you may need to lean your whole body into the rock while holding your boat on edge. You may also need to push yourself laterally off the rock with your downstream hand quite aggressively. Of course every situation is different, but the key is always to keep your upstream edge from catching water. Lean into the rock and give it a big hug!

Rocks that are just below the surface can also wreak havoc on unsuspecting paddlers. With experience, you should never really be caught unawares by a rock that is just below the surface. Your river reading skills should allow you to recognize its signs. If your path does take you over a submerged rock then you should try to hit the rock as straight on as possible, with enough speed to drive over top of it. This is a good reason to keep your kayak fairly straight with the current in the early learning stages, before your river reading skills have developed. Submerged rocks can also do damage to poorly placed paddles. Remember that you need to be

reading the water all around you, not just directly in front of your kayak. Doing so can easily save you the expense of having to buy a replacement blade for your paddle.

The last rocks that we're going to consider are those under the water that can have a real "impact" on an upside-down paddler. Fortunately, these are the most seldom encountered rocks. In fact, many paddlers will never make acquaintances with an underwater rock. In the event that

If you find yourself sideways against a rock, lean into it and keep your boat tilted downstream. You can then push yourself laterally off the rock.

you do meet a rock underwater, there are a few things you need to keep in mind in order to minimize the impact. Of course your first line of defence is to roll up as quickly as possible. The less time you spend underwater, the better.

This is where the back deck roll comes into play, as it provides the quickest and cleanest means of rolling upright. It can even be done without getting the head wet, which clearly has its benefits. Contrary to popular belief, the back deck roll will not expose your head and body any more than other rolls, if it's done correctly. The nice thing about it is that your arms and paddle shaft form somewhat of a cage around your face. Although this cage won't necessarily stop you from hitting a rock with our head, it will take a lot of the initial impact and act as a warning. (For more on the back deck roll, see the "Rolling" segment.)

If the back deck roll isn't an option for a quick recovery, then you need to look at other ways to stay protected. Your most protected position while upside down is tucked forward against your kayak. Your helmet and life jacket will take the brunt of any impact with rock. This is why you learn to move to this protected position when setting up for rolls, waiting for T-rescues, or wet exiting. Problems can arise when you flip while leaning back, as moving to this protected position requires sitting right up and then tucking forward, which puts you in a very vulnerable position for a brief moment. If faced with this dilemma, you need to consider using your paddle shaft and your arms as your shield, and sit up with this shield protecting your face and head as much as possible.

The back deck roll is the quickest roll, and so the best way to avoid underwater rocks. If done correctly, your face can be fairly protected, as your paddle and arms form a basic cage around it.

RIDING THROUGH WAVE TRAINS

When learning to kayak, you're often taught that if in doubt, keep paddling. The reason is simple. Every paddle stroke that you take effectively acts as a brace. When learning, you don't have enough experience to anticipate how the river will push you around, so you're best off paddling and bracing your way through a rapid. As you gain experience and confidence, you gain the capacity to foresee the effects that waves and currents will have on your boat. As this happens, you'll change your approach to running rapids. Continuous paddling will no longer be your "default" action. Your default action will now involve floating downstream sideways with your eyes scanning ahead for obstacles.

There are a number of reasons for this. Firstly, a river's current is usually carrying you downstream at a horse's pace without any forward paddling. Unless you're in a hurry or need to build forward speed to clear an obstacle, then there's no real use in speeding up your descent. Secondly, if you do see an obstacle or a danger ahead, paddling forward is just taking you there more quickly! It also means that you have to turn your kayak almost completely around to establish an effective ferry angle. When floating downstream sideways, just a small sweep stroke will move you onto a powerful ferry angle in either direction. You are also moving the same speed as the main current, so that catching any waves to help you ferry out of the way will be much easier. The key to floating sideways through waves is staying loose at the hips, so that your kayak can follow the contours of the river while your body stays balanced over top.

If the waves start breaking, you need to get a bit more aggressive to pull yourself through. There are a couple of different ways to deal with breaking waves. You can "jump" the wave, or you can pull yourself through. The method that you choose will depend on your personal preference, as well as on your need to set up for future moves. Jumping a wave involves using a small pivot turn to pull your bow up on top of the break so that you skip over it. It's preferable to have some speed when doing

this to prevent your stern from catching and sending you into a vertical stern squirt.

It's also preferable to approach the wave on an angle in such a way that when it's time to pull your bow up, that sweep stroke pulls your kayak to face directly downstream. A potential drawback from using this technique is that you are usually carried very quickly into the following waves, making any quick moves difficult to make.

Pulling through a wave is a slower, but often more controlled, means of getting through a breaking wave. The idea is to float into the wave on an angle, ready with a powerful stroke on the downstream side that will pull you through the break. In this case, you actually use the breaking part of the wave to slow yourself down. You can then come through with more control and more time to prepare yourself for the next move. Float into the wave with a downstream angle and with your boat tilted downstream. In this way, you prevent water from piling up on your stern and squirting you up when you hit the break. This also lets you pre-establish which stroke you'll be using to pull yourself through the wave.

Your "default" action for riding through waves involves floating sideways with a control blade in the water, and scanning ahead for obstacles.

To jump a breaking wave, you'll approach it with some speed, and then use a small stern pivot turn at the last second to pull your bow on top of the break, which lets you skip over the top.

USING BREAKING WAVES TO TURN

As you get more comfortable pulling yourself through breaking waves, you can even use them to turn your kayak in the middle of a rapid. If you position your kayak so that only your stern hits the breaking part of the wave, then your bow will continue moving downstream as your stern gets held up by the wave's break. This effectively turns your kayak downstream into the opposite direction.

The key for all these techniques is to stay loose and let the boat go with the flow. A relaxed paddler spends a lot less time bracing and a lot more time looking ahead and taking effective strokes.

You can use a breaking wave to turn your kayak by letting your stern hit the break and get slowed down.

MANAGING HOLES

Holes provide your most formidable challenge when running a rapid. More often than not, the line you pick through a rapid will take you around the holes, but sometimes this just isn't an option.

There are three main techniques for getting past a hole; you can "boof" or jump over a hole, you can punch a hole, or you can surf out of a hole.

Boofing is a term most commonly associated with running waterfalls, but the term can be used across situations, as it really just describes the action of keeping the bow of your kayak on top of the water. Boofing is the cleanest and most controlled way of getting past a hole. Unfortunately, it's not always possible. It becomes particularly tricky for big holes with large, vertical foam piles. The easiest holes to boof are those with flatter foam piles, like pourovers. To boof a hole, start with some speed and then take a powerful sweep stroke to pull your bow into the air and on top of the foam pile. To get the bow up a little more, edge your boat into your front sweep as you do in a stern pivot, but remember to level off and get your weight forward quickly. A good boof will usually allow you to skip right over the hole. The most difficult aspects of boofing are the timing and set-up of the boof stroke. You need to approach the hole with a slight angle and time your sweep so that it brings your bow on top of the foam pile to point directly downstream (just like the timing of jumping a breaking wave).

Punching a hole is a technique you can use before you have the boat control for boofing, or when the hole's foam pile is so large and vertical that boofing would just land you flat on your back. To punch a hole you need speed, an aggressive attitude, and a well-placed last stroke.

Boofing a hole requires speed on your approach and a well-timed last stroke that pulls your bow into the air and on top of the foam pile.

Speed is important because you're going to be hitting a wall of aerated water that will try to stop you dead. An aggressive attitude is important because you need to keep your weight forward when you hit the hole to prevent your stern from catching and rocketing you up into a vertical stern squirt. Take your last stroke just as you impact the hole and use it to pull yourself through. This stroke is also handy as a brace during impact, acting as an anchor up at the front of the boat. With this in mind, it's a good idea to punch a hole with your boat tilted slightly towards your last stroke. This helps avoid a surprise flip to your non-bracing side and it also helps prevent your stern from catching the green water in the trough.

A final way of navigating through holes is to surf the hole and manoeuvre out the side. Although this won't be your best option for all holes, there are times when surfing a hole makes a lot of sense. In particular, it makes sense when you want to decrease your downstream momentum. By surfing a hole, you can move laterally to the main current without losing any ground. We're not going to look at the specific techniques required for side surfing and exiting a hole right now, as this is covered in detail in the "Side Surfing" segment. For now, you should recognize that it's not written in stone that holes are always to be avoided; hole surfing is an important river running technique that should be practised.

LATERAL MOMENTUM

For most river running moves, lateral momentum is more important to establish than downstream momentum. For example, consider ferrying across the river, pulling into an eddy, avoiding a hole, or breaking through a big reactionary—they all require some lateral momentum.

Once again, we're looking at a concept that goes against your natural instincts. If you need to break into an eddy or punch through a reactionary on one side of the river, it's only natural to want to start on that side of the river. This can be problematic, since the net effect of waves and holes on the side of a river is to push things out towards the centre. In general,

Punching a hole requires speed, and a well-placed last stroke that pulls you through the foam pile.

White kayak: doesn't establish lateral momentum and can't break through the eddy line. Black kayak: starts on the opposite side of the river and establishes the lateral momentum necessary to break through to safety.

to get to one side of the river, you want to start on the other side or at least far enough out to establish enough lateral momentum

to get yourself where you're aiming. This might even mean crossing above the very feature that you wish to avoid, which can certainly be intimidating. However, without adequate lateral momentum, you might not make the move you're going for.

USING THE POWER OF THE RIVER

When we were learning, we were taught that kayaking was all about technique and that you didn't need to be powerful to do it well. Though there's a lot of truth to this statement, we can't pass on these words of wisdom without first clarifying something. Though good technique is integral to good paddling, there are times when it simply isn't enough to get you where you need to go. At these times, you may need to combine your technique with your own power or the power of the river. Building your own power is important, but the focus of this segment is on how you can use the power of the river to your advantage.

There are many ways to take advantage of the river's power, but we're going to focus on a few of the most common. We've already looked at a turning technique that uses the river's power in the "Turning Midstream" segment. In this segment we looked at how you can use the break on a breaking wave or hole to slow down one end of your boat while the other end continues downstream uninterrupted. This effectively spins you at the peak of the wave or side of the hole. Now, we're going to look at how to use waves and holes to help your ferries, and then we'll look at how you can use pillows to your advantage.

Waves and holes are the most common river features, and they can also be the most helpful to kayakers. Waves will give your ferry an added kick and you a quick break. Consider a situation in which you are ferrying from one eddy to another. If there is a wave abutting the top of the initial eddy, exit so that your bow is in the trough of the wave and try to stay up on the face as you surf the wave across the current for a free ride. Be careful when exiting the eddy. If you pull into the current too far above the wave, you risk blowing through it as you come back downstream. If you enter the current downstream of the wave, you'll be pulling onto its backside and risk missing the wave and/or purling your bow underwater.

The backwash or foam pile of holes or pourovers can also be helpful for ferries. Although the aerated water may be quite turbulent, it can provide a great escape from the fast-moving main current. The trick is to stay on the foam pile without getting sucked right into the hole or falling off its backside, which of course takes practice. Each hole has a different backwash, and the real challenge is learning to read this kind of flow. Once you're comfortable, you can use the foam pile to ferry across the river. You can even use the recirculating water to give your ferry a big boost out the far side of the hole.

Pillows are features that can also come in handy. Remember that a pillow is formed as water piles upstream on itself after being backed up by a rock. You can

Waves can give your ferries a huge boost, but be sure to pull onto the face of the wave.

You can also use a hole's foam pile to ferry across the river.

use this slack water to slow your own downstream momentum and help make your ferry more effective.

Using a pillow to get where you need to go.

PORTAGING

"Never lose track of what hooked you on paddling in the first place." (Ryan Whetung)

No matter how skilled a kayaker you become, portaging will always be an important factor in your paddling. Sometimes there's no choice but to walk around a rapid. Other times, you may decide to take the high and dry route because you just don't feel on the ball. Deciding whether or not to portage in different situations can be very challenging. You need to evaluate more than just the feasibility of the rapid. You need to look at how you're feeling that day. Are you tired? Are you a little bit off your game for some reason? There's never any shame in walking around a rapid. Furthermore, it's totally unacceptable to make someone feel bad about portaging. Having said this, there's nothing wrong with a bit of friendly encouragement at the right time. Sometimes we all need a little push from our friends to help us achieve our potential, but a friendly push is very different than pressure. As for general portaging etiquette, it's a good idea to start your portage as soon as you've made the decision not to run the rapid, so that the other paddlers in your group aren't left waiting too long at the bottom.

WATCH AND LEARN

As we mentioned in the beginning of this segment, there are many different ways of using the river's power to your advantage. A great way to learn is by watching the best boaters as they make their way down rapids. They make things look easy by using every river feature to their advantage. Watch and see which eddies they catch, where they leave eddies, which waves they use to ferry, and how they get around or through holes. You should also take note of which strokes they use to do these things. We're not necessarily suggesting that you copy the lines of better paddlers, but there's no doubt that you can learn a lot from watching them. As we've already mentioned, smart paddlers learns from their mistakes, but a smarter paddler learns from other people's mistakes.

No matter how good you get, portaging will always be a big part of the sport.

SEAL ENTRY

The seal entry involves sliding off the shoreline and dropping into the river. The seal entry is a fun way to start your day and, on rivers with steep banks, it can be the only way of getting on the water. If done right, you can seal launch from fairly high up, but the higher you go, the smaller the room for error and the bigger the potential consequences. A botched seal launch from any significant height is a great way to hurt your back or damage your boat.

Seal launching is a skill like any other, and just as you wouldn't start by running a twenty-foot waterfall, you shouldn't start with a ten-foot seal launch. The first order of business is establishing whether or not the potential seal launch spot has a deep

landing zone. Although a good scouting should give you the answer, it never hurts to let someone else go first! Just kidding! You then need to pick your line, which means choosing where you want to slide off the rock. This will of course dictate where you get in to your kayak. Ideally, a buddy can hold your boat and paddle while you get in; otherwise you'll have to find a flat spot or something to brace against. When it comes time to launch, there's a good chance this same buddy will be eager to give you a push off the rock. This can sometimes be helpful, but unless he or she has some experience in launching paddlers, it's probably better to do it yourself. At least this way you'll only have yourself to blame!

When launching, hold your paddle with your control hand and use your other hand to push yourself off. This push-off will play a huge role in the success of your seal launch. The speed and trajectory with which you launch will be different for every situation, but the desired result of your seal launch will be the same. Ideally, you'll enter the water straight, with your kayak on a 70-to-80-degree angle so that you pencil into the river. This slightly off-vertical angle will let the rocker and the buoyancy of your kayak bring your bow to the surface in a smooth arc. If you launch with too little speed, your kayak is likely to stand up too vertically, or even rotate past vertical, which is referred to as "going over the handlebars." If you launch with too much speed, there's a good chance that you'll land flat and hard on the water, which is particularly dangerous for the back with today's flat-hulled boats.

The last thing to consider is where to hold your paddle as you hit the water. The goal is that when you make contact with the water, your paddle doesn't come up and whack you in the face or put dangerous stress on your shoulders. With this in mind, you can hold it slightly over your head (if the drop isn't too high) or along one side of your kayak. Holding it just above your head can be appropriate for small drops, but avoid holding it too high, as this will strain your shoulders. Never hold your paddle right in front of your face, either—you won't be the first paddler to finish a seal launch with a bloody nose! To minimize the risk of anything happening, reach across with your front hand and keep the paddle on one side of the boat as you enter. Seal launching can be a lot of fun and is a great way to spice up a mellower river. Just remember to think things through and do a thorough scouting before launching off anything.

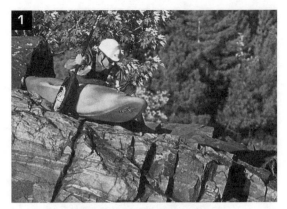

Your push off will play a huge role in the success of your seal launch.

A 70-80 degree angle is the ideal entry angle.

Make sure that your paddle isn't in a position where it will hit you in the face when you hit the water.

8

BIG WATER RIVER RUNNING

EQUIPMENT • GO WITH THE FLOW
KEEP YOUR HANDS ON THE STEERING WHEEL
MANAGING BOILS AND WHIRLPOOLS • PUNCHING REACTIONARIES
BIG WATER SAFETY

"On the river, a little humility buys a lot of longevity." (Scott Docherty)

There's no doubt that big water can be the most intense and committing type of whitewater paddling. When you enter a big water rapid, you have to accept the fact that you may not be in control at all times. You also accept that you might spend a good deal of time underwater and could potentially end up swimming. None of these things is really appealing, but they're risks that you must weigh when deciding whether or not to run a big water rapid. Having conjured up some healthy fear, we can now tell you that big water is absolutely exhilarating to paddle and that there are few activities in this world that compare to it!

We're going to take a look at a few issues that need to be addressed for big water paddling. Of course the fundamental skills and strokes that you use don't change. What does need to change is our approach to the rapids, both mental and physical.

To enjoy big water paddling, you need to accept the fact that you may not be in control all the time.

EQUIPMENT

The equipment you use when paddling big water can have a real impact on which rapids you might run and which you might walk. Your boat selection is obviously very important, but there are a couple of other pieces of gear that you should consider as well.

BIG WATER BOAT SELECTION

The most ideal big water boats are fast, stable, forgiving, and responsive. This translates into a fairly short kayak with more volume than a playboat, yet less than a creekboat, with fairly high edges and a flat hull. The problem with

the smallest playboats is that they're designed with very low edges to make it easy to submerge the ends of the boat. When running big water, these low edges make them very unforgiving. On the other hand, a creek boat has high edges and is designed to be very forgiving. It also has lots of volume, which helps the boat resurface very quickly to avoid any rocks below the surface. In big water, however, you're not too concerned about submerged rocks. You'll be much more concerned about getting stuck in a big, trashy hole, which the additional volume won't help you avoid! This is why for big water river running, you should be looking for a boat that is somewhere between a playboat and a creekboat in size and features. We commonly use a bigger playboat than we would normally use for freestyle. The additional size makes it more forgiving, while the aggressive edges keep it responsive and versatile.

GO WITH THE FLOW

The most important rule for paddling in big water is that you need to "go with the flow" more than ever. This means staying loose and relaxed in your kayak and doing your best to anticipate and roll with the punches that the river throws your way. On a similar note, it's very important that you paddle big water with good posture. Leaning back not only puts you in unstable mode, it lowers your stern edges and makes them much more susceptible to catching. This is very important to understand, as the vast majority of flips in big water are caused by the stern edges of the kayak being caught.

Staying loose and relaxed in big water is absolutely essential for staying upright.

KEEP YOUR HANDS ON THE STEERING WHEEL

Paddling through big water can be kind of like being a pinball in a pinball machine. The river is going to knock you around. To stay in control, you need to keep your

OTHER USEFUL BIG WATER GEAR

There are a number of other pieces of gear that can come in handy for big water paddling. One of the biggest concerns when paddling big water is having your skirt pop. Holes and waves can sometimes break over your kayak and onto your skirts with such incredible force that they blow your skirt right off the cockpit rim. To prevent your skirt from "imploding," it should be supported from underneath. Many skirts now have some form of built-in "implosion bar" that does just this. Now there's even a removable implosion bar that can be used with a standard skirt. The dry top is another good piece of gear for big water, as it's inevitable that you'll get very wet. There's also a good chance of spending time underwater. As well as keeping water out, a dry top will also help keep you warm and energized. Having water in your kayak won't make your run through the big stuff any easier, that's for sure!

A final piece of equipment that we highly recommend is air bags, or flotation bags, for your kayak. These can be invaluable pieces of gear if you go for a swim, as getting a boat full of water to shore is nearly impossible. Flotation bags give rescuers a much better chance of getting your equipment to shore before it disappears down the next rapid.

hands on the steering wheel, which means keeping a blade in the water. When you're actively paddling, this isn't an issue. It's when you're not paddling that it's more important than ever to have an active blade in the water. You generally want this blade on the downstream side of your kayak, ready to brace, sweep, draw, or pull yourself through a breaking wave or hole.

The only way to maintain control in big water is to keep your body weight forward and a paddle blade in the water.

MANAGING BOILS AND WHIRLPOOLS

Boils and whirlpools are right up there with eddy lines among the most unstable spots on the river. In fact, big water eddy lines are often composed of boils and whirlpools, but that's not the only place you'll find them. Whenever water is being constricted or forced to make a quick turn, or when different currents collide, you'll likely find whirlpools and/or boils, along with lots of other nameless, funny water. We're going to take a quick look at how to deal with these features and even how you can use them to your advantage.

BOILS

Boils are formed when water is forced up to the surface at speed. It can be water that is pushed up by a submerged obstruction, or turbulent water that has become aerated and is rushing to the surface like boiling water in a pot. Once it hits the surface, this boiling water peaks and then runs off to the side to the lower lying water around it. Where this shedding water hits the current around the boil, a seam line is created (see the "River Features" segment).

You already know that you don't want to spend time on seam lines or eddy lines, where the water is unstable, so either get yourself clear of the boil or break right across the seam line and on top of the boil. The key to tackling boils is to take them almost straight on (perpendicular to that point on the seam line), with a slight ferry angle in the direction you'd like to go (usually downstream). As you break through the seam line and paddle on top of the boil, it will try its best to push you off to the side. You can use this energy to your advantage by carving a smooth turn on the boil and letting it push you off in the direction that you'd like to go. You'll need

Boil bouncing is a great way to navigate through boily whitewater. As you drive up on a boil, you'll carve a smooth turn so that as the boil pushes you off itself, you can punch through its seam line and right up the side of the next one.

to have turned your kayak enough so that you can break through the seam line at a fairly straight angle. When there are multiple boils grouped together, you can even use this boil riding technique to bounce your way downriver, carving off the top of one boil and then the next.

WHIRLPOOLS

When running a high-volume river, you'll probably spend a lot more of your time avoiding whirlpools than playing in them, and this isn't always easy to do. In many cases, whirlpools (like boils) can be totally unpredictable and pop up in front of you unexpectedly. Fortunately there is a way to deal with them if you can't miss them.

You can actually enter the whirlpool and use its energy to your advantage to get through it. The helical flow of a whirlpool offers you a free ride if you make your way into the right part of the swirling water. If you successfully paddle into the part of a whirlpool's swirling current that is moving downstream, then you can slingshot yourself around and out the other side using this current for a nice boost. This slingshot technique uses a similar concept to that which allows satellites to resist the gravitational pull of the earth and maintain orbit. Of course, this means paddling into a side of the whirlpool and not into its centre.

If for some reason you find yourself in the eye of the whirlpool, your momentum will be lost and there's not much you can do but hold on and wait for the opportunity to escape. If the whirlpool is big enough, your boat will sometimes be pulled completely underwater. This can be nerve-racking (or exhilarating!), but you can take comfort in the fact that the whirlpool will eventually die out. Sometimes it will take only seconds for a whirlpool to grow and then disappear, while others can last ten seconds or longer. Invariably, though, the whirlpool will settle out as it moves downstream. This is nice to know when you find yourself upside down

in a whirlpool, because it can sometimes be very difficult to roll. If you're having trouble rolling, or even moving your paddle into a set up position, try to relax and wait for the whirlpool to dissipate. Unfortunately, the only way to really develop your comfort level with whirlpools is to play around in them. So next time you get to that squirrelly spot on your local river, throw on your nose plugs and start messing around!

PUNCHING REACTIONARIES

Reactionaries are diagonal breaking waves or holes, and are a common phenomenon on big water rivers. Reactionaries usually form when water hits shallow sections or obstacles and is redirected towards deeper

If you can recognize which way a whirlpool is spinning, you can ride the side of it and use its current to sling shot you right on by. If you fight the whirlpool's current, you'll get sucked into its maw.

To punch a reactionary you need to establish lateral momentum directed so that you'll break the reactionary at a 90-degree angle.

A LESSON FROM MOTHER NATURE

by Ken Whiting

Why are many of life's most educational experiences the most traumatic ones? I'm talking about the experiences that turn your stomach to think about, but at the same time had a valuable impact on your life. The thought of what I've gained from such experiences lets me appreciate Conan the Barbarian's philosophy: that which does not kill you will make you stronger. Stronger or not, there are a few experiences I would choose not to relive. One of these experiences took place on the magical Ottawa River on a gorgeous summer day in 1991 . . .

I was fifteen years old, and it was my second year of paddling. My addiction to the sport was quickly turning me into one of the better paddlers on the river, but I severely lacked experience. Sure, I knew the Ottawa River as well as anyone. My buddy Paul and I had done more enders and pirouettes that summer than the river may have ever seen, and we routinely tested the river's tightest lines. After all, it was only the Ottawa River! This was our playground, and we were determined to make the most out of it.

This is how we so easily ignored the warnings of a little voice in our heads (which we later learned to name "Common Sense") and hopped out of our kayaks to swim in the whirlpools at the bottom of "Butcher's Knife." We'd get sucked down, swirled around, then pop back up to the surface like a cork. You can probably guess how these activities became a life-changing experience for me. To put things simply, the River Gods spanked me!

After a few enjoyable times getting swirl-o-grammed in the whirlpools, things quickly went sour. Like a lemming making its final leap, I hurled myself into the river and was immediately pulled underwater as a whirlpool formed around me. The awesomely powerful, yet soft, hands of the river tumbled me about. After a short while, the turbulent waters eased their grip on me, and I was allowed to make my way back to the surface. But, with the surface only inches away, the river trolls grabbed my ankles and unmercifully yanked me down into complete blackness. Running out of air, and without any light to guide me to the surface, panic set in swiftly.

I can still remember the events that followed quite vividly, and even after fifteen years, their recollection sends shivers down my spine. I reached a physical stage that I never thought I would reach. I hovered for far too long at a point where I thought I couldn't hold my breath any longer, until finally, I began swallowing water. The darkness that surrounded me was replaced with an even deeper blackness as I passed out.

Moments later, I returned to my senses in a remarkably calm state after such absolute panic. The buoyancy of my lifejacket was finally allowed to pull me towards the surface, and I watched the first signs of daylight appear as a far-off point. My lungs continued their desperate scream, but I was too confused to focus on that pain. I knew I should be swimming for the surface, but my body was unresponsive. I floated, completely at the mercy of the River Gods, and watched in desperation as the light grew brighter. Before I knew what was happening, I broke through the surface, and was taking the biggest, most welcomed breath of my life. My buds were there quickly to tow me ashore, and I dragged my spent body onto the riverbank.

The events of that day had an immediate and lifelong impact. The nightmares that followed were a nuisance, but most disturbing to me was the effect the experience had on my paddling. I stopped trying new moves and played only in the smallest playspots, as panic would set in as soon as I lost the slightest control. For the first time ever, my confidence was far below my skill level. Fortunately I had a great group of paddling friends that pushed me, and helped to build up my confidence.

I've often wondered whether this was really a necessary experience? Did surviving an experience like this really make me stronger as Conan believed it would? Well, besides scaring the crap out of me, I did learn a new respect for Mother Nature. I also learned a lesson that any whitewater paddler should understand. No matter how good you are, and no matter how well you know a river, the river is always in control. All we can do is play as safely and as responsibly as possible with the awesome and humbling power of whitewater.

THE BIG PICTURE

One of the most important and less understood rules for running big water is staying a step ahead of the game. Because the current is so powerful and things happen so quickly, you can end up in a recovery/survival mode in no time at all. To avoid this, you need to always look ahead to your next move, which at the time might seem like quite a distance away, and follow a line that will set you up for that next move. This of course reinforces the importance of scouting and picking a good line from the beginning, particularly in continuous water. By looking ahead and taking the big picture in like this, you'll find yourself fighting the river less and enjoying your trip a whole lot more.

sections of the river (see the "River Features" segment). Learning to break through reactionaries is an essential skill that requires an aggressive approach.

Ideally you can break through a reactionary using the "boof" technique that was discussed in the "Managing Holes" segment, which lets you skip right over top of the break. Unfortunately, big water doesn't always let you do this. In fact, as opposed to making it over the reactionary, it's likely that you'll take a big piece of the wave in the chest. If you're not prepared for this hit, the reactionary will stop you dead and take you for a ride at its discretion.

The way to prepare for this hit is by establishing lateral momentum directed so that you'll break the reactionary at a 90 degree angle. Once you are lined up properly, your biggest concern is having water pile up on your stern, which would quickly send you into a stern squirt. To prevent this, you need to stay in a fairly aggressive position, tilt your kayak downstream slightly, and plant a powerful last stroke on the downstream side. This stroke will serve as a brace, while at the same time allowing you to pull yourself right through the reactionary.

BIG WATER SAFETY

"Injuries aren't a sign of weakness or getting old . . . just a sign that you're doing something wrong." (James McBeath)

Big volume rivers can present the most difficult rescue scenarios because the shore is often quite far away and the current is moving so quickly that you can be washed downstream at frightening speeds. One result is that as the victim you can't always rely on others to help you. To paddle responsibly in big water, you should be proficient with your self-rescue skills as well as with your rescuing skills. Let's have a look at the most basic self-rescue skill: swimming.

SWIMMING

If you've ever taken a swim in big water, then you know how frightening it can be. It's very hard to get oriented and you can spend a fair amount of time underwater. You need to prepare yourself for this eventually, and the best way to do so is to go for a swim on your own accord, in a controlled environment. As your paddling advances, this practice becomes even more important as you'll be forced to swim less often, but when it does happen, there's a good chance that you'll be in more serious whitewater that requires you to get out as quickly as possible.

When swimming in big water, getting out of the river is usually your main objective and biggest concern, although every situation is different. The only effective way to get yourself to shore is to swim aggressively. Of course there are times when you'll want to assume the body surfing position to protect yourself from rocks, but you're not going to get any closer to shore like this. It becomes especially important to swim aggressively through eddy lines or seam lines, for the same reason that you paddle aggressively through them.

The only effective way to get to shore in big water is to swim there aggressively.

Big water eddy lines are often accompanied by whirlpools and boils, which can pull you underwater for undesirable periods of time. On that note, you can expect to be pulled underwater when swimming in big water, but you can take some comfort with the knowledge that the features that pull you underwater will usually dissipate quite quickly and allow you to resurface. It's important that you stay as calm as possible when you get pulled underwater. Panic is a downward spiral that not only impairs judgment, but causes your body to use oxygen much less efficiently. Fighting frantically against the downward pull is not usually the best course of action, because the river is just too strong. You need to try your best to relax and wait for that downward pull to ease off, at which time you can swim back to the surface.

ROLLING

Your best means of self-rescue is the roll. After reading the swimming section above,

hopefully you are even more motivated to master your roll! Not only does a roll prevent a frightening and potentially dangerous swim, but it saves you an incredible amount of physical and emotional energy. I can't stress enough how important it is to develop a confident and effective roll before tackling serious big water.

There are a couple of things to consider for rolling in big water. Firstly, big water can make it difficult to set up your roll, as strong currents play games with your paddle. Be patient! If need be, wait a moment for these currents to ease off before attempting your roll. The back deck roll remains the quickest and best way to roll upright, but by no means is it the only one that will work. All other rolling techniques will work fine, although the sweep roll can be slightly more effective than the C-to-C roll, as it is less likely to be foiled by funky currents.

Whatever technique you use to roll, be patient and don't give up if your first one doesn't work. Set up and try again, and if need be try a third or fourth time. If you can, try to get a breath in between rolling attempts. There's no rule for how many times you should try your roll, as every situation is different. It's definitely worth trying a few times, though, given the exposure to risk, the time, and both emotional and physical energy you'll save. At the same time, you don't want to wait until you're exhausted and out of breath before deciding to swim.

KAYAK RESCUES

When setting up safety for a big water rapid, you need to identify the hazards and set up rescue systems below, because if a situation does arise, the victim will usually be swept downstream very quickly. You need to prepare yourself by establishing an action plan, then putting yourself in the best position to help.

In some situations, a throw line set up on the riverbank can be very helpful, especially when there is pinning potential and the bank is relatively close. However, since pins aren't very common in big water, it's usually more important to have paddlers in the water ready to help. You then need to consider your priorities. Of course, the safety of the rescuer is always first, as you're doing nobody a favour if you add yourself as a victim. With the safety of the rescuer secured, the top priority is the swimmer.

Other things need to be considered as well. Are you on a continuous river with limited access? If so, retrieving equipment is quite important, and you'll want to have at least two safety boaters below: one to help the swimmer and the other on gear retrieval. If the river is like the Ottawa River, which is composed of big, drop and pool-style rapids, then you won't need to concern yourself as much with the equipment, as it will all end up in the calm pool below where it can be easily collected.

There are a few ways for a rescuer in a kayak to help a swimmer. Simple words of encouragement can be very effective in calming a swimmer. When a swimmer needs more help, he or she can grab onto the grab loop at the back of the kayak and get a tow. If you've ever towed a swimmer, then you know how difficult it can be. If possible, instruct the swimmer to kick and help propel you forward. Be aware that there are situations where having a swimmer holding onto your stern can do more harm than good to both of you. There's no rule for when to tow someone

If there is nothing to worry about below, you can tow in the swimmer and his kayak at the same time, although this is very difficult to do with any significant current.

and when not to, but you do need to evaluate each situation as it arises.

EQUIPMENT RETRIEVAL

Depending on whether the river is continuous or remote, equipment retrieval will vary greatly in importance. We're going to take a quick look at the best way to retrieve equipment, with the assumptions that the swimmer is safe and the river continuous, so time is of the essence.

Getting a kayak to shore in the middle of a big water rapid can be a discouragingly tricky thing to do. Remember that the kayak will be incredibly heavy when filled with water, so you should consider it a danger in turbulent water. You're best off waiting until the river calms down enough that you can safely approach the kayak. For the quickest

recovery, you can empty out the boat mid-rapid using the boat-over-boat technique, and then tow it to shore with a towline.

The boat-over-boat technique involves dragging the upside-down kayak over your own cockpit and rocking the boat back and forth to dump the majority of the water out. After doing so, flip the boat upright and attach your towline to one of the grab loops. The towline is a great tool for moving boats around in big water because it allows you to paddle unimpeded. With the quick-release feature, you can separate yourself from the towline and kayak in a heartbeat if the need arises.

Without a towline, you'll need to use a bump-and-chase technique for getting the empty boat to shore, which involves repeatedly pushing the empty kayak forward and then paddling after it to until you get to shore. This can work if you're close to shore, but it is not effective over any great distance.

A towline is one of the best tools for retrieving boats in big water.

Retrieving paddles is much simpler than boats. You have two good options. The first is to throw the extra paddle into an eddy or onto the riverbank like a javelin. This has the potential of damaging or breaking the paddle, so try to be careful if you can when doing this. The other option is to grasp both paddle shafts in your hand, and paddle to shore with the double blades. This can be tricky for smaller paddlers, or when the blades of the two paddles have very different offsets.

CREEKING

ROCKS ARE YOUR FRIENDS • BOOFING
RUNNING WATERFALLS BY TAO BERMAN • ROCKSLIDES • CREEKING SAFETY

"It's not what you paddle . . . it's why you paddle. Have fun and enjoy the river, otherwise, why bother!" (AJ McIntyre)

Creekboating is as much a game of strategy as it is a sport. Half of your time on creeks is spent scouting, and half of the fun comes from picking lines based on how you predict the river will affect your kayak. In this way, creekboating is a lot like a game of chess, and, like chess, there are some important rules that need to be understood. We're going to look at some of these rules, along with a few unique creekboating skills, techniques, and concepts.

ROCKS ARE YOUR FRIENDS

On high-volume rivers, rocks can create daunting river features such as big holes, pourovers, and undercuts, all of which you generally try to avoid. On lower-volume creeks, the features that rocks create can often be your best friends, such as micro-eddies that break up a rapid, and ramps for jumping over holes. It's important that you begin looking at rocks as your friends on creeks, not as your enemies. If you're scared of rocks, then you'll end up avoiding them at times when you really should be using them to your advantage. We'll be looking more closely at how you can use rocks to your advantage in the next segment on boofing.

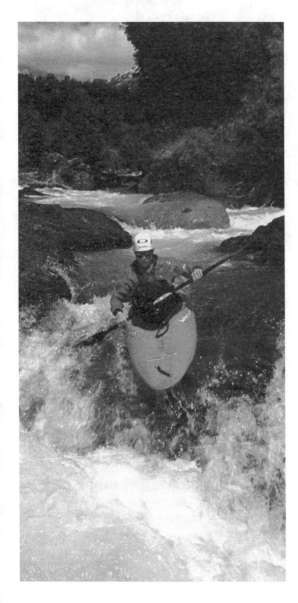

BOOFING

Boofing is the act, or art, of keeping the bow of your kayak from diving underwater, and it is without a doubt the most important skill to learn for paddling creeks. Most notably, you can boof waterfalls and steep drops, but you can also boof holes, pourovers, reactionaries, and even eddy lines.

You should acknowledge from the outset that although boofing is a crucial technique for running drops, it can also be quite dangerous if not done properly. Landing flat from a drop of any significant height is going to shock your spine. This shock has broken the backs of paddlers on surprisingly small drops. Only experience can tell you when, or when not to, boof a drop.

Master waterfall runner and World Record holder Tao Berman takes a closer look at the variables you should consider when running a waterfall, along with the different techniques you can use to do so in his upcoming segment "Running Waterfalls." For now, though, we'll focus

Boofing lets you run drops while keeping your bow from diving deeply underwater.

With lateral momentum, you can sometimes boof right into an eddy.

on the general boofing technique that will take you cleanly over a small, vertical drop. This technique can be modified slightly to boof over many different features.

The success of your boof relies on two key factors: your set up, and your boof stroke. As a general rule, you need forward speed directed at the steepest part of the drop, and away from the centre of it. The forward speed helps you launch far enough to clear the hole at the bottom of the drop, and aiming for the steepest part makes it easier to achieve this goal. By directing your boof away from the centre of the drop, you are avoiding what is usually the stickiest part of the hole below.

In many cases, you can even boof completely out of the main current and into an eddy. This of course requires plenty of lateral momentum on your approach.

This is also a great time to remember that rocks are your friends on creeks. If there is a rock at the lip of the drop, it might prove very useful as a launch ramp. The ideal boof rock is a rock that will give your bow a kick into the air without slowing your forward momentum too much. This means you want to hit the rock with your bow, but not with the rest of your kayak. Do this by establishing lateral momentum on your approach. If you hit the rock with too much force, or approach the rock too directly and

Rocks, or the pillows coming off rocks, provide great launch ramps for boofing.

catch it with too much of your kayak, then you'll be slowed right down and you'll have difficulty clearing the hole below.

Having successfully set up your boof, let's now take a close look at the boof stroke, which is the last stroke that you take as you drop over the lip. The boof stroke requires a combination of timing and power. The timing of the stroke is fairly straightforward. Plant the stroke just over the lip of the drop, where you can get the most

pull away from the falls. On shallow drops, this sometimes means that you actually pull against the face of the falls.

In regard to the actual stroke that you'll use, let's refer back to the "power stroke" that we covered in the "Essentials" segment. The power stroke is a vertical forward stroke that propels your kayak forward without turning it. Since your goal for boofing is to launch yourself over the hole at the bottom of a drop, it should make

1) *Your boof stroke is a power stroke planted over the lip of the drop. 2) As you pull on your stroke, thrust your hips forward to keep your bow up.*

You'll always want to land a boof with your weight forward and a paddle blade in the water. This lets you control your kayak from the moment it touches down.

sense that this "power stroke" will come in very handy. You don't need to worry quite as much about the stroke being perfectly vertical, but make sure it's powerful.

As you approach the lip of the drop, you'll reach forward and then plant your boof stroke just over the edge. At this same time, the bow of your kayak will begin to drop over the falls. Now is the time to pull aggressively on your boof stroke. As you pull on the stroke, you'll thrust your hips forward and past the paddle blade. The further you pull this stroke, the more lift you'll give your bow. This means that when you want to land the flattest, your power stroke will pull right past your hip and your hips will be thrust hard forward so that you end up in a leaning back position.

Contrary to popular belief, you're not done yet! You now need to prepare for your landing. You always want to land in your default body position, otherwise known as the "moderately aggressive" position. Landing like this helps prevent your boat from being back-endered, it helps you cushion the blow, and it allows you to control your kayak from the moment it touches down. For further control, you should land your boof with a paddle blade in the water at your toes, ready as a brace or to pull you forward and completely away from the hole at the base of the drop.

BOOFING NON-VERTICAL DROPS

Boofing non-vertical drops is quite difficult. The key is in the timing of your last stroke. Be patient and make sure that your boof stroke pulls your bow up just before you hit the foam pile at the bottom of the drop. The most common error on non-vertical drops is taking your boof stroke too early, which usually means you won't clear the hole at the bottom.

Tao going big. Photo by Jock Bradley.

RUNNING WATERFALLS

by Tao Berman

"Close your eyes and visualize your line. If you can't create a clear mental picture of yourself running the drop cleanly, don't expect to do it for real." (Tao Berman)

Running waterfalls takes a solid understanding of how and when to boof, body positioning, and timing. I will pass down some important tips I have learned from experience, but remember that no amount of reading will be enough to master the moves. What I have to say will only teach you what you need to do. Then the work comes: lots of practice.

I've been experimenting for years with different body positions and techniques and have discovered a few things that work best for me. The primary goals are to maximize my boat control and minimize the impact sustained, especially on big drops. Have no doubt though: waterfalls are powerful, and even when using these techniques, they pose a significant risk and should be approached with caution.

THE BOOF:

Knowing how and when to boof is essential to good creeking and waterfall-running

Land flat off too big of a drop and you can cause serious injury to your back.

141

technique. Generally speaking, the higher the drop the less flat you want your boat to be when it enters the water. The amount of aerated water at the base of the waterfall will also help you determine how flat you can land your boat. The more aeration, the more cushioned the landing and the less vertically you need to enter the water. Every drop is unique, so knowing what is too high to boof is something you will learn only with experience. A final consideration is an obvious one: the depth of the landing!

Boofing is not rocket science—once you know what to work on, practice will make perfect.

The following are a few important tips. As you approach the edge of the drop, be patient and plant your blade as close to the lip as possible. As you take this last stroke, thrust your hips forward. On average, you'll pull the blade to about your hip. Continuing to pull past your hip extends your boofing stroke, which will be necessary in some situations.

BODY POSITIONING AND BOAT ANGLE:

The hardest part of running a drop is actually being able to successfully achieve the boat angle that you chose. As we discussed above, the height of the drop and the aeration at its base will determine what boat angle you want to enter the water with. The most important factor is your last stroke. A finely tuned intuition will allow you to use this stroke to land flat (or vertically) off about any drop you

Ideally, you should be sitting upright in your kayak while airborne. This allows you to make small adjustments to your kayak's angle, and prepares you for the landing.

choose. However, a general misconception about running waterfalls is that once you are in the air, gravity dictates the rest. This is not the case, although changing the angle while airborne is an advanced skill that develops only through trial and error. As you get more comfortable in the air, you'll be able to focus on making fine adjustments to your body position to make for less of an impact when you hit the water.

For flat (or almost-flat) landings, have an aggressive body position and reach forward to take a powerful stroke as soon as you land. Taking that first aggressive forward stroke will help pull you away from the hole at the bottom of the drop and act as an anchor that prevents getting a big boat back-ender.

For all other boat angles, once you're in the air, continue to sit vertically in your boat so you can brace or even take a paddle stroke if need be (a last-second technique for raising your bow a little). Just

before hitting the water, lean all the way forward over the cockpit of your boat so you're as aerodynamic as possible.

This will do a couple of important things for you. First, it will help keep the water from hitting you in the chest and throwing you on your back deck. Being thrown violently on the back of your boat can cause whiplash or damage your back on the cockpit rim. Second, it will help protect a lot of your body's soft spots if things go wrong. A final landing tip is to try to remember to turn your head a quarter rotation upon landing. This will help prevent a huge nose, lung, and eye douche, and will save you from slamming your nose on the deck of your boat because of the impact.

These are only a few of the basics to work on when running waterfalls. As you get more comfortable with these essentials, you'll develop your own little tricks for handling different situations that work best for you.

Sitting upright while airborne is critical.

ROCKSLIDES

Rockslides come in all shapes, sizes, and levels of difficulty. They're generally best run with creek boats that have plenty of rocker to keep the ends from pinning. It's just too easy for the pointy ends of playboats to catch an unsuspecting rock lip. Running simple rockslides is usually quite straightforward, and your entry into the slide will have the most impact on the success of your run. Once you've entered the slide, it's really hard to make any significant movements because you'll be accelerating very quickly, and the slide is often too shallow for effective strokes. This makes it crucial that you scout the rapid to pick a good approach and line. For longer slides, when there is more room for getting bounced around, it's never a bad idea to

probe the run. The best probes are small logs that will float well. You can learn a lot by how a log runs through a rapid, although it can be somewhat depressing when the log has a cleaner line than you!

Once you've picked your line and entered the rapid, your main concern is keeping your kayak straight and upright, two things that do tend to go hand in hand. The best way to stay in control of your boat is to maintain your posture, which gives you the most edge control and allows you to make the quickest corrections. The surest way to flip or get broached on a rockslide is to let yourself be spun sideways or backwards.

Since rockslides are often very shallow, it's not reasonable to think that you can keep your boat straight by having a rudder planted at the back of the boat. Instead, you need to use small "checking" strokes out to the side

Your entry into a rockslide will have the most impact on the success of your run. Remember to sit upright so that you have the most control over your kayak.

Rockslides are often too shallow for large strokes, so you'll use small "checking" strokes to keep your boat straight and in line.

A LITTLE PADDING GOES A LONG WAY

The half inch of plastic that lies between you and the river might seem like a lot when you're on the water, but when you're bouncing down a rock face, it won't seem like nearly as much. A bit of padding on your seat, and some well padded booties on your feet can save you lots of grief!

of your boat. These can be partial sweeps or stern draws. You need to be careful that these strokes stay small and controlled, because cruising down a rockslide is like driving on ice. As soon as you start to spin out, things can quickly get out of control. It's also very easy to overcompensate and send yourself spinning in the opposite direction.

One thing to watch out for on rockslides is a rooster tail or fan, which is a plume of water sent hurling into the air by rock that juts out. These rocks have the potential of pinning your kayak—or at

least making things very uncomfortable for you. You should also be on the lookout for keeper holes at the bottom of rockslides, which can again be assessed using a test log.

CREEKING SAFETY

The safety considerations for creekboating are somewhat different from those for big water paddling. Pinning now becomes a major hazard, along with the bodily trauma

It's always a good idea to have someone on the water below a drop, but there a number of other safety precautions that can be taken.

caused by hitting rocks. One good thing is that most incidents happen within an arm or rope's length from shore, so rescuers can often play a greater role. This is why it's absolutely vital that all creekboaters be trained in swiftwater rescue and first aid. The skills you'll learn could save someone's life someday, including your own!

ON COURAGE AND GOOD SENSE
By Bryan McKenzie

Helmet? Check. Boat? Check. Paddle? Check. Skirt? Check.
Thirty-five-foot waterfall? Check. Cameras ready? Check.
Balls? They must be around here someplace . . .

Here I am, halfway through a tour of New Zealand. It's a beautiful country, but more importantly, it's full of beautiful rivers. I've been on a grand tour, hitting as many rivers as possible. Every new river brings a different challenge, and the limits of my comfort zone have been pushed day in and day out. I've enjoyed the challenges and have survived them all—so far. Yet all of that still does not quite add up to an explanation of just what I'm doing here, at the top of thirty-five-foot Maruia Falls.

Maruia Falls is a peculiar waterfall. A mellow class I river winds its way out of the countryside, suddenly drops thirty-five feet, and then continues on its merry, mellow way. It is probably the easiest waterfall you could ever find over thirty feet. No moves to make on the way to the lip. A calm pool at the bottom. Yet it remains a waterfall over thirty feet. At this moment, I curse the people who brought up the fact that people have been caught behind the curtain and that people have wound up in hospital with compressed vertebrae. I can only do my best to ignore that little voice inside my head that is telling me, "You are either crazy or stupid. Maybe both."

All of a sudden it is too late for me to listen to the voice—I've left the eddy. With one tentative stroke, I am past the point of no return. Okay, ferry out. Line it up. Just paddle off the lip. A little speed . . . Not too much . . . Not too little . . . Holy s**t! That looks like a long way down. That is a long way down!

The descent passes in a blur—I remember nothing. The landing, too. It must have been quite an impact. The first thing I remember after teetering over the lip is a total sense of shock: I'm at the bottom. I'm all in one piece. I'm upright! I'm so excited to have landed upright, I promptly flip. Oh, well. You can't win them all. The spectators give me some friendly thumbs up, but I am looking for the photographer. Did she get the shots? She nods. Sweet. I've got evidence. All I need now is a pint and a table full of friends with whom I can relive the day, right? You'd think so . . . But you'd be wrong.

Now my first waterfall of any significant size is in the bag. I still think that running it was crazy, stupid, or both. So just what does it say about me, now that I am back at the top getting ready to run it again?

EQUIPMENT

Creek boats are designed to be as safe as possible in steep, shallow whitewater. "Creekboat" is a generic term that refers to any short boat with lots of rocker and lots of volume in its relatively blunt ends; features that cause the boat to resurface very quickly and to bounce off any rocks that it encounters. If you've already spent time on creeks, then there's a good chance you've seen experienced paddlers using playboats on them. It's important to understand that this does not mean that it's a wise thing to do. A playboat simply doesn't give you the same margin for error that a creekboat does.

Unlike big water paddling, creekboating involves a lot of land-based safety. This gives rescuers the opportunity to use a wider range of safety equipment. We'll be looking at different scenarios and how this equipment can be used in the "Rescue" chapter of this book, and it should be re-stated that the best thing to do is take a swiftwater rescue course. With that said, here's a short list of some safety gear that can come in really handy.

- throw bag
- breakdown paddle
- pin kit
- first aid kit
- river shoes
- rescue vest
- elbow pads

"NEVER leave your boat without your throw rope." (Shannon Carroll)

SCOUTING

As we mentioned at the beginning of this chapter, creek boating is similar to chess in that it involves a lot of strategy. You can easily spend more of the day scouting and picking lines than actually paddling. In fact, there are even people who enjoy the scouting and line picking more than the actual paddling! If you've ever done it, then you'll understand why. We wanted to briefly address the subject of scouting, because there are a few valuable lessons we've learned over the years.

As a general rule, you should always scout rapids when you can't see the bottom. It's easy to dismiss this rule when it's a local river that has been run recently, but the fact is that you never know when new wood can appear in a bad place. It's important to understand that the chance of new hazards appearing increases exponentially after rain or fluctuating water levels. Taking a few minutes to ensure that the coast is clear can make a huge difference in your day. You'll also want to wear proper footwear, as bare feet are next to useless in rescue situations. Other good habits to get into are carrying a throw bag at all times and keeping all your safety equipment secured on your body. Murphy's Law definitely applies to kayaking, and odds are that if you aren't carrying your throw bag then you're going to need it. The reality is that everything doesn't always go as smoothly as we'd like on the river, so you need to keep yourself as prepared as possible for whatever situations might arise.

SWIMMING

Swimming in creeks is never really fun. The water is often snowmelt, and consequently nearly freezing in temperature. On the upside, this does manage to numb your body so that the rocks don't hurt quite so much! As we were saying . . . swimming in creeks is never fun, but there are a few things to understand about the topic that could spare you some real grief.

When swimming in whitewater, you can either take a defensive position, or an aggressive position, and you avoid standing at all times. Standing up in current is the best way to become a victim of the dreaded foot entrapment, where your foot gets caught between rocks while the current knocks you off balance and traps you underwater. This hazard is much more of a reality on creeks. Aggressive swimming involves actively swimming yourself to shore or away from a hazard as quickly as possible. You generally only swim aggressively in deeper water, as you are less exposed to serious injury from rocks. The defensive position comes into

play when we're swimming over drops, or when there are rocks around that you need to protect yourself from. This "body surfing" position involves floating on your back, feet first, with the rest of your body as close to the surface as possible.

The defensive swimming position gets used when you are swimming over drops, or when you need to protect yourself.

PINS

Fortunately, pins are not overly common, but they do happen, and have proved fatal in far too many instances. If a pin is going to happen, there's a very good chance it will be on a creek. There are two main types of pins. There are vertical pins (stern or bow), and lateral pins, commonly referred to as "broaches." Both pins represent very dangerous situations that have the potential of becoming lethal. Pins need to be dealt with quickly and efficiently. We're going to look at a few methods for dealing with pins in the "Rescue" chapter of this book, but you also need to know how to avoid pins in the first place.

Unless you see a drop when it's as dry as a bone, you never really know what is under the surface. These small potholes are caused by erosion over many years, and in the wrong place could be dangerous pinning spots.

Why do pins happen? Pins can happen for two reasons. Either you don't recognize the risks, or you miss your line and are paying the price. Recognizing potential pinning spots comes with practice, but there's also a major element of common sense. Unless you see a drop when it's dry as a bone, you'll never really know what kind of rock is beneath the water line. With experience, you learn to predict what is under the surface by assessing the reaction of the water. With or without this river reading experience, you can learn lots from the surrounding environment, since there's a good chance that the character of the riverbed closely resembles the character of the riverbank.

For example, are there lots of boulders lying around that would create big gaps for pinning the end of a kayak, or is the rock quite flat and smooth? It's also a really good idea to make some inquiries before running a river for the first time. The paddling world is a tightly knit community with a common lingo, so if a river has some hazards to be aware of you can be sure that people will happily share that info with you. On-line chat boards can provide great information on rivers if you don't have anyone in particular to ask. It's not a bad idea to ask the chat groups even if you do get some information beforehand. You can never be too well informed.

OH RUTHERFORD

By Ken Whiting

My buddies and I learned a very good lesson a few years back while paddling a creek in the Whistler area of British Columbia, Canada. We were making our way down a section of Rutherford Creek, which one of us had run only a week earlier. The creek had been clear of wood and other debris at that time. About halfway through the run, we arrived at a rapid that was blocked from view by a huge mid-stream boulder. Having been clean the week before, we mistakenly decided to press forward without scouting.

To all our horror, we encountered a river-wide log straight out of our worst nightmares. With no escape, we all ran into the log, one after the other. Just before I slammed into the log, I watched in shock as my buddy Tyler's boat disappeared from view underneath it, while my other buddy Brendan's boat floated upside down on the far side. Focusing my attention on the job at hand, I charged the log in an attempt to boof over top, but was unceremoniously denied and tossed on my side still upstream of the log. I'm really not sure how I got through, but I did, and then immediately picked up the chase for Tyler's gear. As chance had it, Tyler was able to escape from his kayak. In shock from the whole episode, we gathered his gear and made our way to the take out, keen to just get off the river.

About a half hour later, we approached another benign-looking rapid that we couldn't fully see. Our eagerness to finish the day seemed to cloud our already wavering sensibility, and we again started downstream one after the other without scouting. My uneasiness grew as I watched Dave head into the drop first, followed by Tyler, and then Ryan. A quick flash reminder of our earlier episode caused me to abort my run and head to shore for a quick scout.

It wasn't until I got to shore that I heard the yelling. "STOP, KEN!" someone screamed. I jumped out of my boat with my throwbag in hand, climbed over the big rock that obstructed our view, and watched Dave as he was swimming downstream. He had apparently made it past the river-wide log that still had Ryan and Brendan boxed into a nasty little hole. Clawing with bionic finger strength, Brendan pulled himself out of harm's way and into an eddy off to the side. With a quick hand, Ryan was safely in the eddy as well. Tyler was downstream with Dave and Dave's gear. Miraculously, Tyler had made his second trip of the day under a log.

Collecting our wits and the pieces once again, we continued on our way downstream. We encountered one more rapid that required a scout, and although it was very doable, it took everyone in the group no more than five seconds to pick up their kayaks and start the portage. We had all used up our lucky tokens on this day, and quite possibly for the remainder of our creekboating lives! We all knew how stupid we'd been, and knew that we were incredibly lucky to get away with what we had.

In hindsight, our rationale for not scouting wasn't completely asinine. The river had been clean only a week before, and there hadn't been any real water level fluctuation. The chance of new wood was minimal! The bottom line, though, is that we risked our lives to save ourselves the little bit of effort that scouting would have required. This is a mistake that I can safely say I will never repeat, and I hope this story saves you equal grief or even worse.

PLAYBOATING

**PLAYBOATING EQUIPMENT • FLATWATER MOVES
WAVE MOVES • HOLE MOVES • RIVER RUNNIING MOVES**

"Playboating practice will help your overall paddling dramatically. It forces you to become comfortable with waves and holes, with standing your kayak vertically on end, and with rolling quickly and reliably from any position." (Ken Whiting)

Playboating, competitively known as freestyle kayaking, is about surfing, spinning, and having the most fun possible by playing with various river features. Playboating has had an enormous impact on the growth and development of the sport of whitewater kayaking. It has made the river appealing and accessible to more than just the hard-core outdoors enthusiasts looking to challenge the extremes of Mother Nature. There are now more paddlers than ever addicted to the sensation of surfing waves and to the challenge of learning new moves. Thanks to this flood of new paddlers into the sport, manufacturers have been working overtime to bring out the latest and greatest kayaks and gear. This has driven the sport forward even further, and has made moves possible that never would have been considered in the past.

The first freestyle kayaking competitions took place in the late '80s and early '90s, and were very casual in nature. Surfing, spinning, enders, and paddle twirls were the big tricks in those days. These fun and playful events rapidly grew in popularity. Boat manufacturers took notice and new kayaks began appearing on rivers. In 1993, the first-ever Freestyle Kayaking World Championships took place at Hell Hole on Tennessee's Ocoee River, with such legendary paddlers as Scott Shipley, Corran Addison, Bob McDonough and Eric Jackson taking part. Since then, the World Championships have taken place every two years, with warm-up "Pre-World" Championships being held in the between years. In 1995, Germany hosted the World Championships on the Eiskenal River in Augsburg and it set a new standard for Freestyle Competitions with a very professional organization. The World's then moved from Canada's Ottawa River in 1997, to the Waikato River in New Zealand in 1999, to Spain in 2001, Austria in 2003 and are planned for Australia in 2005.

Each World Championship has marked a significant stage in the evolution of the sport, as it provides the best opportunity for paddlers

A freestyle competition in Lyon, France.

from around the globe to meet and learn from each other, and to showcase the latest moves.

Freestyle kayaking is now a very competitive sport that requires an athlete's complete dedication. The limits of what human and kayak can do together have been pushed to unbelievable levels, thanks to the creativity of paddlers along with innovative developments in equipment design.

Playboating continues to grow in popularity and all the new equipment is allowing recreational paddlers to reach their goals far more quickly than ever before. However, even with the best equipment, you need to have a foundation of skills and an understanding of the concepts in order to learn playboating moves. This book has already provided a very solid foundation of skills and techniques, so now we're going to look at some specific playboating moves and how you'll use these skills to perform them. We'll start with a look at some specific playboating equipment, and then we'll get into some flatwater moves, followed by wave moves, holes moves, and finally a few river-running moves. Please understand that we're just taking a look at some of the more popular playboating moves and that there are countless others to learn. Many of the following are actually segments from *The Playboater's Handbook 2*, which thoroughly covers all freestyle kayaking technique.

PLAYBOATING EQUIPMENT

The equipment you use for playboating will have a huge impact on the speed at which you'll learn new moves and even on your ability to perform some of them. Your boat selection will have the largest impact on these things, but there are some other important pieces of equipment that you need to consider.

PLAYBOAT SELECTION

If you're interested in buying yourself a playboat, then we have some good news and some bad news for you. The good news is that we guarantee there's a boat that will be perfect for your body type and

paddling style. The bad news is that you can expect it to take some real investigative work to find, because a plethora of new designs is introduced each year. We're going to do our best to make this sorting process as easy as possible for you.

Your body type is one of the biggest factors when picking a boat, but you also need to make some personal decisions. You need to decide whether you can afford to get a kayak that will be used almost exclusively for play, or whether you're looking for more of an all-round playboat that you can confidently run rivers in. Regardless, you want to choose a boat that meets your needs as you continue to improve. This means choosing a boat that is short (typically less than eight feet), has a planing hull, and is a reasonable width so that rolling and holding an edge are easy.

Exclusive Playboats vs All-Round Playboats

To make this as simple as possible, we'll just say that the smaller the playboat you choose, the more responsive it will be for aggressive, freestyle moves. The larger the playboat, the more forgiving and comfortable it will be, so the better it will be for other types of paddling. An unfortunate reality of freestyle kayaking is that if you have long legs, you can expect to be slightly uncomfortable in a playboat that is the ultimate size for you. This is because the less volume a playboat has in its ends, the less air you need to force underwater for vertical moves, but the less space you have for your feet. A kayak with more volume in the ends will be more comfortable and more forgiving, but harder to throw around. Of course you can go too far in both directions. You don't want to get a boat that's too small for you or too big for you.

Width

As a playboat gets wider, its planing surface grows. A large planing surface will let you flat spin very well, and it will be more stable to sit in. On the downside, as a boat gets wider it also gets more difficult to move from edge to edge and more difficult to roll. You can get away with using a wider boat by padding your seat so that you sit higher and have more leverage, but be sure not to raise your centre of gravity too much or you're going to be flipping all the time. As a general rule, the taller and heavier you are, the wider the kayak you can get away with.

Volume

Your weight will have a major impact on the volume of the boat you choose. As a rule, a kayak becomes easier to throw around as it shrinks in volume, but it also becomes less forgiving. Smaller boats are edgier and sit lower in the water, so they'll flush off waves and out of holes more easily. However, they can be a godsend when you're practising moves on flatwater. Ideally, look for a boat that you can throw around on flatwater, but that provides enough volume to be slightly forgiving.

Length

The effect of a playboat's length is simple. As a kayak gets shorter, it gets slower, but it becomes more manoeuvrable. In general, the shortest boats make the most moves possible, although this doesn't necessarily mean that the shortest boats make all moves easy to perform.

PADDLES

Your paddle has have a smaller impact on your playboating performance than the kayak you use, but it's important to have one that you're comfortable with. Because it can be tricky to move from one paddle style to another, we suggest that you choose one paddle that will accommodate all the different types of paddling you'll do. If you plan on spending a large part of your time playboating, then you should

OTHER USEFUL PLAYBOATING GEAR

Thanks to the popularity of playboating, there are a number of pieces of gear that have been introduced specifically for the playboater.

Playboating Shoes: These flexible, padded, playboating shoes are smaller than the traditional booties and let you squeeze your feet into small places.

Drydeck: The drydeck is a combined skirt and drytop that allows playboaters incredible freedom to rotate because there is nothing tight around the waist.

Overthruster: The overthruster fits underneath your skirt to prevent water from pressing your skirt inward. This lets your kayak maintain a consistent volume of air and also helps prevent skirt implosions when surfing big waves.

Paddle Wax or Tape: A small amount of wax or tape on your paddle shaft can dramatically improve your grip and therefore increase the amount of power that you can apply.

Playboating PFDs: Playboating requires lots of dynamic body movement, and these low-profile life jackets minimize the interference with your movements without removing any flotation. The flotation is simply moved away from the most active areas (shoulders, chest, and sides) and repositioned in the least active areas (stomach, mid-back).

consider using a paddle with minimal offset. Many playboaters even use paddles without any offset, which can come in handy when both blades are in the water at the same time.

FLATWATER MOVES

"The biggest failure you can have is to not try at all." (Cindy Jamieson)

STERN SQUIRTING

The Stern Squirt involves slicing the stern of your kayak underwater and pivoting around with your bow in the air: basically a stern pivot turn initiated with a back sweep. It's often done when crossing an

Many playboaters use paddles with a minimal amount of twist (offset). An offset of 0–45 degrees is most common.

eddy line where the helical flow can help pull your stern underwater and pivot around, but you can also squirt on flatwater. Stern squirting is a great way to practise the skills that are essential for more advanced playboating moves, while at the same time making you more comfortable with being on end. Keep in mind that playboats are designed to get vertical easily, so if you're getting vertical on a powerful eddy line, it doesn't necessarily mean that you're using proper technique. In order to focus on using the proper technique, you should practise your stern squirts on flatwater, or on weak eddy lines that make it a bit harder to get vertical.

Wherever you practice the squirt, your ultimate goal should be to do a full 360-degree turn with a single stroke. Contrary to popular belief, the ideal squirt is not a vertical move! Your bow should be lifted anywhere from 30 to 80- degrees. Keeping it under vertical allows you to stay balanced while pivoting around on your stern. The size of your kayak relative to your body weight will certainly have a bearing on how easily you can get it up, so not everyone can expect to be able to lift their bow high into the air right away.

One of the keys to stern squirting is keeping your weight over your kayak at all times. This is going to require a real separation of your upper and lower bodies.

A stern squirt initiated on an eddy line. Notice how aggressively the head and body lead the way, and how deeply the paddle is engaged in the water.

On flatwater, you'll start with some forward speed, and then establish spin momentum in one direction with a light sweep stroke, while keeping your boat flat so that your stern will slide out rather than carve. Once you've slid out to 90-degrees (about a quarter turn), it's time to initiate the squirt. When squirting on an eddy line, your goal is to initiate the squirt after your hip has crossed the eddy line, and with your boat perpendicular to the main current. This lets you take most advantage of the power of the current.

To initiate the squirt, your head and body must always lead the way, which means you'll turn aggressively to the inside of the spin. This will effectively wind up your body. As you do this, lean back, reach and plant a powerful reverse sweep as far back as you can. Both your hands should be reaching over the side of the kayak and your back arm should be straight. You also need to edge your kayak to the outside of the turn so that your back sweep will push your stern underwater. Start with a relatively small boat tilt, which you can increase as your balance improves. Ultimately, you'll initiate your squirt with your boat tilted at a 15-to-30-degree angle. It's also very important that you plant your back sweep deeply enough in the water so that you can push upwards while at the same time pushing away from the kayak. Pushing upwards with your blade helps to force your stern underwater. As you push on your paddle, you'll receive the support needed for your stomach muscles to pull the bow of the kayak up and around. This

effectively unwinds your body. Your back sweep should be reaching its end once you've turned about 180 degrees from your initial position. At this point, your stern should be underwater and your body should have returned to an upright sitting position. This upright position is much more stable and is absolutely essential for the more advanced moves.

The success of your stern squirt now relies on your ability to avoid "hitting the wall." From the "Pivot Turn" segment, you'll remember that this means levelling off the tilt on your kayak before your stroke has finished. By levelling off your tilt, your kayak will continue to spin around as the stern floats its way to the surface. This is the only way you'll be able to perform a full 360-degree spin from your initial back sweep.

To make the most out of your stern squirt practice, focus on these three elements: winding up and unwinding your body using your stomach muscles, finishing your back sweep with your body in an upright position, and levelling the tilt on your kayak before the back sweep is finished so that buoyancy energy keeps you spinning. Once you can routinely put these elements together, not only will you have a great stern squirt, but you'll have opened the doors to virtually every other advanced playboating move. Finally, practise these squirts on both sides from the beginning so you don't end up with lopsided skills like most boaters!

GETTING VERTICAL

Practising any move in a controlled environment is the best way to develop good technique. Since playboats have shrunk to a point where vertical moves can be performed on flatwater, more and more paddlers are reaching their "vertical goals." Does this mean that you should squeeze yourself into the smallest boat possible to practise vertical moves on the flat water? Absolutely! The smaller the boat that you use on flatwater, the easier vertical moves will be to learn. Of course, when you're cramming yourself into a small playboat, there comes a point when the pain factor exceeds the fun and learning factors.

Whether you've got a tiny playboat to practice with or not, you need to accept that vertical moves require a combination of technique and power. Neither one on its own will do the trick! We'll start by looking at one of the most basic advanced skills called the "double pump." The double pump is a technique you use to throw your bow underwater, which is necessary in one form or another for the initiation of most advanced moves.

THE DOUBLE PUMP / BOW WIND UP

The idea behind the double pump is to pull your bow into the air so that you have more energy to then force it underwater. To pull your bow into the air (often referred to as "winding up the bow"), there are three things that you need to do at the same time: tilt your kayak on edge, shift

Double pumping the bow into the air requires good balance on edge, and upper and lower body separation.

DOUBLE PUMP DRILL

Here's a drill that helps get your legs and stomach muscles involved with the move: It involves alternately sinking your bow and stern, and is commonly referred to as the "bobbing drill." It starts with a double pump, but once your bow is in the air, you don't commit as aggressively to smashing it underwater. As your forward sweep transitions into a back stroke, shift your weight into a neutral position instead of throwing it hard forward. Your body should remain in the neutral position from this point on. Now, use your knees and stomach muscles to pull your bow (feet) downwards. Once it's underwater, turn your back stroke into a forward stroke and pull the bow back upwards. Continue to bob your bow in and out of the water a total of ten times.

The key to this drill is taking very short and powerful strokes with your blade completely in the water. You also need to have the balance to hold a steady tilt on your kayak while your stomach muscles work overtime to pull your legs up and down. Since your body stays in a neutral position, your stomach muscles will be doing virtually ALL the work. It shouldn't take too many of these bobs to get your abs burning!

A common problem is getting the paddle caught under your boat after a few bobs, which tends to pull you upside down. To prevent your paddle from diving, use a sculling technique for each stroke to maintain a climbing angle with your blade. This means curling your wrists slightly forward as you take a back stroke, and cocking your wrists slightly back as you take a forward stroke. This technique keeps your paddle near the surface, about a foot or two out to the side from your hip and knee.

Keep in mind that the goal of this drill is not to sink your bow and stern as deeply as possible! The goal is to feel your knees and stomach muscles actively involved in pulling your bow up and down.

The goal of this drill isn't to sink your bow and stern as deeply as possible. The goal is to feel your knees and stomach muscles pulling your bow up and down.

your weight back, and take a forward sweep stroke. Once your bow is in the air, don't hesitate before throwing it down. The power you need to throw your bow underwater can be gained only through torso rotation. Plant a back stroke just behind your hip and turn your whole upper body so that your chest faces the water. Now as you push off the paddle, throw your weight aggressively forward and unwind your body by pulling your feet down with your knees and stomach muscles.

BOW STALL

Bow stalling involves balancing on the bow of your kayak with your stern in the air. This takes some awesome balance and a lot of practice, but it's a great move to learn because it teaches you about the vertical balance points of your kayak, and it's really fun.

Like any other vertical move, bow stalling is easiest with the lowest volume kayaks. So, the smaller the boat you practise with, the more quickly you'll see results.

Before you can even contemplate bow stalling, you need to be comfortable with double pumping and pulling your bow completely underwater. If you're not there yet, then keep working on both.

The ideal bow stall position has your kayak at around a 70-to-80-degree angle from a side view, with your body in a moderately aggressive position that keeps your centre of gravity low. Your paddle should be completely in the water and as far out from

The ideal bow stall has your kayak on around a 70–80-degree angle, your body in a moderately aggressive position, and your paddle in the water, out from your kayak

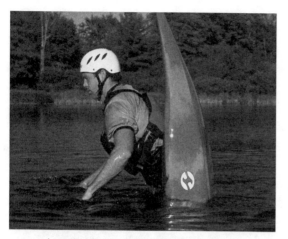

Leaning back while in a bow stall will pull your kayak more vertical.

Leaning forward while bow stalling will flatting out your kayak.

your kayak as is comfortable in a low brace position. Imagine that your kayak and paddle blades form a tripod. The farther these points are from each other, the more stable your tripod will be.

With this ideal stall position as your goal, you'll need to throw your bow down at around a 70-degree angle, and then stop yourself when your kayak is nearly vertical. To stop your spin momentum, put on the brakes by using your paddle as a low brace. Staying stalled is now simply a matter of balance!

Using your paddle blades to brace yourself will help stop your bow from slicing out to the side. Your paddle is also helpful for stopping your kayak from falling forward or flattening out, and this is why you need to keep your blades completely in the water.

Having said that, it's your body position that plays the biggest role in keeping you balanced, and the effects of your forward and backward leans are

actually a couple of the most frequently misunderstood concepts in playboating. When balanced on your bow, leaning back will actually pull your kayak more vertical. This can be confusing, because the natural thing to do when you feel yourself falling forward is to lean back. Leaning forward, on the other hand, will help flatten out your kayak if you're starting to fall over-vertical.

FLATWATER LOOP

The flatwater loop is basically a complete front flip done on flatwater! The evolution of the playboat has made a lot of cool new moves possible, but this move in particular blows us away.

Our first piece of advice is quite simple. If your local river doesn't have warm water, then go to a pool to learn this one! You'll save yourself a lot of headaches!

Before even considering the flatwater loop,

1) Keeping your body as neutral as possible, start bouncing your kayak lightly. 2) Reach down with your paddle and pull your boat as deeply underwater as possible while standing up on your foot pegs. 3&4) As your boat pops out of the water, jump out and away and tuck forward.

you need to have a solid bow stall. Like so many playboating moves, the success of your loop will depend on your set up, and this set-up requires some fine-tuned bow stall control. From your bow stall, the idea is to pull your boat as deeply underwater as possible so that you get popped into the air like a cork. This is one of the times when a paddle with minimal feather comes in handy.

From your bow stall, start bouncing your kayak slightly by pushing off both paddle blades, but don't over-bounce yourself. The idea isn't to push your boat high into the air, but to establish a rhythm and to build up some additional energy for

pulling your boat underwater. It will also help if you keep your body neutral as you bob up and down. Fight the urge to lean hard forward to push your stern into the air.

Ideally you'll initiate the loop on your second bounce. As you approach the height of this second bounce, lean hard forward while cocking your wrists back so that you can slice your blades deep. As your boat bobs downwards pull it as far underwater as possible with a powerful dual forward stroke. As you pull on your paddle, lean back and stand up on your foot pegs. This helps push your boat the deepest while at the same time pulling your kayak to vertical. As your boat starts popping back out of the water, you should be standing up on your foot pegs with your paddle out of the water and your boat should be falling past vertical. As you continue to accelerate out of the water, you need to jump out and away from your kayak and tuck forward.

If you've nailed things to this point, then you're well on your way to stomping a loop, but you're not there yet! There's one more very big trick to the move. As you jump out and away, it seems reasonable that tucking hard forward will bring your kayak around for the full loop, but it won't! It took us a while to figure this one out, but we did! As soon as your shoulders hit the water, you'll actually reverse your body motions. In other words, lean hard backward and kick your legs aggressively away from your body, while also pushing back on your paddle for support. The idea is that opening up your body like this will kick your bow further into the air, allowing the stern to stab into the water almost vertically. If you can get your stern to stab into the water like this, then your boat's rotational momentum will help you finish the move.

When done right, the loop hardly uses your paddle after the initial pull down. More than anything, your paddle provides the support necessary for keeping your boat straight as you flip, and from which you can kick your legs out and push your bow into the air. If you rely too much on your paddle, your tendency is to pull on one blade and you'll always finish by rolling up to one side.

As soon as your shoulders hit the water, reverse your body motions and kick out your legs.

Lean back and push your bow over your body with your feet.

You can also push off the paddle over your head to help finish the loop.

UGANDA
THE LAND OF OPPORTUNITY

by Lisa Utronki

Ugandan kayaking has just exploded (365 days a year, a temperate climate, warm water, countless big waves . . .), and the Ugandan boaters are now showing the world what it's like to have such a special playground in their backyard. Our journey to Uganda's White Nile was a beautiful experience to say the least. On top of everything else, we were able to help pass on some of the opportunities that come along with kayaking to a few locals by doing our part in the creation of the first Ugandan National Freestyle Kayaking Team.

Jinja is a mellow town of colourful, welcoming people. It's situated on the northern shores of Lake Victoria, the source of the magnificent White Nile. Along the riverbanks are villages of mud huts with grass-thatched roofs cut into the tropical jungle where anything and everything grows. It's clear that "river is life" here. The river provides all the daily necessities as well as a place to let go and enjoy. Whether fishing for Nile perch, collecting drinking water, bathing, doing laundry, or just cooling off, the Nile is a focal point of activity here—and not just on its calm sections. One my most vivid images, during one of my first heart-pumping days: three boys of about fourteen years clinging to the only rock (that I didn't even realize existed) in the middle of the river. Then off they go, bobbing down Budjagali Falls, one of the more significant rapids, hanging on only to a jerry can for flotation. Apparently, this is how some of these kids get introduced to whitewater!

As happens so often, I found myself tossed into the depths of a huge river, having accepted the task of videoing a raft trip on a section of which I had only briefly seen bits. Standing on the banks of Budjagali Falls, hoping that I'd positioned myself well, I watched with amazement as the local safety boaters cartwheeled and wave-wheeled their way through the enormous whitewater. The amazing thing is that these local safety kayakers were using leaky, outdated boats; paddles that one might hardly agree have two blades; and anything else that has been handed down over the years. There was no doubting the potential of these men, and having just come returned from competing in the World Championships in Graz, Austria, I felt they really deserved the opportunity to compete on an international level.

That's why I began throwing around the idea of organizing a freestyle rodeo. Shortly thereafter, Jon Dahl and I had gathered the troops and created the "Nile Freestyle Festival," a four-day festival featuring the first-ever Ugandan Team Selections. The event was a huge success. The entire community came together with enthusiasm and support to make it happen. The weeks leading up to the festivities were full of anticipation. I'll never forget the 7:00 a.m. training sessions with the locals, and the gatherings to clarify competition rules and event judging. The excitement was embraced by all.

The Nile Freestyle Festival took off, with 38 kayakers freestyling some of the finest waves on the planet. Sun, big waves, and warm water; and afterwards kegs of beer and music pumping—who could ask for more! The event consisted of a freestyle rodeo, a down-river race, a rolling rodeo over nine km, and a big wave competition. Two nights of camping on "Hairy Lemon" Island ensured that all festivities were pushed to the max. Joining the Ugandans, we had entrants from New Zealand, England, Scotland, South Africa, and Canada (myself—the only female competitor). In everyone's minds, the main focus was the selection of the Ugandan Team. Everyone who was there was blown away by the performances of Geoffrey, Paulo, Juma, Paul, and Alex. The Ugandan boys kicked butt big-time, taking all the top places in the main events.

In the end, Geoffrey, Paulo, and Juma were chosen as the first men to officially represent Uganda. Their stage: the Pre-World Championships at Penrith, Australia. This would be a first opportunity for so many things. The first time out of their village without their families; the first time on a plane; the first time on another river; the first time in the first world; the first beer in a different pub . . . The great thing is that these guys showed some incredible talents, and they deserve everything that is coming to them.

Kayaking is more than just a sport for me. It gives me an endless opportunity to travel and explore foreign lands, cultures, and river communities. It's an alternative way of life that I can share anywhere. I'm ever so grateful for what I've learned through kayaking. This time in the heart of Africa was one of my most special experiences, and it feels so good to pass on some of the opportunities paddling has to offer.

Stand back as Geoffrey, Paulo, and Juma embark on a special journey—and something tells me this won't be the last we see of them.

WAVE MOVES

Waves are truly amazing river features. There really is nothing that can compare to the feeling of carving on a big, fast wave, with the water rushing by at high speed.

WAVE SURFING

Front surfing is a skill at which most paddlers become proficient quite quickly, thanks in large part to great boat designs. Backsurfing, on the other hand, is one of the most under-practiced skills. By practising backsurfing, you not only develop an important playboating skill, you enhance your backward awareness—which will do wonders for all aspects of your paddling! The best way to prepare yourself for backsurfing is to spend time on your reverse eddy turns and ferries. You need to reach a comfort level where your strokes and boat tilts become instinctive, because you won't have time to think them through while surfing a wave!

We're going to look at wave surfing skills from a front surfing perspective to keep things as clear as possible, but it's important to realize that you use these same techniques for backsurfing. The only thing that really changes for backsurfing is the direction that your kayak points and the back strokes that you use instead of forward strokes.

Catching waves

Catching a wave is often the toughest part of surfing. You have two options. You can catch a wave on the fly, or you can ferry onto a wave from a nearby eddy. Ferrying from an abutting eddy is easiest because you have little or no downstream momentum to stop. The challenge is to set your ferry up so you slide right onto the face of the wave. Staying on the face of the wave means you won't have to worry as much about having your bow dive underwater. If you enter the current too far upstream of the wave, you risk being carried all the way up and over it by the fast-moving

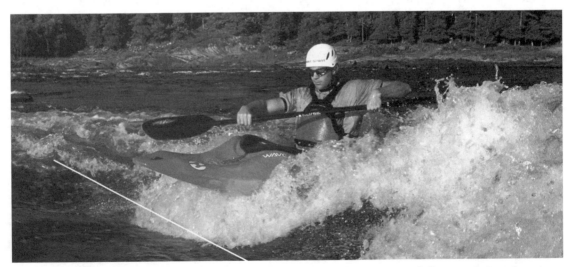

When ferrying onto a wave, aim to keep your bow at, or downstream of, the wave's trough.

DROPPING ONTO A WAVE

Dropping onto a wave (or "catching it on the fly") requires a bit more finesse and power. The toughest part about dropping in is lining yourself up to catch the steepest part of the wave. It's a bit easier to line yourself up by approaching from just off to one side with a slight ferry angle so that you can keep track of your position by looking over one shoulder. When you get close to the wave, slow yourself down as much as possible with powerful forward strokes. When you hit the trough of the wave, lean back to help keep your bow from diving, but as soon as your bow is clear, throw your weight forward and take a few quick strokes so you don't float right past the wave. The steeper the wave, the more important this weight shift will be to keep your bow from diving.

water as you drop back down. You also risk catching your bow under water as you drop back through the trough of the wave.

In order to successfully ferry onto the wave's face, you need to consider your kayak's angle, speed, and its point of entry into the current. Because every wave is different, and the speed of the main current can be very different, there's no single way to catch a wave, but there are a few key points to keep in mind. First, you need to aim your bow at or slightly downstream of the wave's trough. Second, the faster the water is moving, the more upstream angle you need to enter the current with. Whether the wave is right beside the eddy or a short ferry away, you must remember your ferrying technique. As you break through the eddy line, you need to establish some spin momentum into the main current, and then follow up with a forward stroke on the downstream side that pulls you right across the eddy line and momentarily holds your ferry angle. Once you're on the face of the wave, you can start using a rudder to control your surf. If in doubt, you're better off having

too much upstream angle, because it's easier to let your angle go than to recover from losing it.

Surfing

Nice work, you've caught the wave! Whitewater kayaks have become incredibly forgiving for surfing waves. The short, low volume ends allow you to blast in the trough of holes or breaking waves, and their considerable rocker lets you surf on any part of all but the steepest waves without having to worry about your upstream end purling. We're going to start by looking at the fundamentals of surfing, and then we'll move quickly onto more advanced surfing techniques, which will help you surf waves of all shapes and sizes.

First of all, you have to understand that most of your surf time should be spent on the face of a wave. Because whitewater kayaks have been designed to surf so effectively, you can sometimes get away with surfing passively down in the trough. Unfortunately, this won't work on all waves and it won't be useful for setting up other play moves. On mellow waves, you can often surf on the face without any effort whatsoever. In these cases, all you need to do is maintain control of your boat with rudders. On steeper waves, or when a wave is breaking, you need to get more aggressive with your surfing in order to stay on the face. This involves carving back and forth from one ferry angle to the next. The steeper the wave is, the more aggressively you have to do this. Let's look at how the body, paddle and boat are involved in making this happen.

Body position: First and foremost, you need to keep your weight centred as much as possible when you're surfing. Sitting upright puts you in the most stable position and affords you the most control over your boat. This doesn't mean that you can't lean back if you need to. Feel free to be active with your forward and backward leans. If you're sliding into the trough of the wave and your bow is diving, it's all right to lean back if it helps you recover. If you're falling

off the backside of the wave, then lean aggressively forward to slide back down the face. Just return to your default body position as quickly as possible.

The Paddle: Your paddle should be acting as a rudder at all possible times, because the rudder is the steering wheel for your kayak. If it's not in the water, you're not really in control. Your rudder gets planted with your paddle parallel to your kayak, and with your front hand held between shoulder and eye level. Keeping this front hand high buries your active blade deeply in the water. Having your paddle parallel to the kayak ensures that your rudder is not acting as a brake. Though braking rudders can come in useful in aggressive surfing situations, they can easily pull you off the smaller waves. Your chest and belly button should be turned to face your paddle. This winds up your body so that your rudder can act as a pivot from which your stomach muscles can help pull the bow around. Turning your chest towards your paddle shaft also keeps your hands in front of your body, which, as you

Sitting upright is your default body position while surfing, although there are times when you'll need to lean back or forward aggressively.

The best rudders are positioned at the back of the boat with your paddle parallel to your kayak, and your upper body rotated towards it.

already know, helps keep your shoulders safe. Keeping your elbows down will also keep your shoulders in the safest position.

From this ruddering position, you can turn your boat in either direction by simply rolling your wrists. By rotating your wrists upwards, you'll catch water with the power face of your blade and draw your stern towards your paddle. By curling your wrists slightly downwards, you'll engage the back face of your blade and will pry your stern away from your paddle.

The Boat: Your boat will be in one of two positions when front surfing. It will either face directly upstream (12 o'clock), or it will be on a ferry angle to one side. When pointed to 12 o'clock, your kayak will want to shoot down into the trough of a wave, so unless you're on a fairly flat wave, you're going to want to spend all of your time alternating from one ferry angle to the other.

The next big question is how to edge your kayak. Most paddlers' instincts tell them that they should tilt their boats into each turn when they plant the rudder. On flatter, smooth waves this does work quite well, and you can carve some great turns like this just as a surfer does. However, on steeper waves that are breaking, it becomes more important to keep your kayak tilted downstream to prevent your upstream edge from getting caught, which is what we're going to look at next.

Aggressive Surfing

You already know that the key to surfing steep waves is staying on the face, and the best way to stay there is to carve back and forth across the wave. When waves get really steep, cutting back becomes more difficult, and so the shoulders of the wave are the best place to do so. The shoulders are the sides of a wave that are less steep than the rest of the wave. Some waves may not have clearly defined shoulders, but there will always be mellower sections of a wave that you can use in lieu of a perfect shoulder. Once you reach the shoulder, cut back and ferry in the other direction. How far out on the shoulder you should carve depends on the character of each wave and will take some experimenting to figure out. In the case where you're setting up some other play move, then you'll want to cut back a bit harder than normal so that you end up right on top of the wave.

Regardless, you need an active and committed rudder for each successful cutback. There are two types of rudders that you can use. There's a slicing rudder and a braking rudder. A slicing rudder causes the least amount of resistance in the water. This rudder is planted near the back of

Aggressive surfing involves carving back and forth across the face of a wave, with a rudder engaged deeply in the water.

DRILL - FLATWATER RUDDER

You can get a good feel for these stern draws and stern pries on flatwater with a drill very similar to the one we looked at in the "Draws" segment of this book. Start by establishing some forward speed, and then coast with a neutral rudder in the water that keeps you going straight. Now, without moving your arms, rotate your wrists alternately up and down and feel the pressure switching from one side of your blade to the other. It should be immediately clear that prying your stern away from your paddle (curling wrists down) is the easier and more powerful action. This is why it's more common when surfing to alternate between rudders on either side of your kayak. You're actually bouncing back and forth from one stern pry to the next. Each pry is responsible for holding your ferry angle and cutting your boat back into the other direction when the time comes.

By curling your wrists forward in the rudder position, you'll expose the backside of your paddle, which will pry your stern away.

By cocking your wrists backward, you'll catch water with the powerface of your paddle and draw your stern towards it.

RECOVERIES

No matter how good you get at surfing, your upstream end will dive underwater or "purl" every once in a while. To recover from this, quickly and briefly tilt your kayak on edge. This temporarily relieves the water pressure on your bow, allowing it to resurface. You can also recover by spinning out when your upstream end begins to purl. This means that as soon as one of your ends starts diving underwater, you can initiate a flat spin. Instead of your bow being taken directly down, you're providing it with an escape route off to one side. This spin-out recovery only works with a very quick reaction and, of course, only if you're a competent flat spinner. We'll get there!

your kayak, with your body turned to keep your hands in the power position, and with your top hand kept between shoulder and eye level. This is a great rudder to use when you want to keep your speed up. The braking rudder does just the opposite, and gets planted out to the side of your body. It guides or turns your boat, while at the same time acting as a big brake. This is a helpful rudder when you need to pull yourself quickly up a wave or stop yourself from shooting further down. Depending on your situation, use one or a combination of these rudders to cut back at the shoulder of the wave.

BACK SURFING

As we already mentioned, back surfing is one of the most under-practiced skills among both recreational and professional

paddlers. Aggressive back surfing is also one of the most difficult moves, because you really need to feel your way around the wave instinctively as you don't have the same visuals. The only way to develop this sixth sense is through practice and the development of your backward awareness. We're not going to look at back surfing in depth, because it follows all the same rules as front surfing. The only thing that changes is your rudder technique. The back surfing rudder is very similar to the front surf rudder, except that you plant the rudder at the bow of your kayak rather than at the stern. Your top hand should be held between shoulder and eye level to ensure the blade is engaged deeply in the water and your wrist rotated forward so that this rudder blade is parallel to the boat. You need to resist the temptation to roll your wrists back, which allows your rudder to become a brace! You really need to be aggressive and dig your rudder in to grab water if you want to maintain control of your boat. This is the most common problem people display. They're timid with their rudders, which means they don't carve well and inevitably they end up down in the trough where their stern catches and things go downhill.

There's no doubt about it: back surfing is a tricky skill that will require more practice than any other move. At the same time, it has real and significant spin-off benefits and is well worth the time and effort required to learn it. When learning, we highly recommend getting to know a wave by front surfing it first. Learn where the wave's sweet spots and weak spots are and then spin to a back surf or back ferry onto the wave and plug away. Be aggressive and persistent.

FLAT SPINNING

Flat spinning is the motion of rotating 180 degrees or more while on a wave. Now that playboats are designed to be as "loose" (easy to spin) as possible, it really doesn't take much to get them spinning on big, fast waves. It's on the smaller, more finicky waves where proper flat spinning technique makes a big difference. Let's look at the set up, the initiation, and the recovery of the flat spin.

The best place to set up for a flat spin is at the peak of a wave. The best way to get up onto the peak is to carve out to the shoulder of the wave and then cut back

and ferry your way up top. Once you're there, you then need to establish some upstream momentum, which you'll do by pointing your kayak to 12 o'clock, leaning forward and letting yourself slide down towards the trough. You should practise doing this successfully several times on a wave to master it before actually going for the move. When you're ready to go for it, then just as you feel yourself beginning to drop down the face of the wave, it's time to initiate your flat spin!

To initiate the flat spin, you need to pop the entire stern of your kayak out of the water, or "release it." Until you pop these stern edges out of the water, your boat will want to carve a turn. To release the stern and initiate the flat spin, use a back sweep with a slight downstream tilt on your boat, and throw your weight forward. You should recognize this from the basic bow pivot turn that we covered in the "Essentials" segment, where we used a back sweep to pull our bow underwater and throw our stern into the air. Though you're not necessarily looking to pull your bow far underwater when initiating the flat spin, you definitely need to pop your stern out of the water. The amount of boat tilt to use depends on the situation and on how much your stern needs to get popped out of the water. On faster waves, your boat planes very high on the water and it doesn't take much tilt, if any, to release your stern. As waves get slower and smaller, your stern edges sink deeper into the face, so it takes more pop to release them, which means incorporating a stronger downstream tilt into your initiation. On these smaller waves, it's also

To initiate a flat spin, you need to pop the stern of your kayak out of the water.

helpful to push down on your back sweep to help pop your stern up.

As soon as your stern is released, then just like the bow pivot turn, you need to level off your boat tilt in order to keep your spin momentum going. Let's look at this move from the beginning . . .

Make your way to the top of the wave, and just as you start sliding down the face, initiate the flat spin with a back sweep. While pushing down and away with your paddle, throw your weight forward and tilt your boat slightly downstream for an instant to release your stern from the water.

Once your boat is spinning, you have two choices: you can stop in a back surf, or continue with a full 360-degree spin. On the smallest waves, you can only expect to spin 180 degrees at a time because a full 360-

degree spin will usually pull you off the wave. On these waves, a "recovery stroke" is necessary after each 180-degree rotation. A recovery stroke is a back stroke taken on the opposite side of the kayak from your initiating back sweep. This back stroke helps keep you on the wave and establish control in a back surf. To spin back to a front surf, things get a bit trickier. Ideally, your recovery stroke has set you up perfectly at the peak of the wave where you can quickly establish some upstream momentum by pointing your stern to 12 o'clock and sliding down the face. If not, then you need to get set up while back surfing. Obviously, you need to be pretty confident at back surfing before having this type of control. If you can get set up, then spinning back to a front surf is similar to the first part of your spin.

Spinning from a back surf to front surf, you'll need to pop your bow edges out of the water.

Once you start moving down the face, lead the spin with your head and body and use a forward sweep to pull your bow around. This time you'll need to release your bow edges, which you do by throwing your weight back and tilting your boat slightly downstream. Do you recognize this stern pivot turn from the "Essentials" segment? The amount of downstream tilt you use will depend on how aggressively you need to pop your bow edges out of the water. On the smallest waves, you again need to finish with a recovery stroke, which is a forward stroke on the opposite side of the kayak as your initiating sweep.

On faster, steeper waves, you can do full 360-degree spins, which is actually easier than stopping halfway, because you never have to back surf. The key to the full "360" is keeping your spin momentum going once you've established it. You must make smooth and precise edge transitions, lead with your head, and get your second sweep stroke in the water as quickly as possible. For the smoothest edge transitions, you need to tilt your boat downstream just enough to be able to release your ends, but no more. Any extra tilt will just catch more water and slow you down.

The key to doing a full 360-degree flat spin is getting your second stroke in the water as quickly as possible.

You also need to level off your boat as soon as you've released an end, as a level boat will plane out more effectively on the water. To get your second stroke (the front sweep) in quickly, drop your blade into the water at your knees and don't worry about taking the extra second to reach to your toes. By getting this second stroke into the water quickly, your boat doesn't have a chance to stall out and you can continue to pull it around with your stomach muscles.

As your set up improves and your edging transitions become smoother, you'll soon find that you don't even need a second stroke to get yourself around. Full, 360-degree flat spins that are accomplished with a single stroke are called "clean spins."

ADVANCED WAVE MOVES

One of the greatest things about waves is the awesome potential that they provide us with. On big, fast waves, there's an enormous amount of energy just waiting to be harnessed, and the newer playboats are designed to do just this. With aggressive carving edges and hulls that like to be bounced out of the water, a world of aerial acrobatics has opened up to paddlers. Here are a couple of the hottest aerial moves that you'll see on the river today:

Aerial Blunt and Backstab: The aerial blunt is a radical move that involves rotating from front surf to back surf by bouncing your boat into the air and

Ty Curtis throwing an Air Screw at Reversing Falls.

throwing your stern up and over your head. The aerial backstab is the same thing, but done in reverse so that you're moving from back surf to front surf and throwing your bow up and over your head.

Air Screw: The air screw is a horizontal aerial pirouette that doesn't use a single paddle stroke!

The Helix: The helix is an inverted, aerial 360, and is without a doubt one of the most sensational moves out there.

HOLE MOVES

SIDE SURFING

Side surfing is the act of balancing sideways in the trough of a hole. This can be one of the most intimidating skills to learn, but once you've developed the technique, then even the biggest holes can be relatively easy to surf. It's getting out or moving

around that causes the most problems! That's why we're going to take a quick look at each of these skills on its own.

The ideal side surf position involves balancing on your downstream butt cheek and lifting your upstream edge with your knees just enough so that it doesn't catch the downstream flowing water. Any extra boat tilt makes for a bouncier ride as you expose more of your hull for the incoming water to hit. Though it's tempting to lean your body downstream and use your paddle like a crutch, you need to focus on keeping your head and weight balanced over your downstream edge. This way, your paddle is free to move you around in the hole. It's also very important to sit in the moderately aggressive position when side surfing. This position gives you the most edge control and prevents your stern edges from catching water, which is quite common. As a final note, you should spend the majority of your time looking upstream. It doesn't matter if your kayak is facing

Side surfing is a balancing act.

upstream, downstream or sideways, the best way to keep track of your position in a hole is to keep your eyes on what's happening on your upstream side.

When sitting passively in a side surf, your paddle should be ready as a brace. The type of brace you use will depend on your situation, but whether you're using a high brace or a low brace, you've got to keep your paddle below your chin and keep your arms in close. It's when you overreach with braces that your shoulders are put at risk. If you happen to catch your upstream edge, you're gonna flip, so don't fight it! Trying to save yourself with an upstream brace will only jam your paddle into rocks or tweak your shoulders. If you're comfortable with the back deck roll, this is the perfect time to use it. You'll throw your body back and into the flip and roll back up on the downstream side.

Moving around and escaping holes

Once you're comfortable balancing in a side surf, it's time to start moving yourself around. The first rule for moving around in a hole is that all of your strokes are to be taken on the downstream side of your kayak, in the foam pile. Because the foam pile itself is aerated and doesn't provide much substance, you actually need to reach under it to the hard, green water below.

To escape from a hole, or to set up any freestyle hole move, you need to move from the trough of the hole up onto the foam pile. The most ideal places to do this are at the

Blasting is the most powerful means of moving around in a hole, although it's also the most challenging.

weak spots, such as the tongues or the corners of a hole. There are a couple of good ways of getting yourself to these spots. The easiest way is to simply take forward or backward strokes on the downstream side and pull yourself to the tongue or out to a corner.

A more powerful, but slightly more difficult, way of getting on top of the foam pile or escaping a hole is to "blast" your way from the trough of the hole out to the side. Blasting means front surfing in a hole or breaking wave. To pull yourself into a blast, take a powerful sweep stroke while keeping your boat as flat on the surface of the water as possible. In the blasting position, one end of your boat is underneath the foam pile while the other is pointing directly upstream. With a rudder in the water, you can then ferry out to the corner of the wave. This blasting technique requires you to be very aggressive, but it's definitely the quickest and most powerful way to move around in a hole.

Spinning in a hole

Spinning in a hole requires a combination of balance, edge control, and hole awareness. The key to spinning in a hole is using the shoulder or tongue of a hole to get yourself out of the trough and onto the foam pile, where you can manoeuvre. It's also critical that you keep your eyes upstream as much as possible, as this is where the action is, and it gives you the best understanding of your boat's position relative to the hole.

CARTWHEELS

A cartwheel is a smooth combination of elevated bow and stern pivot turns that can be done both on flatwater and in a hole. If done properly, the boat should be revolving around a fixed point at a fairly consistent rate. The cartwheel provides the foundation for virtually every vertical move, both on waves and in holes. Since every hole is different, there's no one method of cartwheeling, but there are some key concepts and techniques that can be slightly modified to fit any situation. We're going to take a look at the set-up, the initiation, and the "linking of ends."

The Setup

Without a good set up, your cartwheel is doomed from the beginning. Your ultimate goal is to initiate the cartwheel at the seam of the hole, with as little upstream speed as possible and with some spin momentum already established. Though the best paddlers have learned to initiate carthwheels from the trough of a hole, it's much easier to start on top of the foam pile. The easiest way to get set up is to ferry onto the foam pile when you enter the hole. If you're trying to get set up from a side surf, then you have to work yourself to a tongue or corner to get on top of the foam pile.

Once there, it isn't easy to remain in place, as the hole's recirculating water will want to pull you right into the trough. This is where your braking strokes come in handy. Braking strokes are powerful back strokes that get planted deeply out to the side of your hip. Using alternating braking strokes, you can stop yourself from being sucked into the trough of most holes. These strokes also help you set up the right initiation angle on your kayak, which is what we're going to look at next.

Braking strokes are very useful for holding your position on a hole's foam pile, while getting set up to initiate a cartwheel.

The Initiation

As we just learned, your ultimate goal is to initiate the cartwheel:

1. with as little upstream momentum as possible
2. with your bow at the seam of the hole
3. with spin momentum already established

You need to initiate with as little upstream momentum as possible because extra upstream momentum will simply drive your kayak deeper into the green water, which in turn will pop you into the air (ender style) or push you downstream and out of the hole.

Initiating your bow at the seam of a hole is a good guideline, because it forces you to use a combination of your own power and the power of the river. If you initiate in too much of the green water, you'll get pushed downstream and out of the hole, whereas if you initiate too high in the foam pile, you'll tend to tumble down into the trough of the hole.

When we say to initiate with spin momentum, we mean that you should already be pulling your bow around and downwards **before** it enters the water at the seam. This forces you to use your own power instead of relying on the current to take your bow downstream. To establish this spin momentum, use braking strokes to set yourself up on an angle slightly off of 12 o'clock. Then, use a small double pump right there on the foam pile to smash your bow down at the seam of the hole. It's important to understand that you aren't looking to pull your bow directly downward, but that you need to slice it down and around, underneath your body just like a bow pivot turn.

As a general rule, if you're intending to initiate a cartwheel to the left, you should set up with a slight right angle (around one o'clock), and if you intend to initiate a cartwheel to the right, you want to set up with a slight left angle (around 11 o'clock).

Initiating the bow at the seam of the hole.

Whichever way you're cartwheeling, the goal is for your bow to initiate at 12 o'clock. You set up slightly off of this mark to account for the small amount that your bow will come around between the set up and initiation. For more vertical ends, your kayak will be tilted more aggressively on edge and your spin momentum needs to be directed more vertically than laterally.

For lower-angle cartwheels, your kayak should be initiated with a tilt between 20 and 45 degrees, and your spin momentum should be directed more laterally.

Now that you understand where to initiate your cartwheel, let's take a closer look at how your body and paddle are involved.

The paddle is responsible for three things:

1. It provides the braking power that will stop your kayak from diving too deeply into the green water.
2. It provides a pivot from which you can pull your bow down and around using your knees and stomach muscles.
3. It acts as a brace, although it isn't a crutch for you to lean on, as your weight needs to stay over your kayak.

To do all these things, you need to plant your initiation stroke firmly in the greenwater under the foam pile, with your

A fairly vertical cartwheel being initiated to the left. The bow is initiated at 12 o'clock, with the boat tilted aggressively on edge.

arms in the power position and with your whole body turned to lead the way. This power position allows you to use the power of your whole torso for the initiation and keeps your shoulders safe. With your body wound up, pull your bow down and around with your stomach muscles and legs, and by shifting your weight forward. As you do so, focus your eyes on the seam of the hole so that you can keep track of your position in the hole. The length of time that you remain looking upstream will depend on the power of the hole and the speed of your cartwheel, because staying ahead of your kayak is the top priority. If you're initiating a cartwheel in a slow hole or pourover, you can look upstream right up until your initiation stroke has finished its job. However, in a powerful hole, you'll have to turn and lead the way with your head right away to keep ahead of your kayak.

Linking Ends

Once you've initiated your cartwheel, keeping it going involves staying ahead of your kayak, keeping your weight forward, making smooth edge transitions, and moving quickly from one stroke to the next. To demonstrate this, we'll take a quick look at the actions of your boat, body and paddle.

The boat: It should be clear now that in order to keep spin momentum going for any move, you need to make your edge transition before your initiation stroke has finished. When practising pivot turns, you were levelling your kayak off; but for cartwheels, you need to make a complete edge transition so that the submerged end slices back to the surface. The amount you tilt your kayak onto its next edge dictates how vertical your cartwheels are. If you're slow in making this transition, your

Watching the seam of the hole lets you keep track of your position in the hole.

cartwheel will usually stall out or you'll get turned downstream in a pirouette.

The paddle: Your paddle has three main functions when you're cartwheeling. It acts as a pivot point, from which your stomach and knees can pull your bow around; it acts as a brake to prevent you from catching too much greenwater in the trough; and it acts as a brace with which you can make small corrections. It's important to note that all these things require that your paddle be planted as early as possible for each rotation, so that you have the maximum time to control your kayak. In small holes, you need more power from your paddle to pull each of your ends through. In big holes, where your cartwheels are quicker and you have less time to reach for your strokes, it's okay, because the water provides most of the power. In this case, your strokes are in close to your body and your focus is more on making smooth edge transitions and staying ahead of your cartwheels with your upper body.

Your paddle also acts as a brake to prevent a powerful hole's recirculating water from dragging you down into the trough. In weaker holes, the recirculating water may not be powerful enough to hold you on its own while linking cartwheels. In these holes, you may need to take small recovery strokes after each end. Recovery strokes are quick, short strokes that move you back upstream to keep you in the hole. For example, after initiating your bow to the left, your recovery stroke would be a small back stroke on the right, which is taken immediately before the forward sweep on the right that pulls your stern through.

The body: There's no one position for your body when cartwheeling. You need to make constant adjustments as each end comes around. As a general rule, though, you want to stay forward and keep your upper body as quiet as possible.

Let's look at your ideal body position in more depth. When your bow is down, your body is best off in a relatively neutral position, or leaning slightly back as you stand up a bit on your foot pegs. If you find yourself falling on your face, then it usually means that you're leaning back too much. Remember the effects of your forward and backward leans when bow stalling? Leaning back actually pulled your kayak more vertical! When your stern is submerged, your weight should be in a

The key to linking ends is getting to your next stroke quickly and early.

Although it's important to keep your weight forward as much as possible when cartwheeling, it's even more important that you always lead the way with your body.

more aggressive, forward position. Though these forward and backward leans play a major role in cartwheeling, the most important job for your upper body is staying "wound up" and leading your kayak through each end. As long as your body leads the way and you get your strokes planted early, your stomach and knees can continue to pull the bow around and you can make any small corrections that are needed.

Cartwheeling is one of the most difficult freestyle moves to master, because it isn't a single move. It requires constant control in a hole and the ability to make quick and effective corrections. But as we mentioned at the beginning, cartwheeling provides the foundation for most other playboating moves, so once you've developed the control for cartwheels, then there's no reason you can't perform any of the more advanced moves!

ADVANCED HOLE MOVES

There are a number of more advanced hole moves that you can learn, but most require a cartwheeling foundation. The best place to practise most of these moves initially is on flatwater, where there are fewer variables. This will require a small playboat and the use of more of your own power as there's no current to help with the moves.

Splitwheel: The splitwheel is a two-ended cartwheel with a 180-degree pirouette between ends.

Clean and Super-Clean Cartwheels: The clean cartwheel is a two-ended cartwheel that is done with only a single stroke. The super-clean cartwheel is a three-ended cartwheel with only a single stroke. Though these are the only named "clean" cartwheels, there is really no limit to how many "clean" ends you can do. Clean ends

A LITTLE EFFORT GOES A LONG WAY

by Ken Glaeser

I think it was my second or third day of paddling on the Fu with the Kayak Futaleufu group. It takes you a few days to get used to the size and feel of that incredible river, not to mention the travel to another hemisphere. On this day, we had a stellar run down the challenging "Bridge to Bridge" section. I even had a clean line through the nemesis, Mundaca! It was mostly by chance, because you had to hit two very large and unpredictable waves and you never knew what was going to happen. Throw in the incredible alpine scenery with crystal blue water, and it makes for one of those runs you'll never forget. But I was itching for a little play. That was why I braved all this big gnarly stuff in a tight, edgy little playboat!

We found a playhole just above the take-out bridge, which I learned had been named "Superclean." A few of us stopped to check out it out, and it was definitely worth staying for. It was a little trashy, and a rock in the middle was painfully visible through the translucent water, but it had potential. Ken Whiting and Kevin Varette were there, so I was anxious to get some pointers on hole riding from the pros. As so often happens, I had one really good ride on my second or third try, but after that I couldn't get back in the groove. At one point, I even found myself getting a bit of a spanking—stuck against the rock in the middle of the hole, upside down, of course!

I started drilling Ken and Kevin for advice: What was I doing wrong? We went through the skills of finding the sweet spot and positioning yourself in the hole. This helped, but I was still having trouble linking ends. I was then reminded to set up my bow at one o'clock and make sure I was always leading with my upper body. Still, I wasn't getting back into the form I'd had a brief glimpse of earlier. Sure, I was getting tired and already had a long day on the river, but that was when Ken gave me the most valuable advice I ever got: TRY HARDER!

I will never forget that invaluable piece of advice. Now you know why Ken Whiting is one of the top instructors in the world!

are accomplished by leading aggressively with your head and torso, pulling hard with your stomach muscles, and switching your edges with precise timing.

Loop: The loop is a complete front flip that is done by popping ender style out of the hole and into the air. The best loops are actually completely airborne and are one of the most dynamic moves that you'll see on the river. An ender is done by ploughing your boat deeply into the greenwater of a hole with your boat pointed firmly at 12 o'clock. Your boat is rejected by the water once it hits the wall and you get shot straight back up into the air.

Tricky Whu: The tricky whu is a funky move that involves linking a splitwheel with a stern pirouette. The move uses a single paddle blade and requires great balance and edge control.

Ty Curtis hucking an aerial loop.

RIVER RUNNING MOVES

River running moves are performed while travelling downstream, unlike all other playboating moves, which are executed while surfing on a wave or in a hole. These moves can be done using rocks, waves, holes, and most other river features. They're a great way to spice up rapids and add some fun to your day. Whichever river running move you attempt, make sure that the river is deep enough both at and around the feature that you are using.

THE WAVE WHEEL

The wave wheel is an airborne cartwheel that is done with a well-timed launch downstream off the peak of a wave. Freestyle paddlers sometimes use it as an entry move into a hole, but more often than not, the wave wheel is a way of spicing up a simple wave train. The bigger the wave you use, the more dynamic your wave wheel will be. With a big enough wave, you can even get your entire kayak out of the water! Learning to fly this way is remarkably easy once you're comfortable with the flatwater cartwheeling technique. The trickiest part of the move is actually lining up your approach and timing your initiation stroke.

So what's the best type of wave for wave wheels? The most ideal waves are relatively steep (but not breaking, as this will stall you out) and deep on their downstream side.

On the approach to your wave wheel, it's important to have some forward speed, but your focus should be on timing a powerful launching stroke on the face of the wave, just before you reach the wave's peak. This launching stroke is used to do two things: pull your bow into the air, and pull your hip past the wave's peak. This stroke is a cross between the "power stroke" we covered in the "Essentials" segment and the "double pump" we covered in the "Flatwater Playboating Moves" chapter.

Here's how it works. As you climb the face of the wave, tilt your kayak right on edge and plant the launching stroke at your toes with your top hand at shoulder level. Pull down on this stroke to lift your bow, and pull forward to launch yourself downstream off the wave. As soon as you've taken this stroke, continue with your double pump motions. This means rotating your head and upper body aggressively downwards and turning your launching stroke into a back stroke that gets planted behind the cockpit and at the peak of the wave. With your body wound up and your back stroke planted, throw your weight forward, push your stern into the air and pull your bow down aggressively with your stomach and knees. After hitting your first end, you can keep the wave wheel going with your standard flatwater cartwheeling technique. In a wave train, you can even keep using wave after wave to do several wave wheels in a row. Wave wheels aren't limited to standing waves, either. They can be done on virtually any kind of wave. For instance, a small roller above a hole or a reactionary at the top of a rapid both make great wave wheeling ramps.

The wave wheel.

ADVANCED RIVER RUNNING MOVES

Any river running move requires a good launching platform, which is ideally a consistent standing wave with minimal break. The steeper waves will usually work best. Although speed is nearly always an asset, the timing of your last stroke will always be more important, so take your time and be precise in setting up. It may even take a few trial runs to get your stroke rhythm worked out. We've spent hours doing laps at a good wave just trying to get

Initiating a kick flip while launching off a wave.

A free wheel.

some techniques nailed down. Here are some of the more impressive moves that you can then consider trying.

Kick Flip: The kick flip is an airborne, horizontal pirouette that is done while launching off a wave. Landing a big kick flip is an awesome feeling. This has always been one of our favourite moves!

Macho Move: The macho move is a downstream loop done while launching off the peak of a wave and is one of the trickiest moves to learn.

Freewheel: The freewheel is a wave wheel done off the lip of a waterfall, which results in an airborne cartwheel. Yee haw!

WHITEWATER RACING

SLALOM • EXTREME RACES

"A little time spent running gates pays for itself in all around paddling skills." (Tyler Lawlor)

SLALOM

Slalom is the oldest and most established form of whitewater competition, as well as the only whitewater sport to have a presence in the Olympic Games. In slalom racing, paddlers negotiate their way through 18–25 "gates" that are hung over a 250–400-metre-long section of rapids. The objective of slalom competition is very simple: navigate, without fault, through all the gates in the shortest amount of time.

Paddlers are required to go through some of the gates in an upstream direction (which are coloured red) and others in a downstream direction (which are coloured green). Faults result in time penalties and are incurred for touching (two seconds) or missing gates (fifty seconds). Touching faults are given for any contact with the gate by boat, paddle or body. Missing a gate means not completely manoeuvring the head and at least part of the boat through the gate. Decisions on these faults are made by judges positioned along the riverbank. A full-length slalom course will usually take around two minutes for an experienced racer to complete. In a standard race, competitors are given two runs through a course and the times are combined to give a final score.

Slalom boats are quite different from other whitewater kayaks, as they're designed to be as quick and responsive as possible, yet they must meet certain dimensional requirements. They're extremely light and rigid, being made of composite materials such as Kevlar, carbon fibre, and fibreglass, and are not designed to withstand the same abuse that their plastic cousins do.

Slalom racing is an incredible test of strength, endurance, precision and planning. For some, the adrenaline rush of racing and physically pushing oneself is a lure to the sport, while many recreational

paddlers spend time running through slalom gates to improve their overall paddling. Racing through gates, either casually or competitively, will develop your boat control, timing, and stroke efficiency. In the end, it can have a fantastic impact on your paddling and can make those tight, must-make eddies a lot

Slalom racing is a demanding sport, requiring an incredible balance of power, technique, and timing.

easier to hit when you're pushing your limits in more adventurous whitewater.

EXTREME RACES

Extreme races are the latest craze in whitewater competition, both for paddlers and for the media. These races take competitors down a short and intense section of class 5 whitewater that usually involves at least one major waterfall. Unlike slalom, there's no set of strict rules for extreme races, as each location has its own challenging variables that competitors need to negotiate. Sometimes small groups, or "heats," of paddlers will race "head-to-head," fighting their way through the mob in a mad dash to the finish line. In some races, the winners from each heat will keep moving onto the next round, and time is not a concern. This is a form of round robin that leaves one winner at the end of the final heat. In other races, competitors will have to race one at a time against the clock. Those with the top times move onto the proceeding rounds, which may either be timed or head-to-head, until a final winner emerges.

Make no mistake; extreme races are just as they suggest: extreme! These are races designed exclusively for the expert whitewater paddler who is willing to take an already challenging piece of whitewater and make it more difficult by racing his or her way down it. Needless to say, these races amazing to watch and absolutely exhilarating to take part in. They're the ultimate test of nerve, technique, precision, and power.

Extreme races involve short and intense sections of whitewater, where errors made by the competitors often have consequences.

SURF KAYAKING

"The quickest means of progressing is by paddling with those better than you." (James McBeath)

Surf kayaking is an amazing spinoff sport from whitewater kayaking. There really are few feelings that can compare with shooting down the face of an ocean wave and carving a hard turn. If you've ever been kayaking in the ocean surf then you know what we're talking about. You'll also be able to appreciate it when we say that playing out in the ocean can be very intimidating. This is probably a good thing, because although the ocean is a wonderful natural playground, it can be very dangerous and should be treated with the utmost respect.

Surf kayaking began in the 1950s, but the first true surf kayak wasn't built until 1968, which caused the sport to boom in popularity. Equipment continued to evolve through the '70s, but it wasn't until the '80s that competitions really began to take form, and the first World Surf Kayaking Contest was held. Since that time, equipment has been constantly improving, and the limits of what can be done in the surf have been pushed to awe-inspiring levels.

THE FORMATION OF WAVES

To make the most of your time on the water, you need to understand how surf waves are formed. It all starts when the winds from offshore storms churn up waves. These waves can be huge, but very choppy, erratic, and not great for surfing. As these waves move through the water, friction causes them to lose some of their energy. If the storm didn't give them enough energy to begin with, then the waves will flatten out before reaching our beaches. If the storm was strong enough, the erratic waves will hit each other and their energy will combine. If this happens enough, swells will be created and make their way to beaches on opposite sides of the ocean. Along the way, friction

SIZING UP A WAVE

Waves are measured differently in different sizing up a wave communities. Most surfers refer to the size of the wave's face, from crest to trough, but some use the backside of a wave as their measure, resulting in smaller perceived sizes of the same waves. Make sure you know what system is being used in the area that you'll be surfing. The difference between five feet on the front side and five feet on the back side is substantial! There's nothing more frightening than being caught in surf that is beyond your ability to deal with.

will work out the small and choppy elements of the wave, leaving a smooth, glassy face that is ideal for surfers.

Tides also play a major role in the development of surf waves, although there is no general rule to follow. Each beach has a "break zone" where waves crest and surfers surf. The depth of the water at the break zone varies with the tide, and the unique characteristics of each beach dictate what part of the tide cycle provides the best surfing. Local knowledge is of utmost importance.

TYPES OF BREAK

Break is formed when ocean swells reach shallower water, which causes them to slow down and pile up on themselves. This is why waves grow in height and steepness when they hit break zones. The type of waves that we get at break zones depends on the speed, power and direction of the swell, along with the tide height and configuration of the ocean floor. The more quickly the ocean floor becomes shallow, the more quickly the waves crest and break, and the steeper they become. An ocean floor that becomes shallow more gradually will create less steep waves that build and crash more slowly. There are three common break zones.

Beach Break

Beach break is the most common type of surf. Waves build as the ocean floor becomes shallower closer to the beach. You find a wide variety of waves at beach break and so you may spend some time finding the areas that offer the best surf on a particular day. Shore break more accurately describes the zone where waves crest a final time and roll into the beach, providing minimal surfing potential. At a beach, you often have an initial break further out and then a shore break as the waves hit the shallowest water. In big swells, the shore break can be a very challenging barrier to paddle through as you try to get out to the smoother break for a surf.

Point Break

Point breaks often provide surfers with the best surfing, and of course will usually be the busiest surf spots. Point break waves are caused as swells refract (or bend) around a point and into shallower water. This has the tendency of creating waves that steadily break outward as opposed to just dumping. As such, they can provide sustained, high quality surf zones. To the outside of the point break you can usually find a calm zone for paddling back out, which makes life much easier and saves your energy for the surf.

Reef Break

Reefs are shallow spots in the ocean and reef break is caused when swells hit this shallow zone. The great thing about reef break is that it is usually surrounded by calm water, which makes paddling out to the drop-in zones very easy. On the flip side, reefs are composed of sharp rocks and coral, which can spell disaster for the out-of-control surfer. Depending on the site, a reef may form a dumping break or a sweeter point break.

CURRENTS

Rip tide/current

Rip tides are the primary cause in over 80% of swimmer rescues at surf beaches, because they can be tricky to detect and are surprisingly powerful. These rip currents are formed when water that has been pushed up on a beach by breaking waves is pulled back out by gravity. Because waves may continually push more water up the slope of the beach, there can be a lot of water searching for the quickest way back to fill this void. Under certain conditions, this outflowing water can be concentrated into a channel, which becomes a strong underwater current moving away from the beach. When in

A rip current is formed when water that has been pushed up on a beach by breaking waves is pulled back out by gravity through a concentrated channel.

control, you can use these rip currents to help you paddle out past shore break, but if you find yourself swimming, these rip currents can be very dangerous. A rip can be recognized in a few ways. It may create especially rough or choppy waves, be a darker colour because of the deeper water, or leave a foam trail. To escape from a rip current, you must swim perpendicular to it until you're free. Again, local knowledge is very important.

Longshore currents

The same forces that cause rip currents also cause longshore currents. These currents are most obvious when waves hit the shore at an angle. This causes water to be pushed laterally along the beach away from the oncoming waves. You've probably found yourself swimming at a beach and after a short time wondering how you ended up so far away from your stuff! Longshore currents are generally less

dangerous than rips because they don't pull directly out to the open sea, but it should be noted that they can feed water and swimmers into rip currents. Longshore currents can be a pain for surfers, as you now need to fight against them on top of fighting your way through the shore break.

EQUIPMENT

One nice thing about surf kayaking is that you can use your whitewater equipment for it. Of course, it's not ideal, so if you were going to spend a lot of time on the ocean, you'd probably want to look at buying a surf kayak. The difference between a surf kayak and a whitewater playboat is largely in the hull design and length. Surf kayaks are longer and designed for speed and carving ability, whereas whitewater boats are designed to turn quickly, to be easy to get vertical, and to be forgiving. What this means is that whitewater boats are typically slower and

Surf kayaks are slick-looking machines. They have little to no rocker in the stern, which makes them faster on waves and better at carving turns.

A LESSON FROM MOTHER OCEAN

by Kevin Varette

In December of 2000, I accompanied my mom to Santa Barbara, California, for a week. She was attending an executive coaching course and would be turning 50 during the week. Since I also have an interest in that field, and didn't want her to be alone on her 50th, I tagged along. By pure chance, there also happened to be a surf kayaking festival happening that week at Jalama Beach, about an hour north of Santa Barbara! One of my sponsors, who lives outside of Santa Barbara, told me about it and offered me a boat and a ride up for a day of ocean surfing—yahoo! Yah right!

When we pulled up to the beach, it became clear pretty quickly that the playboat I had borrowed from Reed wasn't the ideal tool for the day. The waves were enormous and dumping hard all over the place. I stopped and talked to a few friends who had their ten-foot composite surf kayaks laid out on the ground and were busy switching from three inch to five inch fins for more control! I looked out at the waves and sighed. What the heck! Here I am in California, it's freezing at home, and the sun's beating down here; I have nothing to lose and a sponsor to impress!

I geared up, put my boat at the edge of the beach, got in, and paused for a second to watch a massive wave explode just twenty feet away! I pushed along the sand until a huge wave rode up on shore and dragged me out. On the way out, part of my hull got caught in the sand and I spun sideways, but it was too shallow to put a strong enough sweep in to straighten out. Wham! Upside down, moving back up the beach and trying to roll against the sand—a great start!

Well, I finally managed to battle out past the shore break and join a few more appropriately outfitted locals where the big swells were. I watched them for a while, my heart fluttering out of both excitement and anxiety. With their speed, they were able to catch the wave when it was pretty flat, carve some nice turns as it steepened up, and then either cut back stylishly off the lip before the wave dumped, or shoot way down the face and into the trough, leaving the monstrous break behind them.

I toyed around with a few flat swells, but knew that my boat was too slow and I would just keep falling off the backside unless I went for something steeper. Tired of waiting (more like tired of looking like a wimp!), I moved in about 20 feet and awaited my fate. Before long I saw a set coming toward me—wow, it was one of the biggest of the day and I would be committed with only a couple of strokes!

Silly me. It didn't take more than two strokes before this huge wave took hold of me, its power making me feel utterly puny. It started off well enough, and I even mustered up the courage to spin once, but that was the end of the controlled portion of my ride, and the end of my day! As the rip sucked into the bottom of the wave, it instantly grew in size and turned into a vertical nightmare. My only chance was to point straight down the face and get as far away from the break as possible, so I did. The thing about playboats is that they aren't designed for this kind of speed, so it was like flooring the gas pedal on one of those lame go-karts that have speed governors—a disappointing lack of acceleration!

Most incredible was the sensation of actually moving backward as the wave pulled me up into the air, but the rest truly sucked! I was thrown like a rag doll face first along with the break, crashing hard at the bottom and enjoying the feel of my paddle snapping across my forehead under the force of the impact. Rolling up with one half of my paddle and my skirt partly blown off, it was an ugly finish that included another flip and unwanted side surf. I finally jumped out of the boat, pulled it up on shore and collapsed in the sand—very impressive, Kev!

Blurry from the beating, blood trickling down my face, and embarrassed by my defeat, it was definitely uplifting to hear a few hoots and hollers in the background. I've had many great days of ocean surfing in my playboat since then, but when the break is huge and dumping like it was at Jalama, give me ten feet and fins any day!

can lack the speed to stay ahead of the break on big dumping ocean waves. As such, they will often get caught in the break and side surf into shore; or in bigger surf, can get thrown bow over stern! Most of the time however, whitewater boats let you have a super fun day at the beach.

Other pieces of gear to consider when surfing in the ocean are a good paddle and a good skirt. The power of the ocean can only be compared to the power of a big volume river. Big ocean waves have the ability to break your paddle in your hands or to pop your skirt right off your cockpit rim. You can dramatically reduce the chances of either of these things happening by using a good quality paddle and skirt. You don't need to look at the top of the line by any means, but you also don't want to rely on an entry-level paddle that might break much more easily.

Swimming in ocean surf can be a terrifying and dangerous game, and you should do your best to avoid it. On that note, an implosion bar or some type of device that will help prevent your skirt from popping is a very good idea at the beach.

PADDLING OUT

One of the very first challenges of surf kayaking is getting on the water and paddling out past the shore break to the surf break. The best place to get into your kayak is somewhere where one of the bigger waves will wash enough water up the slope of the beach to lift you off the sand and let you paddle out. This means you should take a minute and watch the shore break before picking your spot. When you decide the time has come, set your boat down, climb in, and get your skirt on before the next wave takes you away. You can expect to have to push yourself further into the surf using your hands after getting into your boat. You can also expect that waves often appear erratically and grab you before your skirt is on!

Paddling out past the shore break requires a combination of aggressive paddling and wave reading. Look ahead, watch the waves roll in, and try to pick out where the weak spots will be. The weak spots are parts of waves that haven't yet broken, or that have broken far enough ahead that most of their energy has dissipated by the time you encounter them. You can also use rip currents to help pull you out.

The best way to get through waves that have broken or that are breaking, is to use the boofing technique that we covered in the "Managing Holes" segment of the "River Running" chapter. This means approaching the wave with a slight angle, then taking a powerful last stroke that pulls your bow to 12 o'clock and on top of the foam pile. Using this boofing technique, you can bounce over some amazingly large breaking waves, but you had better have some forward speed and an aggressive body position to do so.

The worst-case scenario involves hitting a wave just after it has crested and has begun to break. In this case, there's not much you can do to avoid taking a hit from the ocean gods. By leaning forward and placing one of your arms in front of your face and body you can sometimes split the wave and deflect some of its impact. Leaning forward will also protect your

skirt. A large wave can easily blow your skirt if it's allowed to dump directly down on it.

CATCHING WAVES

The secret to catching waves is choosing the right wave and positioning yourself correctly for it. Both these things require that you learn where the best break zones are by watching earlier sets, and that you read the waves as they come in. Before the next set arrives, you should have a good idea of where the sweet spots are, how many waves to expect, and which waves are likely to be the best. When you've chosen a wave, turn your boat toward shore and accelerate with some quick and powerful forward strokes. As the wave picks you up, you need to lean forward to help establish your position on its face. If you've timed it correctly, the wave should just be steepening up and about to peak. Gravity will then take over and send you screaming down the face of the wave.

SURFING

You surf ocean waves just as you would big river waves. Most importantly, this means that your time should be spent carving on the face, where gravity is working on your side. The higher on the face of the wave you carve, the more room you have to accelerate. If you let yourself shoot down into the trough, you'll lose all your speed and therefore your ability to

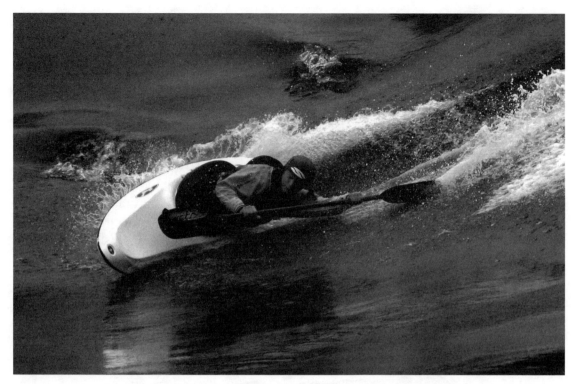

Carving a huge turn on the face of a wave. Photo by Andrew Watkinson.

move around on the wave. If the wave is breaking and you're in the trough, it is very probable that you're going to get creamed. The rudders you use to carve on ocean waves are no different than those you use on river waves, although you're not going to need braking rudders very often. Your focus should be on using rudders at the back of your boat that don't slow you down at all. Something else to consider is how to get the most performance out of your kayak. Whether you're using a surf kayak or a whitewater kayak, it's important that you use the forward edges of your kayak to carve on a wave, which means keeping your weight forward as much as possible.

SURF KAYAKING ETIQUETTE

Wherever there's surf, you'll find surfers; so you need to follow some surfing "road rules" to avoid collisions and confrontations on the water. Unfortunately, there's a high rate of "road rage" in surf zones. For some reason a lot of this tension exists between board surfers and kayak surfers, and much of it comes from our lack of understanding of surfing etiquette and a lack of appreciation for the board surfers' feelings toward us kayakers. We're going to take a quick look at some issues that will help you avoid conflict in the surf.

Due to the speed and power involved with surfing ocean waves, collisions can be catastrophic; so the single most important rule in the surf has to do with the surfing "right of way." It must first be understood that this rule dictates the right of way on unbroken waves only. A surfer has no right of way on broken waves. Two factors determine who has the right of way on ocean waves.

First and foremost, the surfer who catches an unbroken wave first has the right of way. If it's questionable as to who caught the wave first, then the right of way goes to the surfer closest to the break. A surfer is considered to have caught the wave once he

or she has stopped paddling, kicking, or stroking, and is moving down the face of the wave due to the force of gravity alone.

It also must be understood that it's a surfer's responsibility to avoid all swimmers, surfers, or paddlers encountered while surfing a wave. Having said this, those paddling out should do their very best not to interfere with surfers. This might mean taking the long route out and paddling around the surf, or it could mean paddling directly into the broken sections. Something we need to consider is that we kayakers don't have the same ability to carve free from a wave once it's breaking. This means

This dude has right of way.

The right of way goes to the surfer who caught the wave first, or the surfer closest to the break.

we have less control than the surfers at this point, and have become a risk in their eyes.

Another thing to consider is the advantage that kayakers have over other surfers. We can catch waves earlier than board surfers, and it's easier for us to paddle back out after each surf. What this means is that surfers will often consider their rides more valuable than those of kayakers and will easily get frustrated by a kayaker who repeatedly takes the right of way by catching waves first. If you're aware of this issue, then common courtesy should dictate when you sit back and let other surfers grab a few waves.

On a final note, surfing has a territorial issue that isn't as prevalent in river communities. Local surfers often believe that they have more right to "their waves" than others. Though we may have trouble understanding this logic, it's not something that you should fight. You need to respect these territorial feelings, consider yourself a "guest" at their surf spots, and provide the local paddlers with a wide berth. It goes without saying that a friendly greeting and an "after you" mentality will go a long way to making your time in the surf more enjoyable, even if you do end up getting a few less surfs than you'd like.

SQUIRT BOATING *by Brendan Mark*

WHY SQUIRT BOAT? • **CHOOSING A BOAT** • **GEAR** • **TRICKS**

"Making stupid moves in a marginally buoyant boat will not only make you unpopular with your fellow squirtists, it will probably get you killed." (Scott Docherty)

The first squirt boats popped up in the late 1970's, thanks to the creativity and the 'out of the box' thinking of the now legendary Snyder brothers and Jesse Whittemore. Since then, squirt boating has developed a cult like following of die hard whitewater enthusiasts, enchanted by a slightly different aspect of paddling than the average kayaker is.

Squirt boats are kayaks designed specifically for playing with the currents below the waterline. This is accomplished by having the kayaks made as small as possible, while still allowing them to float; albeit just barely. To do this, squirt boats are custom built to suit a paddler's body weight, leg length, foot size, and paddling style, in order to get rid of any unnecessary volume. This makes for a very tight and often uncomfortable fit, but it's deemed a worthy sacrifice by the squirt boater, as it allows them to ride low in the water and tap into currents that other paddlers wouldn't even notice. This intimate

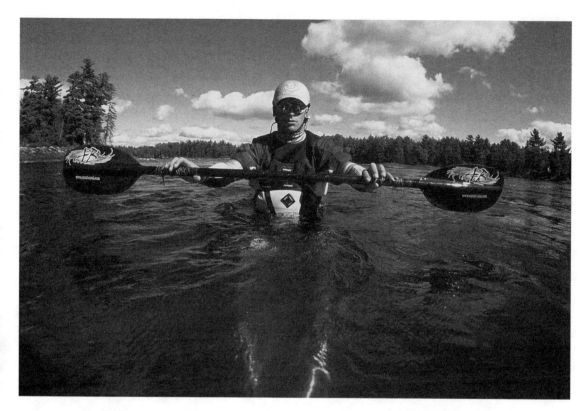

connection that is developed with the water is one of the reasons that squirt boaters are some of the most devoted and obsessed whitewater paddlers.

WHY SQUIRT BOAT?

Aside from being really fun, the concept of how squirt boats can benefit absolutely any kayaker is simple. The average paddler is not fortunate enough to have a world-class learning river at his or her doorstep and even if they are, that river becomes way too cold to paddle during the off-season. Squirt boats are very versatile and can be used almost anywhere—from eddy lines and waves to winter pool sessions, or on the lake at your cottage. On top of this versatility, squirt boats can be very effective tools to help teach paddlers the technique necessary to perform virtually any freestyle move. Whether it be your first cartwheel or a more advanced move, such as a super clean or a tricky-whu, a squirt boat can help you master it. With the streamlined design and minimal volume, learning new moves is much easier with a squirt boat. By minimizing the force necessary to submerge the ends, they allow you to concentrate solely on your technique and not so much on power. Once the technique is mastered, adding power is much easier.

Squirt boating is incredible practice for all other types of whitewater kayaking.

CHOOSING A BOAT

Squirt boats are custom made kayaks, and are very labour intensive to build. It takes a minimum of twenty-four man-hours of precise craftsmanship to build one of these boats, and considerably more time when intricate graphics are requested. A base model squirt boat is made from six to seven layers of fibreglass. It increases in value and decreases in weight as fibreglass is substituted with carbon and/or Kevlar.

To appeal to a growing number of paddlers, squirt boat designs have changed radically over the past few years. They are shorter and easier to use; and there are numerous designs to choose from.

A paddler's inseam initially determines what boats are appropriate for him to use. From this assortment of models, the paddler must then consider what his most common use of the boat will be. Similar to choosing a plastic boat, if you wish to run

rivers you would purchase a more river-running friendly design, and if you want to play you would purchase a playboat.

In the world of squirt boating there are two main disciplines—downtime and freestyle. Briefly, downtime is the use of eddy lines and specific currents to work yourself below the surface of the water and then resurface further downstream. Longer squirt boats, those nine feet or more, are better suited for performing downtime, as they have more surface area for the currents to work on. In general, shorter squirt boats are better suited for performing all the latest freestyle manoeuvres. A proper-fitting squirt boat should be comfortable and float so that the cockpit is almost even with the surface of the water and the stern is approximately one or two inches below the surface.

GEAR

The two pieces of gear that are unique to squirt boating are the *spray deck* and the *paddle*. Skirts are generally smaller and require a larger "lip" to create a tighter seal

Brendan Mark on his way to some big downtime.

around the cockpit. A limited number of manufacturers make squirt-specific decks. Traditional squirt paddles are made of wood, have smaller blades, and are shorter in length. These features allow for increased manoeuvrability when performing both freestyle moves and downtime. An alternative to the traditional wooden paddle is one made from composites with a zero degree offset. I personally use a composite paddle with zero-degree offset and small blades, since I find it offers superior performance, especially underwater. Another optional piece of gear for squirt boaters is hand paddles. These are either webbed gloves or plastic circles you strap on your hand that make it easier to manoeuvre underwater.

TRICKS

Many generic tricks are easier in a squirt boat, since they have less volume. However, all moves rely 100% on technique as opposed to muscle. When getting in a squirt boat for the first time it will seem very tippy. Take the time to get comfortable and semi-stable before attempting any moves. On the positive side, squirt boats are the easiest boats on the market to role, so if the elusive hand role has been a challenge, a squirt boat could be your solution. I've designed a unique progression for teaching basic and advanced paddling skills through the use of squirt boats and have found that the results are very positive for all levels of students. The following is a brief look at some of the techniques you can perform in squirt boats.

DOWNTIME/MYSTERY MOVE:

Probably the coolest move you can perform in a squirt boat is the "mystery move." You disappear under water and resurface further downstream ten, 20, and even thirty seconds later. The ability to do mystery moves is what really differentiates squirt boats from plastic playboats. To do them, you'll need a crisp eddy line or seam line, a pourover or a steep breaking wave. The idea is to purl your bow under water (approximately one foot), slice the stern down the same distance, and then level the boat so that it's flat. At this point, the forces of the river can act on the flat deck to push it down. A reverse sweep is generally the easiest way to sink the stern and then there is a variety of strokes you can use to "screw" yourself deeper underwater, ultimately completely submerging.

The most common place to do mystery moves is on a crisp eddy line. To get down on eddy lines after the initial purling of your bow, it's easiest to follow with a sequence of forward sweeps that turn your boat in the same direction. When surfing a wave, or paddling into a pour over, it's easier to use a reverse sweep stroke. Keeping your paddle in the water as much as possible, you'll corkscrew yourself deeper and deeper underwater. The key through all of this is to *keep your boat level*; as soon the kayak is not flat (i.e. if you lift

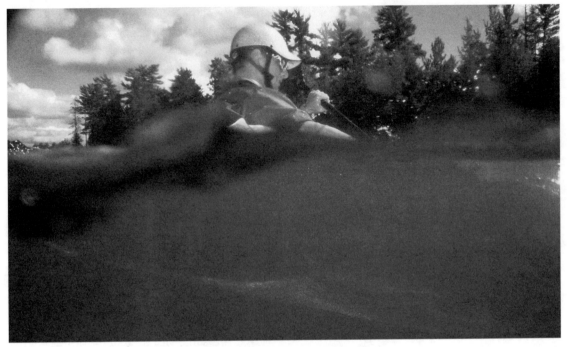

Initiating a mystery move on an eddy line.

your knee, or your body position shifts forwards or backwards), you'll quickly resurface. Advanced squirt boaters can control the speed at which they descend, level off at a certain depth, and even ascend to a desired level when too deep.

BOW STALL

One of the easiest moves you can perform in a squirt boat is the bow stall. To do this, extend your hands straight in front of your torso, lean forward, and *voila*! Your bow will slowly sink and you'll be in a perfect bow stall. Maintain your balance by adjusting your body weight: counter-intuitively, you should lean back if you are losing verticality

and lean forward if you are falling over vertical. Keep your paddle in the water to control side-to-side movement by pushing on the blade you are falling over on.

BOW SCREW

A true bow screw is a pirouette when the stern of your kayak is over your head, or simply, when the kayak is over-vertical. Once in a bow stall position, use a forward sweep to pivot yourself around. Keep sculling that blade back and forth to maintain the screwing motion; make sure your blade doesn't leave the water. Keep your weight forward and look in the direction you want to turn.

The stern screw.

STERN SCREW

A proper stern screw will pirouette the boat over a vertical 360 degrees on its stern. Wind up your body and plant your blade deep in the water at the back of your boat. Unwind your body while doing a powerful back sweep. As you begin unwinding, aggressively lift, and pull towards your chest, the knee on the same side as your back sweep. Just to be sure, with a left back sweep, you would lift the left knee and vice versa for the right side. One stroke should be sufficient to bring the boat vertical. If you're still not vertical, repeat the steps above with another big back sweep. As your kayak passes vertical, continue to lead with your head by looking in the direction you're turning. To finish the move, you'll use the standard sweep roll as your bow falls toward the water.

FLATWATER CARTWHEEL

Begin with a reverse sweep followed by a forward sweep. Continue doing this until you are comfortably spinning in a circle. The next step is to edge your boat by lifting the opposite knee from the blade you are sweeping with. With a back sweep, you'll be knifing the bow of your boat underwater, and with a forward sweep, you will be pulling the stern of your boat underwater. It's really important to wind your body up before each sweep in order to harness the power of unwinding your torso. Take a moment to visualize this. At first, you'll be doing low-angle cartwheels. However, the more you really concentrate on lifting your knees, the more vertical your ends will be. Advanced squirt boaters can even perform past vertical flatwater cartwheels by aggressively lifting their knees.

SUPER CLEAN FLATWATER CARTWHEEL

Super cleans are complete cartwheels without using a paddle. To do this, you need a shorter squirt boat (eight feet and under), at least mediocre stomach muscles, and good balance. Begin as you would a bow stall: lean forward and let the bow of your boat sink approximately a foot under water. Next, edge the boat on the side on which you are most comfortable cartwheeling—if you prefer left, then you will lift your left knee. Aggressively turn your torso to the left, and the bow of the boat will then shoot out of the water. Now you want to dive the bow back under by

lifting the right knee (for a left cartwheel), cranking your torso around to the left again and leaning forward. As you repeat these steps, you can rock your body forward and back to help sink each end. The more aggressively you lift your knee, the higher your ends will be out of the water.

WASHOUTS

Washouts are bow screws done without your paddle touching the water. To perform this trick, you'll need to have mastered your bow screws and flatwater cartwheels. Begin with flatwater cartwheels. As you pull your stern through the water, lift your paddle out

The washout.

so it is at face level. Let the bow of your boat initiate without smashing it under, using a back sweep. Keep your body position back and aggressively look in the direction you are spinning. If you're cartwheeling to your left, look over your left shoulder. Your boat will pirouette around on the bow, so be certain to keep the paddle in the air in front of your face. As with the bow screw, the boat should go over vertical. When you're near the end of your pirouette, reach around with your trailing blade (in this case the right blade) and recover from the spin by pulling the stern of the boat through the water, like the second end of a cartwheel.

RIVER SAFETY AND RESCUE

GROUP DYNAMICS • KAYAK RESCUE • BASIC RESCUE FOR GROUP LEADERS
RESCUE GEAR • RESCUE TECHNIQUES • ADVANCED TECHNIQUES

"Rivers aren't going anywhere. It never hurts to say no I'm not ready." (Woody Callaway)

With some common sense and attention to basic safety principles, you can effectively avoid most trouble on the river. The unfortunate reality is that rivers are dynamic and somewhat unpredictable, so sometimes things that are out of your control just happen. In this chapter we take a look at some basic safety principles, some safety equipment, and a variety of rescue techniques. Hopefully this sheds some light on the options that you have in dealing with issues that arise on the river.

The bottom line, though, is that no amount of reading can prepare you for dealing with the rescue situations that will pop up. You need to make informed decisions on what safety equipment to carry with you, learn how to use it all correctly, and then practise these techniques. We've said it before and we'll say it again: the best thing any paddler can do is to take a swiftwater rescue course—because on the river, knowledge is power.

Scouting on the Ottawa River.

GROUP DYNAMICS

Whatever type of river you're running, you've got to be comfortable with your paddling group. Too often, paddlers cruise down the river without consideration for the other members in their group, or for other groups on the river. First of all, you've got to be sure that you can count on your paddling partners to make wise decisions, because they can have a major impact on everyone in the group. Your group also has to acknowledge that they're only as strong as the weakest paddler. Don't expect to move downstream any faster than is comfortable for the weakest paddler.

river. Lack of communication is a very common and preventable cause of accidents. There are some universal signals that everyone needs to know, such as "stop," "go ahead," and "I'm okay," but many paddlers will have a number of other signals that they use on the river. Make sure you discuss these signals before hitting the water.

SIGNALS:

Make sure that everyone in the group understands the signals that you use on a

Paddle signals: 1) Stop 2) all is OK 3) Go ahead

SPACING:

Crowding can be a major problem on some rivers, so be careful that you aren't pulling out in front of someone who's upstream of you. Remember that upstream boats have the right of way. When heading downstream, it's nearly always best to move one at a time. This is especially important when there are holes to negotiate that can stop a paddler and cause a pileup, such as at the bottom of a waterfall. Collisions between paddlers create some of the most potentially dangerous scenarios and need to be avoided. Don't let your anxiety on the river get the better of you. Be patient; don't rush ;and make sure things are clear below before setting out.

Spacing is also very important on tight rivers with small eddies. You never want to put on a river like this with a large group. If you're in a large group, split yourselves into smaller groups. There's nothing more frustrating than finding yourself crowded into a small eddy, and there's nothing more frightening than not being able to fit in an eddy and having to run the following rapid blind.

GROUP AWARENESS

When paddling challenging whitewater, it's easy to get caught up with what's happening in front of you, so don't forget to keep your eyes on the paddlers behind you. If you're not watching them, who is? Make sure that you pull over whenever

possible and set yourself up in a position of safety from which you can help the next paddler through the rapid. Keep in mind that the less confident paddlers usually hang back. The most nervous paddler will often opt to run a rapid last, but this should never happen, because if they get into trouble, it may only be possible to help by moving to them from upstream. For this reason, the strongest paddler should always lead the group and the next strongest paddler should be last, in what is called the "sweep" position.

Less confident paddlers tend to hang at the back of the group, so make sure they aren't left behind.

KAYAK RESCUE

Before we delve into rescue, it's worth emphasizing again that prevention through safety-minded paddling should always take priority. However, just like in any other sport or even some daily activities, accidents do happen on the river. When they do, it becomes all too clear to those involved that river rescue training is a worthwhile investment. The river presents unique rescue conditions that require specific knowledge and practice to deal with effectively. A basic river rescue course, particularly one tailored to meet the needs of kayakers, is one of the most useful, responsible, and enjoyable ways to prepare yourself for incidents on the river.

In a rescue course, you'll apply basic rescue principles to realistic scenarios and learn to use a variety of equipment. You learn to tie important knots, to swim effectively in whitewater, to deal with strainers and shallow water crossings, and to rescue victims from a variety of situations. We'll have a look at some basic river rescue gear for paddlers, and some fundamental skills as a useful reference, but the most valuable thing about a course (which we can't provide here) is the physical and mental practice. Kayak rescue usually involves the application of some pretty basic techniques, but you don't want the real thing to be your first time applying them!

BASIC RESCUE FOR GROUP LEADERS

As a group leader or instructor, you often have a different relationship with the paddlers in your group than if you were with a bunch of similarly skilled friends. Here are a couple of basic rescue techniques that you'll likely find yourself having to perform.

AIDED RE-ENTRY

On small rivers, the best option for rescuing swimmers is to get them to shore with all their equipment so that they can leisurely get themselves ready for the next

An aided re-entry is a great option when the shore is a long way off, and there is little to no current.

round. In the calmer areas at the bottom of rapids on big-volume rivers, or when teaching on lakes, the shoreline can be a long way off. In these cases, you may be better off getting the swimmer back into his or her boat on the water. This is what we call an aided re-entry.

The first order of business is getting the water out of the kayak and flipping it upright. To do this, use the "boat-over-boat" technique we discussed earlier. The boat-over-boat technique involves dragging the upside-down kayak over your own cockpit and then rocking the boat back and forth to dump the majority of the water out. Ideally, there are air bags in the back of the kayak that you're emptying. If there are, then it is easiest to pull the bow of that kayak over your own cockpit. If there aren't airbags in the kayak, then it won't matter which end of the kayak you start with, but with all the water in the upside-down kayak, you may need some help from the swimmer to get the boat pulled up onto your lap. In this case, the swimmer can help by pushing from the far end. Once you've emptied most of the water out, flip the kayak upright and bring it alongside your boat.

The next step involves the rescuer holding the kayak stationary as the swimmer climbs back in. To hold the boat steady, the rescuer should lie on the front deck of the empty kayak and hug it. The swimmer can approach the kayak from the stern, grab the cockpit rim, and pull himself up into a sitting position just behind the cockpit. The weight of the paddler on the back deck of the kayak will sink the stern and lift the bow into the air, so one of the rescuer's biggest jobs is to keep the bow down. For playboats, this can be very tricky. If the playboat is small enough and the paddler heavy enough, then it may not even be possible. Once the swimmer has reached the sitting position on the back of the cockpit rim, he should swing his legs into the boat and slide himself back in. At this point he'll probably need to sponge out any water left in his boat before snapping on his skirt, grabbing his paddle, and heading off. Ta-dah!

THE T-RESCUE

The T-rescue involves a rescuer offering one end of his kayak to an upside-down paddler for to use for support as she hip snaps her boat upright. The T-rescue is the most basic form of kayak rescue and will only really come into play when there is a special teacher/student relationship between the two paddlers. Otherwise, it's unreasonable for any kayaker to expect to receive a T-rescue when out on the river. It's also crucial that the one getting rescued has practised and become comfortable with the skill of hip snapping, which we've looked at in depth in the "Rolling" segment of this book.

The T-rescue starts with the "victim" upside down and the rescuer close by. Because the victim knows the rescuer is there to provide a T-rescue, the victim calmly tucks her body forward while upside down to protect her face and body. She then reaches up to the surface with both hands, one on each side of her kayak. The first thing she should do is slap the

The T-rescue is only a real option when there is a special teacher/instructor relationship.

bottom of his boat three times to let the rescuer know he needs help.

He will then proceed to run his arms alongside the kayak to create as large a target area as possible for the rescuer. The rescuer will then approach the victim at 90 degrees and offer her bow for support. This usually means running lightly into the side of the upside-down kayak in the area that the arms are sweeping. The victim's arm will soon bump into the rescuer's kayak and then he grabs that end with both hands. On occasion, the rescuer is dead on target and the victim gets a little jolt of pain from the impact on his hand, but in the big picture, we can't worry too much about this!

The success of the T-rescue now revolves around the victim's ability to hip snap the kayak upright. Hip snapping refers to the action of rotating the hips to upright the kayak. Without a good hip snap the victim will naturally try to push his head and body back over his kayak, which won't do anything but sink the rescuer's bow and maybe even scare the rescuer off! Once upright, the rescuer can help recover the lost paddle, and then both can continue to head downstream.

On top of being a rescue reserved for situations where there's a special student/instructor relationship and the clear understanding that the rescuer will be looking to provide a T-rescue, it's of course very important that the T-rescue be practised and used in deep, safe whitewater in which a paddler isn't subjecting himself to further danger by hanging out upside down. If in doubt, get out!

HAND OF GOD

The "Hand of God" is a very useful rescue technique for dealing with beginner or novice paddlers who are stuck upside down, or for any paddler that has been knocked unconscious while upside down. The Hand of God is a means of flipping a victim upright while in your kayak. Let's look at how this works.

The natural thing to do when trying to flip someone upright from your kayak is to pull her head up towards you. You can get a paddler's head out of the water like this, but it is very hard to completely turn the kayak upright. Instead, try to simulate the same motions we go through in a roll: start by rolling the boat up and finish with the head. Move in beside the victim's boat, drop your paddle in between your two boats, and reach with the closest hand across the hull of her kayak to grab the cockpit rim that's furthest from you. It's a long way to reach, so you'll need to lean on the upside-down kayak. Once you've grabbed that far cockpit rim, place your other hand on the closest edge of the

The hand of god is a great rescue technique, but it requires a highly competent rescuer, and practice.

upside-down boat. Now push down on the close edge, and pull the cockpit rim up and toward you aggressively. The trick is committing yourself to the move, and using the victim's kayak as a brace while you roll it up. It should be noted that smaller paddlers will have a harder time reaching across the hull to the cockpit rim, especially with the wider, flatter-hulled kayaks. It will require somewhat of a lunge over the kayak to grab the cockpit rim, which makes it even more important to practise this technique before trying it in a real rescue situation.

The Hand of God will work for beginner to intermediate paddlers who are in a situation where a swim should be avoided. In this situation, the T-rescue will usually be the first choice, as it provides the rescuer with more room to manoeuvre, and less direct contact with a potentially panicky victim. If there isn't enough room, or the victim doesn't have the awareness to do a T-rescue, then the Hand of God will work. If you do have to use the Hand of God to pull a paddler upright, be sure to cover your face, as this rescue tends to surprise victims, and paddles can flail around uncontrollably as they're roll upright. An unconscious or injured paddler will roll much more easily, and won't pose as much of a threat to the rescuer. The actual type of injury sustained will dictate the precautions that need to be taken so as not to cause further injuries, but the first priority is always making sure a victim can breathe and is out of danger's path. This means getting him upright immediately. Once he's up, you can then worry about further first aid, such as stabilization for potential neck and back injuries.

RESCUE GEAR

With today's shorter boats, the increasing variety of paddling activities, and the growing diversity of people getting into the sport, there's some lack of clarity and agreement around what gear paddlers should carry. Does it depend on the situation? Maybe, but it's probably best to always pack a basic rescue kit in your boat that you can beef up if a particular excursion calls for it. The effect of an extra two or three pounds will never extend beyond the psychological, and the gear isn't too expensive, so why not have it there just in case?

There have been times when we've felt great to be able to contribute to a rescue, and there have been others when we've felt and looked pretty unprofessional and irresponsible, not having even the basics for a rescue. The latter were situations where we either weren't informed about what we should have, or we just made the decision not to bring any rescue gear because it was very unlikely that anything would happen. It's pretty simple to us now: if you always have at least the basic gear, you'll never be left wishing you had it.

So what should a basic kayaker's rescue kit look like? There's a plethora of name brand variation in rescue products, but the essentials are all very similar. The equipment you bring down will depend heavily on the type of river you're paddling. Here are some of the most important pieces of gear to choose from.

Throw rope: Tightly woven polypropylene or spectra cord, 55 to 75 feet in length, with a wide opening for easy repacking. The exposed end should be "clean," i.e. have no handle or pre-tied knots or loops, which present potential entrapment hazards. A throw rope is one of the most versatile pieces of gear you can carry, and it's worth having a good one. Also, take the time to hang your rope up to dry in the shade whenever you can, as it will mould if left wet in the bag.

First Aid Kit: A first aid kit is always a great thing to carry in your boat; it will need to be held in a waterproof bag or container of some sort. But just having it isn't enough; you need to be trained in the use of the tools. If you haven't taken a first aid course, sign up for one now.

Tow line: A towline provides the greatest means of towing a boat around and is especially valuable on big-volume rivers. It's attached to your body by a quick release belt that wraps around either your

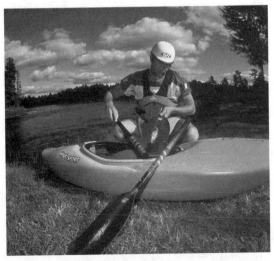

Breakdown paddles come in 2, 3 and 4 piece models, and are the only way of carrying a backup paddle down the river

waist or life jacket and has a relatively short piece of webbing with a carabiner on the end that can be hooked onto another boat very easily.

Breakdown paddle: Breakdown paddles come in two, three and four pieces. A four-piece breakdown paddle will always fit best in the smaller boats that now dominate the river. These paddles can easily ride along in the back of your boat and can come in very handy should someone in your group break his or her paddle. The number of breakdowns you should have within a group is determined by the remoteness of your river trip. Is walking out an option? If not, then you should probably have a couple of breakdowns in your group, just in case.

Whistle: You need a loud enough whistle to hear over the noise of the river—not one that relies on those little balls, or that is made of anything that might rust.

Duct tape: Not an entire roll. You can wrap some around your water bottle, paddle shaft, or just around itself. This wonderful stuff will come in handy more often than you'd ever think.

Pin Kit: A pin kit is comprised of all the tools that you'll need to set up a simple Z-drag with your throw rope. Of course, a pin kit is next to useless if you don't know how to use it, so take a swiftwater rescue course and prepare yourself for all the situations that can arise on the river. A basic pin kit should include the following tools, which should be carried in a small, waterproof bag.

Carabiners—At least two "beeners," made of either stainless steel or aluminum so they won't rust. These come in handy for many

A pin kit: 1) carabiners 2) tubular webbing 3) prussic 4) pulleys 5) throw bag. Not shown: knife.

middle of a rope and not one that you have to feed the end of the rope into. Pulleys allow for the frictionless redirection of a rope in a rescue operation.

Knife—Whether you carry this in a secure holder attached to your PFD or in your rescue kit, you'll want to have something sharp to cut through rope or other material if necessary. Good scissors can also do the trick.

PFD: Your PFD can also be an important piece of rescue gear. A good rescue vest will have a quick-release harness system. The chest harness is secured around the centre of your PFD and should tighten independently of the straps that secure the PFD to you (i.e. the tightness of the PFD should not rely on the chest harness). The harness should have an easy quick-release system up front. You might also have a leash or "Cow's Tail," which has its own steel O-ring attached to the back of the harness and a lightweight carabiner at its other end, which should clip into a quick-release point on the front of the PFD.

The leash is usually stretchy tubular webbing so that it hugs your body and does not interfere with normal movement. It's intended to use as a quick means of clipping into a rope. Many people use the leash for towing boats, but the use of rescue gear for this kind of thing is not highly recommended. If you're going to use your leash for towing boats regularly, it's probably best not to use it in dangerous tethered rescues.

rescues as well as towing, and hanging and clipping things into your boat.

Tubular webbing—At least three metres (ten feet); long enough to wrap around a tree. The ends can be pre-sewn together to form a loop or "sling," which makes for a quicker anchor set-up.

Prussic—At least one; can be a low-diameter rope (at least one metre or three-and-a-half feet) or a newer self-jamming pulley (quicker and easier to use). A prussic is a device that will either slide along a rope or grip onto it securely, depending on the force applied to it.

Pulley—At least one; make sure it's one that you can put on the

RESCUE TECHNIQUES

Because of the dynamic nature of the river environment, the first goal of kayak rescue is to keep things as simple as possible. As a rule, you should try the easiest and lowest-risk solution first, and then move to more difficult approaches if necessary. The very worst scenario would be to add yourself as a victim in the situation, so always consider your level of training and ensure your safety before proceeding with a rescue.

The risk assessment of a particular situation will be based first and foremost on the urgency presented: the less time you have, the more risk you might accept as the rescuer. For instance, if it's an equipment retrieval or even body recovery situation, the level of risk you accept as the rescuer should be reduced significantly. The problem with making yourself a victim is that you then put other rescuers in danger who have to rescue you, not to mention that the initial victim is no better off.

The following is a list of rescue techniques in order of increasing difficulty and risk. The value of practising these techniques cannot be overemphasized.

SELF-RESCUE

"There are only two types of paddler: those who have swum and those who are going to swim." (Kevin Varette)

Swimming

There are two ways of swimming through a rapid. You can swim defensively or offensively. Defensive swimming is also referred to as "body surfing," and involves floating downstream in a protected position: lying on your back, feet downstream, arms out to the side and with your whole body floating as close to the surface as possible. This is the best swimming position to assume if your goal is to ride out a rapid, or if you're in shallow water and worried about hitting rocks. You can also back ferry from this position, but it is not an effective way of moving in whitewater.

If you need to get somewhere fast, then you'll adopt the offensive swimming technique. Offensive swimming involves getting on your stomach and swimming hard with the front crawl technique. You swim aggressively to get to shore in deep enough water, cross eddy lines and to stay afloat in boils or whirlpools.

The 'body surfing' position is the most protected way to swim through a rapid.

Swimming in whitewater can be a frightening experience, especially if you're not used to doing so. The best way to prepare yourself for an unexpected swim is to practise by jumping in the river and deliberately swimming through a safe rapid.

Swimming through holes

If you find yourself swimming into a hole, you need to understand that the only way you're going to get through the hole is to hitch a ride with the greenwater that flows beneath it. If you try to stay on the surface, you'll run into the foam pile and you could get stopped and stuck there momentarily or longer. This means that when you float into a hole, you want to stay low and let yourself slide under the foam pile. If the hole looks nasty enough, you may even want to give yourself a little push underwater. Of course, you need to be careful that you don't push yourself too deeply, because holes often indicate relatively shallow areas. If you push yourself too deeply you could end up bouncing off the river bottom.

To swim through a hole, you need to hitch a ride with the greenwater that flows underneath the foam pile.

Swimming out of holes

Although a swimmer will get washed downstream quite quickly out of most holes, there are some holes that have the potential of holding a swimmer for extended periods of time. If you find yourself caught swimming in a nasty hole, then you again need to remember that the escape route is below you, in the greenwater that is flowing under the backwash and downstream. This means that you need to fight the urge to stay on the surface and should aggressively push yourself downward or tuck into a ball and let yourself sink.

Swimming over strainers

Strainers are obstacles, or collections of obstacles, such as trees, which let water through but stop large objects, such as paddlers or swimmers. If you were ever to find yourself in a situation where you'e swimming into a strainer and it can't be avoided, you need to get on your stomach and swim hard towards it. When you reach it, lunge with all of your might and crawl your way over the top. The key is being aggressive and not wavering. Once you're washed under a strainer, things are much harder to control.

Rolling

Your best means of self-rescue is the roll. The roll will save you a load of grief and an unbelievable amount of energy. You're also much safer in your kayak, as it acts like a huge life jacket to keep you afloat. If

COMMUNICATING IS THE KEY

The most preferable type of rescue is one where the rescuer communicates instructions to the victim to help him or her complete a self-rescue. From your perspective on shore or in a boat, you can shout or signal to the person, encouraging her and directing her in the best course of action. You can use your whistle to get her attention if need be. Use a minimum amount of simple words and clear signals to avoid confusion. This type of rescue avoids all physical contact with the victim, which decreases the risk factor significantly.

you don't have a roll yet, read the rolling segment then get yourself to a pool clinic with professional instruction and learn it. Your confidence will soar, your paddling will improve dramatically, and you'll enjoy your time on the river more than ever!

REACHING

Still a lower-risk technique, reaching involves making contact with the victim from a point of safety, most commonly using a throw rope, or perhaps a paddle or stick. Regardless of the method, the first priority for the rescuer is to make sure he is secure and ready to handle the load.

Throwing the Rope

There are several different ways to throw the rope, and the decision is based on your personal preference for a given situation. In general, an overhand or sidearm toss is usually best for longer distances, while an underhand throw can be effective for quick, short rescues. Regardless of which

type, to become proficient with a throw line you need to practise. With its odd shape and the drag of the uncoiling rope, it's much different from throwing a ball. On top of this, you often have only one shot—so accuracy is crucial, and anticipating the river's flow makes aiming more difficult. For this reason it's best that at least some of your practice be on a river, where hitting the target is more challenging and realistic. The first thing to do is alert the victim to your location and to the fact that you're throwing him a rope. You can do this by shouting or using your whistle. With regards to the toss, start by pulling out an arm-length or two of rope to give you the freedom to wind up. Hold the free end in one hand and the bag in your tossing hand. Ideally, you want the bag to land right in front of the victim. With that said, it's also good to keep in mind that it's better to throw the bag too far and slightly upstream of the victim than too short and downstream. The reason is that with more line out and the bag just upstream of him, the victim still has a chance to swim to the rope before it starts to pendulum into shore. Once the victim has the rope,

Throwing a rope underhand is effective for quick and short rescues.

quickly brace yourself for the tug and get rid of any slack (if you have time).

Positioning

In the best-case scenario, you've taken the time to set up safety by positioning someone with a throw line in a good spot downstream. In other cases, you may have to act quickly by running down the bank or even throwing from a boat. On the bank, the ideal placement has the rescuer within reasonable reach of the swimmer above a relatively safe landing zone to pull him or her into (an eddy or slower water near the shore). Be sure that your footing is solid, both for the toss and the pursuant

Where would you set up safety? Answer on next page ...

IF YOU'RE THE VICTIM

As a knowledgeable swimmer, you can make the rescue go much easier. When you are swimming, be alert and look around for the rescuer. When the rope lands, try as hard as you can to get to it, because it might be your only chance for rescue before being washed downstream. Grab the line, not the bag, as the bag may have forty more feet of cord in it! Once you have the rope, hold on tightly with both hands and get ready for a very strong pull. Roll onto your back (in the defensive swimming position) and place the rope over your outside shoulder (the one furthest from shore). In this position, it's easier to keep your head above the surface, and with the rope over your outside shoulder you're maximizing the pendulum effect.

rescue. It's best to use a rock or something else to help brace you. Another technique is to crouch or sit down, brace your feet, and use a hip belay, which is achieved by bending the rope around your waste to add friction. Notice that we said bend.

It's important never to wrap the rope right around any part of your body—the forces are strong! Lastly, consider the angle at which the rope will be pulling on the swimmer. The idea is to throw the bag out to her so it pendulums them back in toward you. Once the swimmer is directly downstream of you, the rope will be serving no use but to hold her stationary.

In some cases, it you may need to move further in from the bank as she gets closer to shore to maintain the pendulum angle.

Towing

The next step up the risk ladder is paddling to the victim in a boat and towing him to safety. This technique comes along with obvious risks: having a potentially panicking victim clinging to anything he can with superhuman strength can be disconcerting to say the least. It is, however, probably the most common form of kayak rescue on the river.

THROW BAG POSITIONING ANSWER

1. No. If the paddler were to swim out of the hole, they would likely be too far downstream to receive a rope.
2. No. By setting up near a sticky hole, you could easily pull the swimmer right into it.
3. Yes. Setting up below the nasty features gives the swimmer time to get oriented before receiving the rope. Setting up immediately upstream of an eddy allows the rescuer to swing the swimmer into the eddy.
4. No. The swimmer will grab the rope and get swung over the falls of doom.

Before rescuing someone this way, you should consider the situation and his potential reaction. Is there a bad hole or boulder garden just below that you wouldn't want to enter into with a swimmer? Will he panic and try to grab you? Will he listen to what you tell him? Will he let go when you ask him to? The decision of whether or not to let the victim grab hold of you is important and must be made quickly. If you feel that the risk of direct contact is too high, then you can paddle close to the swimmer and guide him with instructions.

The most common tow has the victim hanging onto the rescuer's stern grab loop. Towing a swimmer will slow you down tremendously, especially if he's holding onto his gear, so beware of this if you're in a rapid. If possible, get the swimmer to kick his feet as hard as he can. If the water is very shallow, the swimmer might be better off letting go and getting into the body surfing position. If it's not too turbulent and the swimmer is under control, you might have him slide up the stern on his belly and hang onto your waste to reduce drag and risk of injury. If a bad hole is unavoidable, the swimmer should let go and you should spread out as much as possible. You are both better off negotiating the hole alone, and then regrouping below. Finally, never tie a swimmer to your boat or your body, as this could put you both at risk if something went wrong.

GOING

A final rescue effort could involve going to the victim yourself and freeing her from danger because either she is unconscious, or the situation is not appropriate for a rope or boat rescue. Usually this will mean swimming out to the victim on a tether and then being pulled back to shore. As we discussed in the section on rescue gear above, many PFDs are rigged for tethered rescue with a quick-release chest harness system. If you own one of these vests, make sure you're very familiar with the quick-release system before you consider using it. The bag end of a line would be securely attached to the back of the rescuer's vest as a tether. One person should use a hip belay to manage the free end of the line, which should have no knots or loops in it at all. Anyone else present could be used to help secure the belayer, communicate with the rescuer, or provide safety down below. If anything happens to the rescuer, the person on shore can pull him or her back to safety. On the other hand, if the situation becomes too threatening, the rescuer can release from the tether at any time. It really depends on the situation.

Swimming out to the victim will be more difficult the further away she is because of the drag created by the tether. Keep this in mind when planning the rescue! The main risks to the rescuer are being injured while entering the water, or getting to the victim and becoming entangled in excess slack in the rope. The rescuer should be a very strong swimmer and the person on belay must be experienced so as not to hinder or endanger the rescuer. Finally, make sure there's nothing that the line may get hung up on and that other river users know it is

A tethered rescue: a rescuer, attached by a quick release harness to a rope, swims out to the victim, grabs hold of them, and then they both get pulled in to shore.

there. Have a predetermined exit spot and, if possible, other rescuers downstream in case something goes wrong.

The objective is to reach the victim and get her to safety as quickly as possible. Turning the victim on her back, the rescuer can hug her from behind and under the arms while both are being pulled to shore. This will provide a secure hold, with the rescuer taking the force of the river and keeping the victim's head above water. It also makes it possible to keep the neck relatively stable if there is any suspicion of a cervical spine injury. If the rescuer must release from the line, the best technique is

to swim backwards with one arm while reaching under one of the victim's arms and hugging her so her head is resting against the rescuer's PFD. This is very difficult and tiring; remember that the rescuer should always give priority to his or her own safety.

ADVANCED TECHNIQUES

When you take a good river rescue course, one of the most beneficial, challenging, and enjoyable things you will do is practise a variety of rescue scenarios. The following are some of the techniques you can use in certain situations. They're all potentially dangerous and should be learned formally and practised thoroughly before being put into use.

USING A DIAGONAL LINE TO CROSS THE RIVER

Crossing the river or getting to shore from an island can be very difficult and high risk, especially with a victim. In some situations, this process can be facilitated by tensioning a line across the water at a downstream angle. The angle will depend on the situation, but in general, a slower current will require a greater downstream angle. The bag end should be anchored securely on shore and the free end is belayed by someone downstream and on the other side. This diagonal line allows rescuer and victim to more safely cross, and takes advantage of the river's force to help ferry them.

Once you've tied the rope off, often the most challenging part of the process is to get it across the river. In the best-case scenario, you can throw it across. Otherwise, have a strong swimmer or paddler tow it. Remember that adding a victim to the situation won't help anyone, so keep your safety a priority. In this regard, narrow crossings are much easier to deal with than wide ones. We've had experience with both, and the rescues were indeed very different.

If you're the rescuer, clip into the rope with your Cow's Tail leash or another piece of webbing attached to the back of your PFD. This will keep your head up and free your hands. Depending on the situation and on the condition of the victim, you can either clip him in the same way on your downstream side, or you can grab him securely in the towing position we discussed in the section on tethered rescue. Never tie the victim to you. If you get stuck or are not moving well, the person belaying should make his or her way further downstream. Always account for this possibility when setting up the rope—there's often sag towards the end of the crossing, which means you need more room than it might first appear. Also keep in mind the length of your rope; it could all be going very well until the rope sags and there's none left for the belayer to run downstream with!

Quick release harness

A diagonal line allows a rescuer and victim to safely cross the river, while using the river's current to do the bulk of the work.

USING A TAG LINE TO RESCUE A VICTIM STUCK IN A HOLE

Some hydraulics are strong enough to hold you even when you come out of your boat. Rescuing victims from these "keepers" can be a high-risk affair, even on a tether. The water is very aerated, so you don't float very high in it. Along with this, the turbulence and recirculating flow make it hard to both breathe and get oriented, and there is the risk of becoming entangled in the rope. If the victim is unconscious, you have no choice but to swim to him. If he is conscious, however, and the location permits, you can use a tag line to reduce the risk.

A tag line is a rope tensioned across the river or channel that has been walked upstream on both sides until it reaches the victim. It offers stability and a possible escape route. To establish it, either two people can hold it across the water and

walk upstream, or it can be tied off (upstream of the victim) on one side and walked up on the other. In a hydraulic situation, the line would be kept at water level and walked up to the victim in the hole. Once the victim has grabbed hold of the tensioned line, there are several options to get him out of the hole. Probably the most sensible is for the rescuers to pull one end towards the desired bank while line is gradually let out at the other end, allowing the victim to be pulled right into shore. With this in mind, if you're tying one end off to establish the tag line, make sure it's on the same side that you plan to pull the victim into. As with all rescues, a contingency plan should be in place in case something goes wrong. It's always a good idea to have safety set up below the rescue location.

USING A TAG LINE TO STABILIZE A PINNED OR ENTRAPPED VICTIM

A tag line can also provide crucial stabilization in some vertical pin or foot entrapment situations. For an explanation of what a tag line is, see the section above on using a tag line to rescue a victim from a hole. In a vertical bow pin, the bow of the victim's boat is lodged in an obstruction and the force of the water hitting the victim's back can make it impossible for her to get out of the boat.

Similarly in a foot entrapment situation, the victim's foot is lodged in an obstruction and the water is forcing her downstream

A tag line can be useful to extract conscious victims from sticky holes.

A tag line can provide crucial stabilization in some vertical pin situations.

with too much power to overcome. For either one, the idea is to get the tag line under the arms of the victim and then lift the line and stabilize her in a position that allows her to breathe and possibly free herself from the entrapment. Often just stabilizing her will give her the ability to wiggle free. If not, a decision must be made based on the circumstances about whether to go to her and help.

FREEING A PINNED BOAT

The power of water grows exponentially with volume, so it doesn't take much to build substantial forces on a pinned or broached kayak. To free the boat in these situations, the rescuer will generally try to attach a rope to an exposed end of the boat and pull it loose. The biggest challenge is often in getting this accomplished. If the victim is still in the boat, he should get out if it is safe to

do so. If he can't, he should be stabilized if possible (see the section above on using tag lines to stabilize pinned victims).

In some situations, the victim can't be stabilized and the boat must be freed. The first choice is to throw him the rope and try to get him to attach it to the boat. If he's unconscious or unable to move, the rescuer will have to swim or paddle to the boat to attach the rope. This can be one of the most difficult parts of any rescue, and is occasionally impossible. Which end you attach it to and which direction to pull will depend on the situation. In general, for a broached boat, you want to attach the rope to the end furthest away from where you are pulling and from a point slightly upstream. This way, you're peeling it away from the rock in a way that is deflecting water off of the boat, giving the river less and less surface area to exert force on. For vertical pins where the victim is in the boat, the situation needs to be assessed very carefully as pulling on the boat may put the person at further risk.

USING A VECTOR PULL AND MECHANICAL ADVANTAGE

Quite often, the power of the river makes it impossible to free a pinned boat with just the strength of one person. In these situations, vector pulls and mechanical advantage (sometimes referred to as "Z-drag") systems can be used to substantially increase the pulling force.

A vector pull is quick and easy to set up and is great for situations where you don't have the right equipment to set up a Z-drag. Tension the rope as much as possible, and

(A) The best way to free a pinned boat is to peel it off the rock, with a rope attached to the furthest point from you. (B) A vector pull lets you increase the force exerted at the load, without extra equipment.

then tie it off (a tree is best). Pulling on the centre of this tensioned line at a 90-degree angle will create a vector that multiplies the force at the load (which is the boat, since the tree isn't moving!). The best way to do this is to clip another line onto it using a carabiner and slide the carabiner out to the middle of the tensioned line. The second line is the one you pull on.

Mechanical advantage is a basic concept that can be applied to rescue systems far beyond the scope of this book. We'll keep this simple by looking only at the most basic Z-drag, a 3:1 mechanical advantage system. The general idea is that by redirecting the free end of a loaded rope through an anchored point (a pulley is the most effective) and then back again through another pulley attached to the main line, it multiplies the effect of your pulling on it. The 3:1 ratio indicates that

a system such as this multiplies the pulling force by 3. For example, if you can pull with a force of 100 newtons (N), this system would allow you to exert 300N, minus some small amount due to friction.

To set up a 3:1, you'll need to draw from your rescue kit. Wherever we indicate the use of a pulley, a carabiner can be used as a replacement—it's just not as effective because it creates a sharper bend and more friction in the line. The first step is to make an anchor. This is usually as simple as wrapping a piece of webbing (or a sling) around a sturdy tree or rock and attaching a carabiner to it. For a stronger anchor, you can double wrap the webbing, but make sure it's not too tight. Remember our vector pull? Well, this applies to anchors as well. If you wrap the sling too tightly, then pulling on it can act as a vector pull and unnecessarily multiply the forces being applied to the anchor. Also, position the webbing so that the knot or seam holding the ends together is away from the carabiner that will be loaded.

Once the anchor is ready, attach a pulley to the carabiner, if you have one, and feed the rope into it. Now, attach a prussic as far back down the main line as possible. Today, you can buy pulleys that have a prussic function built into them, which is preferable because they're much faster to set up; and prussic cords can create enough friction heat to melt the sheath on a polypropylene rope. If you don't have either a prussic cord or a mechanical prussic, you can use an overhand knot to create an attachment loop. However, this is not the best set up as you'll have to untie and retie it as you pull the rope in; and any knot in a loaded line presents a weak point. Attach a pulley at this point along the main line and feed the rope into it. You know you're on the right track if you are pulling on the end of the rope in the same direction as the main line is pulling on the load. This makes sense, since you should have made two directional changes in setting up the system. Et voilà, you've created a Z-drag, just like that!

This technique has the capacity of tensioning the line to dangerous levels. By hanging a wet skirt or PFD over the loaded line, you can reduce the potential recoil hazard if the line did ever break. One other safety consideration is that whenever you use a system such as this, the load is securely attached to the rope with no quick-release system. Always have a plan for after the victim or equipment is pulled free.

RIVER ETIQUETTE

RIVER RUNNING ETIQUETTE • PLAYBOATING ETIQUETTE

"A good paddling buddy knows when to push and when to back off." (Jim Sullivan)

As our rivers have become more and more crowded, the potential for conflict between paddlers has grown. Fortunately, paddlers are generally very thoughtful and courteous, which helps us all avoid a lot of problems, but it's still important that we discuss some universal river etiquette. It's also worth mentioning that this etiquette section doesn't cover all the issues that you need to consider. Rivers are like pool halls, in that every river has its own unique paddling community and its own "house rules." We must all appreciate that the rules accepted on our home river aren't always the exact same rules we'll find on other rivers.

RIVER RUNNING ETIQUETTE

The single most important rule of river etiquette is a very simple one that is too often broken. Pick up your trash! If you don't have any trash to take with you off the river, that's great! It means that you have room for trash that some lesser being has left on the ground.

The second most important issue has to do with the right of way on a river. The rule is very simple. The boater going downstream has the right of way. This has always been the case, and despite all the changes in the sport, this is still the case. Of course it's this boater's responsibility to be courteous to those paddlers downstream of him or her. For example, if someone is on a wave below you, then you should do your best to avoid that wave, or wait until he or she is done. On this same note, eddy lines are like stop signs. When you're thinking about leaving an eddy, look both ways and make sure the coast is clear before proceeding into the main current.

The way to deal with rafts on a river is also very simple. Rafts have the right of way. They're bigger than we are, less manoeuvrable, and are usually on a tight commercial schedule. Often the best thing you can do is pull over and let the rafts go by. The sooner they pass by, the sooner you can continue paddling without having to worry about getting blind sided by a big, rubber, floating undercut!

PLAYBOATING ETIQUETTE

The growth in playboating has resulted in the formation of eddy line-ups on rivers around the world, and that's just a part of the sport we have to accept. Although each play spot has its own unique issues, we're going to look at some guidelines that will ease tensions on the river and could

Two paddlers, one hole… trouble.

actually let you enjoy your time in the eddy. Personally, I think eddy line-ups provide paddlers with an amazing learning opportunity. It gives you time to think about what you did wrong on your last ride, and what you have to change for your next. It also gives you a chance to watch and learn from the other paddlers.

Dropping Onto Waves

If there's a line, be courteous and either avoid the hole altogether and get in line, or wait until the coast is clear and go for a big entry move or a very quick ride. Remember that the paddlers in line may have been waiting for their turn for quite some time and won't be ecstatic about every paddler coming down the river just dropping in ahead of them.

Multiple Eddies

If there are multiple eddies from which to enter a play feature, and lines in both, alternate back and forth between them. Sometimes there is a more difficult eddy to catch, which will then have a much smaller line. Those in the short line need to acknowledge that this doesn't give them an excuse to get more rides in than other paddlers, and they should let through a couple at a time from the longer line. Don't worry, by being in that harder eddy, you'll inevitably get more rides; but what we're saying is to maintain some form of etiquette while you're at it.

Double Features

On some rivers there are multiple play waves that can be accessed from a single eddy. In some cases, there will be separate lines for the features. Paddlers who have taken their turn on the upstream feature are not free to drop onto the second feature, but should return to the eddy and get back in line.

Time's Up

If your ride lasts much more than one minute, you can be sure there will be some ticked-off people in the eddy. The grumblings from the eddy can be held off a bit longer than normal if you're getting trashed and providing those in line with entertainment; or if you're pushing your limits and trying very cool new moves.

Line-up Etiquette

Eddy line-ups can get messed up very easily, especially if there's any significant current to contend with. It can sometimes be very hard to keep track of whose turn it is. The best thing to do is remember whom you were after. This is also a great way to approach paddlers who might be taking liberties with their position in line. Don't just sit in the eddy and grind your teeth if you think someone is butting in. Ask them who they're behind. Though they honestly might not know, there's a good chance they'll keep track of whom they're behind for next time.

Many play spots have a calm eddy to the side of the river and a swirly, midstream eddy closer to the play spot. Paddlers will naturally want to jam themselves into the swirly eddy to assure they don't lose their spot in line, but will then spend the next few minutes bumping into each other and fighting the current. It makes a lot more sense for the line to form in the calm eddy and for the swirly eddy to be reserved for the on-deck paddlers only.

TIPS FOR WOMEN *by Anna Levesque*

**GEAR FOR WOMEN • OUTFITTING TIPS FOR WOMEN
THE EMOTIONAL SIDE OF KAYAKING**

"Kayaking is a very individual sport in that you make your own decisions as to which rapids you'll run, and which that you'll walk." (Shannon Carroll)

GEAR FOR WOMEN

Ladies, you don't have to settle for gear that doesn't fit right or look good! Almost every manufacturer is now making gear specifically designed for women. There's a variety of women's PFDs that fit the shapes of your upper bodies, helmets with funky designs, sport tank tops and other comfy underlayers in groovy colours. So shop around and have fun picking out your gear!

OUTFITTING TIPS FOR WOMEN

Since whitewater kayaks are designed mainly by men, they're made with a man's body shape and performance potential in mind. For this reason, some female paddlers have a frustrating time in playboats that are not small and narrow enough for them to consistently perform tricks. As the industry progresses, boat manufacturers are designing more boats with women in mind, and you should now be able to find a suitable boat from most of the major companies. Each company makes boats that have their own unique shape and slightly different performance characteristics, so be sure to test drive as many as you can and don't settle for a mediocre fit.

To help create a better fit for comfort and performance, try the following outfitting tips.

1. Raise your seat. Raising your seat will counteract the sizeable depth of the kayak and give you more leverage, which translates into more power. You can achieve this by placing foam under or on top of your seat. Choose the thickness of foam depending on your height and comfort level. Usually one or two inches of additional height will be enough. The higher you raise your seat, the more leverage you'll have. Remember also that the higher you raise your seat, the more unstable you'll be! If you feel too tippy after you raise your seat, take some of the foam out to lower it a little. Trial and error is the best way to find the balance point between stability and leverage for you.

2. Move your seat forward. Most production kayaks come with the seat moved all the way back. It's important for women to move their seats forward so that their body weight is centred over middle of the boat. This aggressive position makes it much easier for women to sink the bow of the boat when performing tricks like the cartwheel. It will also make it easier for you to maintain or regain control of the boat, because less of your weight will be towards the stern.

3. Be sure to have a strong, supportive back band. Having a good back band that keeps the body in a forward position is especially important for women, because they often find themselves being thrown backwards. Be sure that your back band is snug and supportive.

"Believe in yourself. Know that you can, and you will succeed!" (Ruth Gordon)

THE EMOTIONAL SIDE OF KAYAKING

Kayaking is a relatively intense sport, and all paddlers experience emotion on the river. Sometimes it's the excitement of completing a challenging river or a new freestyle move. Other times it's frustration that comes from failing to attain a goal, fear in the face of a difficult rapid, or intimidation when sitting in an eddy full of skilled paddlers. There are many articles and resources in the kayaking world to help paddlers improve their paddling technique, but very few have addressed how to manage the emotional side of kayaking. During the creation of Girls at Play, my instructional video for women, I conducted interviews with over twenty female paddlers on their approach to the emotional side of kayaking. Combining my personal experience with information collected from these interviews, I've come up with some helpful tips on how to approach and deal with the emotions we face on the river.

Fear

- Face your fear. Admit that you are afraid or nervous.
- Identify the source of your fear. It's important to separate "irrational fear" from "rational fear." Rational fear is fear that comes from a real hazard on the river: an undercut rock or a big recirculating hole. Irrational fear is fear that comes from preconceived notions we have about the dangers of the river and our own ability to successfully tackle them. An example would be someone who won't practice their roll in a pool with an instructor because they're afraid of drowning. The chance of that person really drowning in that situation is very small. Yet they may have been told that practising the roll is dangerous. Or they may have previously had a bad experience in water.

Recognize the source of your fear to determine how best to approach the situation. If the fear you're dealing with is rational, then you might want to walk the rapid. If the fear is based on something someone else has said, or on irrational fear, then you should try to evaluate the situation objectively. Only after doing this can you determine what is best for your particular skill and confidence level.

- If a rapid makes you nervous, break it down. Focus on the class 2, 3 and 4 moves you have to make and not on the "big, scary rapid."

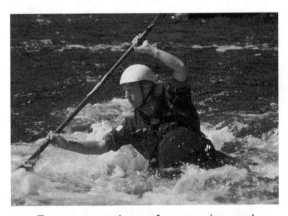

Everyone experiences fear on a river, and everyone also deals with it in a different way.

- Paddle with people who will allow you to go at a pace you feel comfortable with.
- Breathe! Remember to breathe deeply, take the time to relax and assess the situation with a clear mind.
- Paddle for yourself. Don't do something because someone else wants or expects you to. If you don't feel comfortable doing something, then don't do it. Ultimately, you are the one who has to deal with the consequences of your actions.

Intimidation

- Remember that feelings of intimidation exist only in our own minds. Most paddlers are friendly people who like to see new faces on the river.
- Remember that every paddler has felt intimidated by someone at some point in his or her life. It's something that everyone experiences.
- Be kind to yourself. Focus your attention on what you're doing and what makes you happy, not on who is around you and what he or she is doing.
- Try to get to know the person that intimidates you. You will probably discover that you have a lot in common.
- Smile and be friendly to other paddlers. Chances are that some paddlers are intimidated by you.

Crying

- It's okay to cry on the river. Crying is a normal emotional outlet for people, especially for women. In most cases, the person feels much better after crying. Her head will be clearer and her emotions calmer. Healthy crying usually happens in short bursts. If you give a person the space and the time to cry, she will feel much better and your day will go much more smoothly. If, however, a paddler is crying uncontrollably and often, it's probably a good idea to get her off the river.

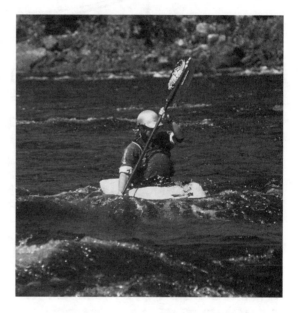

In some paddling circles, showing emotion on the river is sometimes frowned upon. The notion that you're "hardcore" if you can "keep it together" on the river is misguided. Kayaking doesn't have to be hardcore. There's something for everyone in kayaking, from class 2 to class 5, from eddy lines to enormous waves. Accepting the emotional aspects of kayaking will help create a more comfortable and supportive environment for all paddlers.

TRAVELLING AND KAYAKING *By Dunbar Hardy*

**CHOOSING A DESTINATION • DO YOUR HOMEWORK
TRANSPORTATION PLANNING • AIRPORT STRATEGY • FINAL THOUGHTS**

"Kayaking is the ultimate vehicle for seeing the world!" (Brad Ludden)

STRATEGIES FOR PADDLING BEYOND THE BACKYARD

The hazy, humid sky of Marrakesh was filled with blowing sand and dust. We waited. . . . Eventually we were the last ones in the baggage claim. Everything was in Islamic and unreadable. I went over to the non-English-speaking Moroccan airport worker and tried to explain our situation to him. I tried describing and acting out what exactly it was we were missing. It definitely amused him, but it did not help our cause in locating our kayaks. Just another reminder of the real adventure it is to try and paddle far away from home.

For some paddlers, the season never ends. With lots of curiosity, a little research, and a healthy problem-solving attitude, it is possible to paddle year-round in exotic locations all over the world. As winter approaches, it is time to bust out the map and start planning—there is so much water in the world waiting to be paddled.

Dunbar with a fan in Peru.

Chasing good weather and good levels requires extensive travelling, but they are the rewards for exploring rivers beyond your backyard.

A genuine desire to explore this world we live in is needed when undertaking a foreign paddling trip. The farther from home you go, the more the differences you will experience; this cultural diversity should be enjoyed and appreciated. A deep curiosity for the unknown is also recommended. There is suspense in not knowing, and the real excitement is in going through each experience and learning, gaining answers to new questions. True adventure lies in the unknown . . .

CHOOSING A DESTINATION

For your initial excursion abroad, it might be best to select a location that is well known. A place that has been paddled or rafted extensively will more readily provide useful information on rivers to be explored. In these places there will most likely be an in-country contact available as a resource for river levels, gear rental, shuttles, guiding, and lodging. Established local contacts can be invaluable for pre-trip planning. They know the local language and customs and may have extensive firsthand experience on the river(s) you are wishing to paddle.

The lesser known or more out-of-the way destinations can make for very rewarding journeys and cultural experiences, but they can also be very frustrating. The more "out-there" and off the beaten paddling path a destination is, the more of a logistical challenge it will be. There are places still out there where the locals have never seen kayaks, let alone

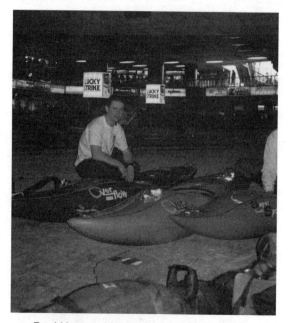

Paul Harwood happy to see his gear at the Guatemala City airport.

know what the whitewater is like. This "foreign-ness" to kayaks in these locations can make for great interactions with the local people, but it can also lead to paddlers having to create their own way. Being a true paddling explorer can lead to lots of "wasted" time dealing with permits, shuttles, logistics, and general transportation arrangements. These details can add up to day after day of not paddling at all, and can become the activity you spend the majority of your time doing.

DO YOUR HOMEWORK

What is that quote . . . "prior planning prevents . . ."? It doesn't actually matter, because things will not go exactly according to plan when foreign paddling. It is recommended to begin planning a foreign paddling trip by having some clear goals and objectives before leaving home. A simple plan of a couple of rivers that you wish to paddle, or even just one on your "must-do" list can help you be organized ahead of time.

Once you have a "list" of rivers, it is a good idea to gather information about how difficult they are, where are they located, how to get there, and when is the ideal time (flow-wise and weather-wise) to be there. Getting answers to these initial questions in regard to the specific rivers listed will give you a more solid game plan. Some of these initial answers might rule out a few rivers right away, based on your timeframe, their difficulty, and differences in goals within the group.

Asking a few more questions can further refine the "hit list." The next level of research is to look into things like what language is spoken there, what gear is available for rent, and what must you bring? What are the costs of getting there and living in this location for the duration of your trip? At this point it is also important to begin looking more closely at the budget of the trip, and see if the expenses to get to certain countries and rivers will further refine the to-do list. As for most true paddlers, we have big hearts and grand plans, but small wallets with little money!

TRANSPORTATION PLANNING

Once you have worked out where to go and when, next is to figure out how to get there. A longer overland road trip to some foreign country will be perhaps the most convenient way to travel. If time is unlimited and there is a somewhat reliable vehicle available, and you are willing to risk it, then overland travel may be the preferred mode of transportation.

It is recommended to travel in a vehicle that can be serviced with parts obtainable in a foreign location. The newer and nicer the vehicle, the more difficult it will be to get it worked on and get parts for it; not to mention that it becomes more of a target for vandalism. Driving, however, allows you to transport all of your own gear and boats. It will also provide a vehicle for shuttles, and can be used for accommodations. Driving

Travelling by bus through Peru takes you on some nerve racking roads.

will also allow you to gain a more intimate knowledge and view of the landscape and culture as the miles pass by.

For further-to-reach places, overseas destinations, and folks with limited timeframes, air travel is an obvious mode of transportation, but it is not without it's own hurdles and obstacles. A plane will get you to a foreign country, but how will you then get around and transport boats and gear while there? In some locations it is possible to travel and paddle exclusively using public transportation such as buses, taxis, and hitchhiking. This can be cheaper on the budget, but not so time efficient when trying to paddle the rivers on your list. Most likely you will need to arrange your own transportation, either through an in-country contact that has been previously arranged, or by renting your own vehicle. It might be cheaper to land in the country then price shop around and find a vehicle in person,

rather than attempting to arrange something through long distance communications before leaving home.

When getting ready to finally commit to renting a vehicle, answer a few more questions. The number of people in your team and the amount of boats and equipment will determine how big a vehicle is needed. Know ahead of time where you will be travelling and whether you need a two- or a four-wheel-drive vehicle. Does the vehicle come with roof racks, or do you need to provide your own? Is it possible to rent a trailer? Does the vehicle come with a driver or do you need to know exactly where you are going and will you be doing all of the driving?

Many foreign vehicle rentals will come with a driver. This can be a good way to learn more about the country and benefit from local knowledge, as well as get help with shuttles. Be aware that these drivers can

James Roddick and Tyler Curtis take a float plane shuttle in northern Ontario, Canada.

also be unwilling to rally the vehicle up dubious roads getting to that "must-do" run. It is important to be as clear and patient as possible when dealing with these folks. Know that the plan can change due to the driver's caution in protecting the vehicle and themselves, or their excitement about exploring their own country with loco gringos. Just driving around can be the most hair-raising part of the trip.

AIRPORT STRATEGY

If flying with a kayak, buckle up because there can be turbulence ahead! It has become harder and harder, as well as more expensive, to fly with a kayak. It is important to show up at the airport up to two hours early and prepare to do battle. Try to pick a less stressed-out, more smiley ticket agent to help you. Don't forget to be polite, friendly and smiling—attitude goes a long way in this interaction.

When flying with a kayak, how it is packed can help get it on board the plane.

It can be recommended to put a boat in a bag so it becomes less obvious what it actually is. You are then able to employ a slight amount of forgivable dishonesty to your advantage. With a covered boat, you have the ability to call it a surfboard, surf ski, or windsurfer, for which all flights have a luggage category at an additional charge. Some flights will not carry a "kayak" on board, thus the need for this resourceful attitude.

Another note here when attempting to fly with a kayak. The words "air cargo" are to be feared, and you must vehemently fight against this reality from occurring. Air cargo means that your boat will not fly on the same plane as you, and this will be a much more expensive "service." There is no definite timeframe when your "cargoed" luggage will actually arrive in the country; it is usually much later than when you have arrived. Of course, it is possible to air cargo your kayak days before you get on your plane and fly, so that it is waiting for you upon your arrival. Again, a very expensive fee will be charged for this "service."

Generally, once the luggage is all classified, the added fee is paid, and all is put on board, you are on your way! My motto is to get my butt in the seat and then I can relax. An adventure awaits . . .

FINAL THOUGHTS

Foreign paddling trips are a great adventure. It is important to be aware of the fact that travelling can be how the majority of the time is spent, rather than paddling. I take the approach when travelling in a foreign country, that if I actually wind up paddling something I will be pleased and surprised—getting on the water is a bonus. Flexibility and patience are keys to surviving the tumultuous and oftentimes inconvenient world of international travelling and paddling.

Somewhere out there in the world right now it is summer, and the water levels are prime! Seeing the world from the seat of a kayak can be one of the most rewarding experiences, and it is undoubtedly worth all of the effort to get there.

IF THE VOYAGEURS COULD SLEEP IN THEIR...

F. MASON

18

OVERNIGHT WHITEWATER TRIPS *by Phil DeRiemer*

**CHOOSING YOUR BOAT • A PACKING LIST • HOW TO PACK
ATTITUDE/ DECISION MAKING**

*"The joy is in the journey." (*Brad Ludden)

To do a self-contained trip is to experience the ultimate freedom that a kayak can offer: easing into river time where the outside world slips from your thoughts as you become focused on the moment. You challenge yourself to see how little you can do without, while experiencing the river on a much more intimate level. Group size can be small, camps out of the way, and your choice of rivers as remote as you'd like. You can make your experience a relaxing two-day flatwater cruise, or an intense 20-day exploratory suffer-fest. Regardless of the type of trip you choose, here are a few variables to consider that will help secure the outcome of your experience:

- Difficulty of the run
- Length of the run
- Remoteness
- Weather/climate
- Food

You should keep coming back to the above items as you plan your trip. It affects the boat you take, the amount and type of food you eat, the clothing and other equipment you bring, as well as your pace. Let's look at each of them and how they should be considered.

Difficulty of the run: You want this to be a great first experience. Let your skills be your guide. If you have never run class 5, perhaps doing it with a fully loaded kayak isn't a good starting point. Under this should also be mentioned the type of run: is it big water or creeky, pool/drop or continuous?

Length of the run: I suggest if you're doing a self-contained trip for the first time that you ease into it with a shorter trip. This gives you a great chance to shake down your systems, fine-tune your equipment

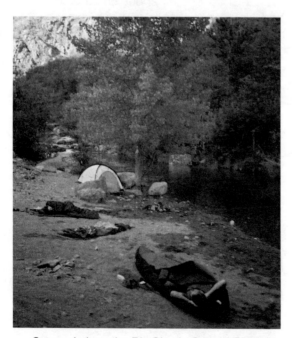

Camped along the Rio Sico in Central Chile.

choices, and see how much you really like it. If you are doing runs of similar difficulty, terrain, and climate, but one is longer than the other, the only real difference in what you carry will be the amount of food. Your kayak, no matter how big, can only carry so much. Where possible, you can arrange for food drops or caches to stretch out the length of your journey.

Remoteness: The game gets more serious when you take it into the back country. You are further from everything—outside help and the nearest road—and you face a long walk out, should you bail on your trip or lose gear. Some changes I might make on a remote trip include: a beefed-up first aid kit; more than just duct tape in my repair kit; maps; good boating shoes, should I turn from boater to hiker; and the number of breakdown paddles for the group.

Weather and climate: This is big. It not only comes into play with regards to food and shelter, but it could determine your pace. If you're doing a run where the water could come up in hours or within the time you are on the river, then you had best pay attention to the weather before and during your trip. Clothing gets tricky, too. If you are going to elevation it is easy to get fooled by hot days that could turn cold at night; so plan accordingly.

Food: I'm not a nutritionist, so I won't even attempt to tell you what to eat, but I can suggest some things to consider in choosing your foods. This is probably the single heaviest group of items in your kit, so where possible, go for the lighter choices. At the end of a long day you are usually not too fired up about cooking.

Keep it simple from that standpoint: one-pot glops and pastas. You can get by on lean rations on a shorter run, but if you're hard at work on a longer run, you need calories; and if you're in a cold climate, then you need more calories.

My earliest travels abroad to paddle not only included a mountain of gear, but one enormous duffle full of freeze-dried food. Upon our arrival in our destination country, while we didn't find freeze-dried, we did find packaged food that was more than adequate for our needs. Ask around if others have been to the area where you intend to travel; that could save you hauling unnecessary supplies with you.

Finally, you can have a lot of fun with the food on a trip. I've done runs where I went lean and mean, but others where I was fat and happy. From soup to steaks, or water to wine. Your imagination, size of kayak, and willingness to carry it are the limits.

CHOOSING YOUR BOAT

By now the topics discussed above have probably helped you narrow your choice of kayak. Unless you're willing to take a small boat and unload at every play spot

LEARNING TO DO WITHOUT

Because of the limitations involved, self-contained trips are all about doing without. This can range from what you eat, wear, and sleep in, to what you can expect of yourself and your kayak. Obviously the Dutch oven is out, as might be the cold beers and wine at the end of the day. If you're doing a run that you know has sandy beaches, maybe you can do without a sleeping pad. A tarp may do where you were considering a tent. Try to make your equipment as multi-purpose as possible. If your paddle jacket can serve as your raincoat, or you can get by with using your river shorts in camp, you'll shed important ounces and hopefully pounds from your load. At the same time, it feels good to the body and soul to slip into something warm and dry on a cold or rainy multi-day. Treat yourself where possible. The items listed below are just suggestions to get you started.

A PACKING LIST

Besides the paddling gear you'll use on your trip, here are some suggested items to consider. What you bring is based on personal wants and needs as well as climate.

Sleeping bag (synthetic is probably the better choice for the watery world, while down is lighter and more compressible)

Sleeping pad (here I often use a 3/4 length ultralight thermarest)

Tarp/ bivy sac/tent (depends on the climate)

Cook pot
Lighter
Bowl (my bowl is also my cup)
Fork or spoon
Food

Camp clothes (could be as simple as a dry shirt or as luxurious as a full set of dry clothes)

Extra insulating layers (light tops and bottoms to fine-tune your warmth; if cool at night, bottoms are nice to have)

Dry bags (There are some great ones available commercially, but if you want a cheap alternative, use trash compactor bags inside stuff sacks. The thicker plastic of the bags will last you for many trips. You simply tie them off at the top to keep water out. The stuff sacks help prevent the accidental tearing of a hole in the plastic bags as you slide them in and out of the boat.)

Breakdown paddle (number depends on difficulty of run and size of group)

Sponge (Before shouldering your boat for a portage it's nice to get every last drop of water out.)

Water bottle
Water purification system (chemical treatments are lighter than pumps)

First aid (What you carry is up to you. Think about where you're going and how long you'll be out. I really recommend carrying at least tincture of benzoine and steri-strips. Will you need antibiotics?)

Repair kit (this may be as simple as duct tape, but could include a sewing kit or more)

Throw rope (70 feet ideal)

Prussics

Carabiners

Optional
Headlamp

Stove/fuel (This is weather dependent. If you can't count on dry wood, then a stove becomes essential if you plan to cook.)

Map

Camera

Leatherman-type tool

Additional clothing (This is weather dependent. If you anticipate bad and/or cold weather, then being comfortable both on and off the river is important. I'll often splurge and bring a raincoat, extra layers of clothing, and perhaps a change of footwear.)

(providing you can get all you need into it in the first place), you may want to set aside any thoughts of throwing intentional ends, or blunts, and bring a bigger boat. I have one boat that I do most of my self-contained trips out of. In choosing my kayak, I know that the performance will be changed because of the extra weight I'll be carrying. For this reason I go with a boat that is forgiving, predictable, and comfortable.

Because I don't know when or where I will be jumping out to scout, portage, or help someone in a bind, I also wear shoes in my boat. On this latter point, I do know of at least one story where a kayaker hiked barefoot eight miles out of the Grand Canyon of the Stikine after a bad swim that washed his boat away with his shoes stowed safely behind the seat.

HOW TO PACK:

Four of us once did a 22 day trip on Baffin Island in the Arctic. While we had scheduled a food drop, we were forced to carry upwards of 12 days' worth of food and supplies in our boats at the start of each leg. Two of us had stock plastic boats that required that we cut a foot off of each end of the pillars, along with trimming an inch off the width just so we could get all of our gear in. We spent most of a day in an airplane hanger packing and sorting our gear so we could figure out how to fit it all in. Packing was like a Chinese puzzle: first one piece, then another, all in essentially the same sequence each time we loaded or

unloaded. The kayaks weighed in excess of 90 pounds. Portaging was probably the most dangerous part of our journey, as stepping over and around boulders and walking on uneven ground could easily have resulted in a fall and a broken ankle. You may never suffer a momentary lapse of judgment such as we did and venture off on a three-week-long journey. But if you've never done a self-contained trip before, you can burn up a lot of time at the put-in figuring out how to make it all fit. If you get a chance at a dry run at home, that is best.

The majority of your gear is going to end up in the back of the boat. If you have an adjustable seat, you may want to look at moving it forward so that your boat will be more balanced from front to back. When packing, I try to run the day through in my head and figure out what I am likely to need and in what order. I then combine this with the desire to keep the heaviest things, such as food, as close to the back of the seat as possible. This keeps the ends of the boat light, which translates to more control in the water.

Some items, such as food for the day, water purification, film, and perhaps an extra insulating layer, I'll carry in a small "daybag" dry bag so I don't have to get into the main store of food and equipment each time to retrieve something. This adds up to time saved at each break. If you have access to the front area of your boat; be it foot pegs or a bulkhead, this can be a good place to store light, bulky items such as a cooking pot (I put it in upside down so water drains out.), or a compact sleeping pad.

Playboats definitely aren't a wise choice for overnight trips.

Many dry bags/stow floats are conically shaped like the back end of your kayak. For this reason I rarely use stuff sacks inside a dry bag. This allows the contents to conform better to the shape of the storage system. A breakdown paddle usually goes in the back of the boat, either all of it on one side, split between the two sides, or shared amongst the participants. Either way, try to tape the pieces together so they aren't bouncing around in there when you take your bags out.

Wherever you store your throw rope, make it the last thing to be loaded, so it can be the first and fastest item to remove.

Clip it in: If you can't afford to lose it, make sure it is secured in the boat somehow; this includes your breakdown paddle. Besides swims, I've seen boats get away on scouts and portages. If they're in

PADDLING WITH A LOAD

With your boat loaded, you're going to notice a difference in how it handles. While it won't be as bad as strapping a sack of potatoes to your backside and going ice-skating, it will require an adjustment. It will spin out more readily when you don't want it to, and be more difficult to turn when you do want it to. You'll learn the new handling characteristics shortly, but in the meantime, take this difference into consideration about what you do and don't run. One good thing about the extra weight is it gives you remarkable punching power, so as you're getting pushed toward that hole that you would have missed in an empty boat, take comfort in knowing you just might make it through.

the water long enough, they can begin to unpack themselves on their downstream run.

ATTITUDE/ DECISION MAKING:

Get yourself in, get yourself out. I've always tried to follow this simple rule on all of my wilderness outings. I suppose you could throw in a cell and/or satellite phone for a little insurance, but you shouldn't use them as the reason to push things a little further. You are your own best rescue, and that begins with making good decisions.

Along those lines, another rule I've come to learn is "bad experiences make for good judgment." It's not my first choice, but I've made mistakes in many facets of my paddling, and treat them as important learning opportunities. I file them away and draw on them in hopes that I won't repeat mistakes. The unexpected can happen, but a lot of incidents in the backcountry could be avoided with better decision-making; be it water levels, running rapids without scouting and/or carrying, or doing a run that you aren't yet ready for. This goes for the people I paddle with as well. If someone in your group is making poor decisions and something happens as a result, everyone is affected. Chances are you will put a lot of thought into the gear you take with you—why not the folks you paddle with as well?

Enjoy the freedom and enjoy the journey. Once you do your first overnighter, it will only leave you wanting more.

GLOSSARY

12 O'clock: An indication of the bow's position when it is pointing directly upstream. All other hours of the clock use this as a reference point.

Aerial: A move that involves getting the complete boat and body out of the water.

Aggressive Swimming: Actively swimming, usually with the front crawl technique, to move from one point in the river to another.

Brake: A surfing stroke that causes maximum resistance with the main current, used to pull the surfer downstream on the wave.

Back band: A padded, adjustable lower back support attached to the seat.

Back Face: The opposite side of the paddle blade from the power face, used for reverse strokes and usually convex with a spine along its center. (also non-power face)

Backside (of a wave): The part of a wave downstream of the peak, where water flows downhill.

Blast: Front surfing in the trough of a hole, with the stern under the foam pile.

Blunt: An aggressive spin from front surf to back surf that throws the stern into the air.

Boat tilt: The balancing of your weight on a single butt cheek or hip, which leans your boat on edge.

Body Surfing Position: The position assumed when floating through whitewater; feet downstream, arms out to the side, and the whole body as close to the surface as possible.

Body wind-up: The rotation of your upper body in the desired turning direction.

Boil: The feature created when water is forced directly upwards to the surface.

Boil line: The point on a hole's foam pile at which the water on the upstream side flows upstream, while the water on the downstream side flows downstream.

Boofing: The technique used to prevent the bow of your kayak from diving underwater when you paddle over a drop.

Bow: The front end of a kayak.

Bow draw: A technique used to turn the boat aggressively by planting the blade near the bow and pulling the bow toward it.

Bow pivot: A pivot turn where the pivot point is forward of the center of the boat, achieved by slicing the bow under water, which frees the stern to come around in the air.

Bulkhead: A specific adjustable foot brace system that moves as one unit and lets you apply pressure with most of your foot.

C-Stroke: A combination stroke using the bow draw and forward stroke. Turns the boat while maintaining forward momentum.

Cartwheel: A standard, advanced playboating move done on flatwater and in holes, in which the bow and stern rotate around the body, staying 45 degrees or more past horizontal.

Clean: A playboating move that involves a full 360-degree rotation with only a single stroke.

Closed face: In the context of a draw, rotating the blade so that the power face is facing toward the tern.

Cockpit: The opening at the center of the kayak.

Corner: The side of a hole that can be used for spinning, setting up advanced moves, or exiting.

Defensive Swimming: Passively swimming on your back, keeping as flat and shallow as possible with your feet downstream to fend off obstructions. (also body surfing)

Diagonal Line: A rescue line that spans the river, angled downstream so that a rescuer and victim can travel from one side to the other using the current to propel them.

Displacement hull: A rounded or V-shaped hull that creates a channel in the water.

Double pump: The action of winding up the bow.

Downstream: The direction in which the water is flowing.

Downstream V: The shape formed by the main current in most cases, usually indicating the deepest and safest route.

Draw strokes: Dynamic strokes that either pull water towards or push water away from the side of the boat at any point along its length for a variety of effects.

Dry top: A nylon top with a variety of possible water resistant coatings and latex gaskets at the wrists and neck to keep water out. A smart choice for cold water or cold days.

Duffek Stroke: An open face bow draw used to stop the forward momentum of the boat and turn aggressively toward the blade.

Eddy: A relatively calm section of water in the river, formed by the deflection of current around an obstruction.

Eddy hopping: Working your way down the river by moving from one eddy to the next.

Eddy Line: The point along which the eddy current and the main current collide.

Edge: Where the sidewall meets the hull.

Face (of a wave): The part of a wave upstream of the peak and downstream of the trough, in which water is flowing uphill.

Ferry: The technique used to move laterally across the main current

Flat spin: Using a flat hull's planning capabilities to change your kayak's direction on the green part of the wave.

Flatwater: Water without current.

Foam pile: The aerated, re-circulating water that forms the white part of a hole.

Greenwater: The non-aerated water that flows into and under a hole.

Gliding draw: A draw planted at the hips while the boat is moving to act as a keel, allowing the boat to carve a smooth turn as opposed to spinning out.

Grab loop: A handle made of webbing at both the bow and stern of a kayak. Used mostly to carry with, but also in some rescue situations.

Gradient: The amount that a given section of river drops vertically over a given distance. Generally measure in feet per mile or meters per kilometer.

Hand-of-God: A rescue technique wherein the rescuer reaches over the upside-down boat and flips it back up.

Helical flow: The circular, spiraling or tumbling motion of water that results from one force acting on it in one direction while another force acts on it in an opposing direction.

Helmet: A plastic or composite piece of head gear designed to protect a paddler's noggin against impact from rocks, large fish or rafters. (also lid)

High brace: A technique using the front face of the blade to either recover from a moment of instability or as support to help prevent flipping over.

Hole (Hydraulic): A type of wave in which the water piles up on itself, forcing aerated water back upstream and into the trough.

Hull: The bottom of a kayak.

Hydraulic: A feature formed when water flows over a ledge and recirculates back into its own trough, become aerated and lighter in color. (also hole, stopper)

Kick flip: A horizontal pirouette performed while launching from the peak of a wave.

Laminar Flow: The streamline motion of water as it moves along a consistent, predictable path, such as the main flow in the center of the river.

Loop: An airborne flip, done either forward or backward.

Low brace: A technique using the back face of the blade to either recover from a moment of instability or as support to help prevent flipping over.

Mechanical Advantage: This is the added force applied to the load in a rescue situation, gained by redirecting the rescue line so that it is pulling from multiple points on the load.

Open face: In the context of a draw, rotating the blade so that the power face is facing toward the bow.

Peak: The highest point on a wave.

Peel-Out: The action of pulling out of an eddy, into current.

Peel-In: The action of pulling into an eddy, from current.

Pirouette: Spinning a kayak around on its end.

Pivot turn: An efficient change of direction that involves slicing one end of the kayak under water, freeing the other to come around in the air.

PFD: Personal Flotation Device. Designed to float a swimmer in the water, but not necessarily with the face out of the water. (also life jacket)

Pillow: The area of still water that is piled against the upstream face of a rock.

Pin: The entrapment of a boat in current, by rocks.

Pin Kit: A kit containing the basic rescue gear, including carabiners, pulleys, prussiks, and webbing. It is used to free pinned kayaks in a variety of situations.

Planing hull: A flat hull that does not displace water. When surfing, this feature allows the boat to spin on the water's surface with minimal friction. (also flat hull)

Pogies: Mitten-like attachments to a paddle shaft, used to keep cold water off the hands. Nice alternative to gloves because they allow direct contact with the shaft.

Pool-Drop: A type of river that is characterized primarily by distinct rapids separated by calmer sections of water. (also ledge-drop)

Pour-over: A sticky hydraulic formed by water flowing over a vertical or nearly vertical drop. Because the water pours straight down, it makes a deep depression in the river. This causes more water to recirculate from further downstream

Power Stroke: A vertical or past-vertical forward stroke that has minimal impact on spin momentum.

Powerface: The side of the paddle blade that is used for forward strokes. It is generally concave and smooth. (also front face)

Reactionary: A diagonal wave formed when the water 'reacts' off of and obstruction of some sort (for example, a boulder or a hole).

Re-circulating: Refers to the action of the aerated water in a hole that is moving upstream.

Rescue Vest: A specialized PFD with a quick release chest harness for tethered rescues and various other rescue-oriented features.

Rocker: A design feature whereby the middle of the hull is lower than the two ends. The more rocker, the greater the difference between the middle and ends.

Roll: A technique, performed in a variety of ways, used to right an overturned kayak.

Rooster-tail: A spout of water that is being deflected into the air by an obstruction just under the surface.

Rudder: A blade that is planted in the water to control a front or back surf.

Scouting: The act of looking at a rapid, from shore or in your boat.

Scull: The action of taking strokes with paddle blades angled so that they continuously work their way to the surface.

Seam (of a hole): The point in the trough of a hole at which the foam pile meets the greenwater.

Seam (of a pillow): The line dividing the current that flows into the rock from upstream and the rock's pillow.

Shoulder (of a wave): The sides of a wave.

Side surfing: Establishing a balanced position on a single hip in the trough of a hole, while being held perpendicular to the main current by the hole's re-circulating water.

Sidewall: The side of the kayak, between the deck and hull.

Sieve: An underwater passage that allows water through, but that often stops larger objects.

Skull cap: A neoprene or fuzzy rubber cap worn under the helmet to prevent ice cream head aches in cold water.

Splash top: A nylon top with a variety of possible water resistant coatings. May have neoprene gaskets or not, but does not keep water out completely. (also paddle jacket)

Spray skirt: Made of neoprene or nylon, it is worn around the paddler's waste and fits securely around the cockpit rim to prevent water from entering the boat. (also spray deck, deck, skirt)

Squirt boat: An ultra low volume kayak designed to work with the currents below the surface.

Stall: Balancing a kayak on end.

Stern: The back end of a kayak. (also tail)

Stern draw: A technique used to turn or steer the boat by planting the near the stern and pulling the boat toward it or prying the boat away from it.

Stern pivot: A pivot turn where the pivot point is behind the center of the boat, achieved by slicing the stern under water, which frees the bow to come around in the air.

Stern Pry: A modification of the stern draw, used to steer the boat, primarily as a rudder while surfing. The bck face of the blade is used to pry the stern away from the paddle.

Stern squirt: A 360-degree pirouette with the bow in the air that is initiated with a back sweep.

Strainer: An obstruction in the river that allows water through, but stops larger objects.

Surfer's left: The left side of the river when looking upstream (from a surfer's perspective).

Surfer's right: The right side of the river when looking upstream (from a surfer's perspective).

Surge: A fluctuation in the size of a water feature.

T-Rescue: The rescuer offers an end of their kayak to an upside down paddler for their use to hip snap themselves upright.

Tag Line: A line spanning the section of river where a rescue situation is in progress, used to stabilize the victim by lifting them clear of the water.

Tethered Rescue: A rescue situation wherein the rescuer swims out to contact and retrieve the victim while attached by a quick release system to a rope (the tether).

Thigh brace: Contoured padding attached to the sides of the seat inside boats to create a snug fit, allow better control and prevent the paddler from slipping out when upside down. (also thigh hook)

Throw Rope: A coated polypropylene or Spectra cord between 50 and 150 feet long in a nylon bag, used in a variety of rescue situations.

Torso rotation: Winding up the torso to involve major muscle groups in strokes as it unwinds.

Tongue: A weak spot in a hole that water flows through freely.

Tow Line: A short line attached to a rescuer by a quick release system, typically used to tow a kayak to shore.

Trough: The lowest point in a hole.

Turbulent Flow: Less predictable than laminar or helical flow, this refers to disturbances in the water that last an instant or not much longer.

Undercut: A rock whose underside has been eroded over time, and which water is forced to flow underneath.

Upstream: The direction from which water is flowing.

Vector Pull: A basic technique for multiplying forces in a rescue situation, achieved by pulling the centre of a rescue line perpendicularly to the direction it is moving the load.

Volume: The amount of water in the river, measured in terms of how much water flows past a given point in a given period of time. Generally classified as high, medium or low and measured in cubic feet or cubic meters per second (cfs or cms).

Wave train: A series of waves.

Wave wheel: A cartwheel initiated as one launches from the peak of a wave.

Wet Exit: Exiting an upside-down kayak in the water. (also swimming)

Whirlpool: A section of downward spiraling current that forms where opposing flows collide.

Z-Drag: A rescue system that gains mechanical advantage by redirecting the rescue line several times. The more redirections, the higher the multiplication of forces achieved.

Astral
buoyancy company

Since 1994, we are responsible for developing the current industry standards for PFD design, materials, and utility. We guarantee everything we make to function perfectly and be of the highest quality materials and ethical workmanship available.

2000 Riverside Dr.
Asheville, NC, 28804
828-255-2638
www.astralbuoyancy.com

straight shaft since '91

whitewater paddles by Aqua-Bound

long time aquabound paddler tyler curtis at ease on his home "turf". photo: ruth gordon

www.aquabound.com

SHRED carbon
carbon blades/carbon shaft
34oz
7.75" x 18" blades
tough, affordable performance

canoe
&kayak
ACCESSORY
MANUFACTURER
OF THE YEAR
2002 & 2003

DIESEL

THE SUV OF KAYAKS

photo - luke hopkins / www.localpaddler.com

Great Falls, Potomac River, MD @ 20,000cfs

WAVE SPORT

	DIESEL 65	DIESEL 75
LENGTH	7'6"	8'0"
WIDTH	25"	25.5"
DEPTH	12.5"	12.75"
VOLUME	65 GAL	75 GAL
WT. RANGE	100-200 lbs	140-240 lbs
WEIGHT	39 lbs	41 lbs

Tanya Shuman
Ken Whiting
Jed Selby
Brooke Winger
Tyler Curtis
Bryan Kirk
Jimmy Blakeney
Deb Pinniger
Luke Hopkins
Karyn McMullin
Bill McKnight
Nate Helms
Jamie Cooper
John Grossman
doubleyouess.com